ORGANIZATIONAL THEORY AND INQUIRY

SOME OTHER VOLUMES IN THE
SAGE FOCUS EDITIONS

ORGANIZATIONAL THEORY AND INQUIRY

The Paradigm Revolution

Edited by

Yvonna S. Lincoln

SAGE PUBLICATIONS
The Publishers of Professional Social Science
Newbury Park   London   New Delhi

Copyright © 1985 by Sage Publications, Inc.

For information address:

SAGE Publications, Inc.
2111 West Hillcrest Drive
Newbury Park, California 91320

SAGE Publications Ltd.
28 Banner Street
London EC1Y 8QE
England

SAGE Publications India Pvt. Ltd.
M-32 Market
Greater Kailash I
New Delhi 110 048 India

Printed in the United States of America

Library of Congress Cataloging-in-Publication Data

Main entry under title:

Organizational theory and inquiry.

   (Sage focus editions ; v. 75)
   Based on papers presented at a conference held
at the University of Kansas in November 1983.
   1. Organization—Congresses. 2. Organization—
Research—Congresses. 3. Paradigms (Social sciences)—
Congresses. I. Lincoln, Yvonna S.
HM131.O683 1985   302'.072   85-8137
ISBN 0-8039-2494-1
ISBN 0-8039-2495-X (pbk.)

THIRD PRINTING, 1989

CONTENTS

FOREWORD: FUTURE DIRECTIONS FOR RESEARCH IN POLICY STUDIES

The process by which innovations become adopted and diffused among potential users is a complicated one, and the innovations in research described in this book are not exceptions. Salient elements of the innovation process are the following: No single individual or group generally is responsible for getting an innovation routinized in an organization (Yin, 1979), although there generally are policy entrepreneurs, catalysts, or fixers who play large and important roles in the adoption and diffusion process (Bardach, 1980; Doig, 1981; Palumbo, Musheno, & Maynard-Moody, 1985). It usually is impossible to fix the exact date when a particular innovation began, and the innovation will be reinvented a number of times or modified to fit into the specific neeeds of those who will use it (Rice & Rogers, 1980). Many years usually pass for the diffusion process to unfold, and along the way a number of unanticipated consequences are likely to occur, so that the end results are likely to be quite different from those anticipated earlier in the process.

The paradigm shifts now occurring in a number of separate disciplinary areas discussed in this book (i.e., organization theory, evaluation, research, policy analysis) are analogous to the process of innovation adoption and diffusion. Various scholars are playing the role of catalyst or entrepreneur (i.e., Guba & Lincoln; Reichardt & Cook; Miller) and the innovations that are occurring will no doubt be reinvented several times before the innovation process completely unfolds. Nor can it be doubted that the process will take a long time to be implemented and have numerous unintended consequences.

There are a number of different strands to the paradigm shifts occurring in what Harold Lasswell called the policy sciences, but they all seem to be coalescing in a specific direction (or causing the soccer field to tilt in a particular direction; see Weick). It is the direction of that tilting and what it means for policy studies that is the subject of this introductory essay.

Policy studies are not a single entity; they involve a bundle of different disciplines (not necessarily "interdisciplinary") and research methods including all of the social and behavioral sciences and, specifically, organization theory, implementation, evaluation, research, policy analysis, and public administration. Developments in these diverse areas are loosely coupled, and so it is not easy to predict the likely outcome or shifts now occurring, but certain outlines appear vaguely on the distant horizon, and I would like to focus on these. Specifically, the major developments I see are in (1) implementation research and in organization theory (which involves things such as the discovery of the macro- as distinct from the micro-implementation process, the complexity of joint action in organizations, the impossibility of anticipating consequences of action, and the difficulty of having good policy design as well as good implementation in such a complex setting); (2) evaluating social programs (including the difference between policies and programs, the convoluted utilization process, and the difficulty of injecting prospective as opposed to retrospective rationality into organizational action); and (3) methods of researching organizations (including the question of resonance between methods and processes, the place of values such as "objectivity" in research, and the compatibility of naturalistic and positivistic epistemology). I will address each of these changes in turn.

DEVELOPMENTS IN IMPLEMENTATION RESEARCH AND ORGANIZATION THEORY

Prior to the rise and use/nonuse/misuse of policy research by public agencies, public administration was approached primarily as a micro- rather than a macro-concern. It focused mainly on the problems that are internal to public agencies (i.e., micro-organizational behavior) rather than on the relationships of agencies with the multitude of other organizations and actors that are part of the environment in which agencies operate. Of course, organization theory, particularly contingency theory (Emery, Marek, & Trist, 1965; Hickson, Henings, Lee, Schneck, & Pennings, 1971; Perrow, 1972; Hage, 1980) had long ago focused on the environments of organizations, but these ideas did not really seep into

public administration until the discovery of the implementation problem (Hargrove, 1975; Pressman & Wildavsky, 1972). Leading texts in
public administration (such as Dimock, Dimock, & Koenig, 1961)
recognized the existence of the "politics" of administration, but after a
short chapter on this topic, attention was turned entirely to micro-organizational questions.

Macro-organizational behavior encompasses the vertical relationships among organizations that exist in the federal system (in which
influence flows as often from the bottom up as from the top down) but,
more important, it also encompasses the horizontal relationships
among the numerous public and private organizations required for the
implementation of most social programs.

What is crucial about the focus on macro-organizational behavior is
the complexity of joint action. The large number of participants, perspectives, and decision points necessary for the completion of a program
brings into stark relief the problems associated with injecting prospective rationality into organizational behavior. As successful implementation in such ambiguous circumstances requires mutual adaptation
among the actors involved, the only kind of rationality that seems to
exist in organizations is retrospective as opposed to prospective. Retrospective rationality involves explaining events *after* they have occurred,
whereas prospective rationality is an attempt to predict and control
events *before* they occur. Although at times organizations attempt to be
rational in the prospective sense, most often they are rational only in the
retrospective sense. Hence, organizational behavior is rational, but only
in the sense that organizations act first, then analyze what they did,
rather than the other way around (Palumbo & Nachmias, 1983). As Karl
Weick (in this volume) explains, intention seldom, if ever, controls
action; but because we assume that what appeared to happen did
happen, we often conclude that rational models actually work when, in
fact, they do not.

An equally important development in implementation research is the
finding that programs must be modified or adapted to fit local needs and
that street-level implementors play a crucial role in this process. Michael
Lipsky (1980) pointed out that street level bureaucrats (i.e., those who
act as the interface between the organization and the "clients" or target
groups) participate as much in the making of policy as those at the top.
From a prescriptive position, the role of street-level bureaucrats is
desirable because they have greater ability than those at the top to know

which parts of a program are working and which are not (Elmore, 1982). This also enables organizations to learn from and correct their mistakes (Wildavsky, 1980). Hence, program implementation and program design are highly interrelated activities. Because it is impossible to anticipate all of the consequences of organizational action (and, therefore, impossible to be prospectively rational), it usually is impossible to design programs completely before they are implemented. As lessons are learned during implementation, programs are adjusted, and this is or should be a continuous process.

There is an ambiguity here in that if organizations can learn from their mistakes, they are goal-directed and, therefore, rationality and order in organizational behavior ultimately may be possible. However, the rationality that is achieved is primarily retrospective, and this applies to goals as well as to processes of implementation. Thus, as organizations or actors achieve a particular goal, they can say that this is the goal at which they were aiming all along and, if the goal is one that is supported by important stakeholders, they can say they scored a point in the game (which gets us into the question of who determines what the slope of the soccer field should be, and the answer is the crucial stakeholders).

Simultaneous with and complementary to the developments in implementation research, organization theory also was undergoing changes. The top-down, Weberian view of organizations, coupled with the rational model of decision theory, was being supplanted by the concepts of loosely coupled systems (Weick, 1976), garbage cans (Cohen, March, & Olsen, 1972), and reticular models (Dunsire, 1978). In traditional public administration theory, departures from the rational model were considered anomalies that could be corrected by following principles such as unity of command, matching authority with responsibility, centralization, and proper delegation of authority. However, communications are distorted as they are transmitted down the organizational hierarchy. Subordinates add to and subtract from the messages they receive. By the time directives reach the lower level, there are major differences among the versions received by comparable lower echelon members in different parts of the organization (Meltsner & Bellavita, 1983). This "leakage of authority" (Downs, 1967, p. 134) is in close accord with the idea that organizations are loosely coupled systems, for the discretion of street-level bureaucrats cannot be controlled or abolished. Thus, the view of organizations that is most consistent with implementation research is, "Goals are discovered by acting. Action precedes intent. Solutions search for problems. Subordinates specify spheres of work to superordinates" (Clark, this volume).

CHANGES IN OUR UNDERSTANDING
OF PROGRAM EVALUATION

The changing perspectives of organizations and implementation of public policy have enormous repercussions on evaluation. How do we evaluate loosely coupled systems that are not prospectively rational? How do we evaluate a game in which goals are scattered haphazardly around the field, and in which people enter and leave the game at will and can lay claim to any goal they want? Certainly not by beginning with the assumptions of micro-economic theory or with the assumptions of positivist, empirical research.

Evaluation as a form of disciplined inquiry was originally strongly positivist and based on the same assumptions as micro-economic theory, but it has since made a number of important shifts. One of these is the recognition that the process of program implementation is important. Because it often may take a long time for a program to be implemented, it is essential to assess the extent to which and how a program has been implemented before it can be evaluated for impact; otherwise, we may wind up evaluating a program that has not been implemented (Patton, 1978; Musheno, 1982).

There are a number of different patterns of implementation, each of which requires a different impact assessment. Figure A depicts four possible models of implementation (McCain & McCleary, 1979). It is obvious that if implementation is gradual and temporary, but we use an impact assessment model based on the assumption that it is abrupt and permanent, we will understate the extent to which the program has achieved its objectives. For example, in a process evaluation of Minnesota's decriminalization of a public drunkenness law, Aaronson, Dienes, and Musheno (1978) found a 37% drop in police pick-ups of street drunks when a public health mandate replaced the criminal mandate for public drinking. They assumed that implementation was abrupt and permanent. But McCleary and Musheno (1980) reanalyzed the data, assuming that implementation was gradual and temporary, and found that there was a 64% drop in police intakes—almost twice the original figure.

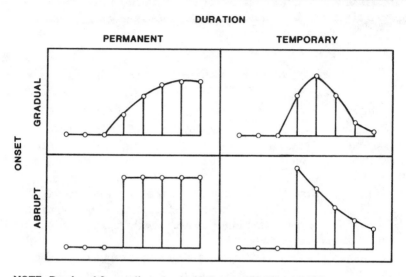

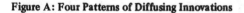

NOTE: Developed from a discussion by McCain and McCleary (1979).

Figure A: Four Patterns of Diffusing Innovations

Thus, evaluating impact cannot proceed in the absence of process evaluation (Palumbo & Sharp, 1980). But when process evaluations are conducted, we often find that goals and objectives change in the process of implementation. Similar to Chinese baseball, in which the bases are moved after the pitcher releases the ball (Siu, 1984), program goals are adjusted and made more realistic when it is discovered that the goals assumed when the program was adopted cannot be achieved or have become outmoded. For example, Kress, Koehler, and Springer (1981) found that a California program that originally was perceived to be a rehabilitation program for blind vendors changed into a business program to provide opportunities for business enterprise. Another example is the food stamp program that, although originally adopted as a farm support and nutrition program for the poor, ultimately became a welfare reform program (Nathan, 1976). Few if any congresspersons realized in 1964 that they were creating a program that would develop into an in-kind, guaranteed income (Berry, 1984, p. 145).

So people can move bases or lay claim to different goals after the game starts. This is desirable if organizations are to be self-correcting and learn from their mistakes. But what goals should be used in an impact assessment? In answering this question, we need to distinguish between a policy and program.

> Policy refers to the general intentions or principles that guide specific actions, such as a program, and may only be inferred from specific legislative acts, statutes, programs, or court decisions. Policy is not implemented; it is the statute or programs that are implemented. (Palumbo, Maynard-Moody, & Wright, 1984, p. 46)

Moreover, it is possible to move toward the achievement of policy goals even if statutory goals are not achieved (Guba, 1985). This is similar to the distinction between the letter and spirit of the law. The letter of the law can be followed faithfully and the spirit still not obeyed.

Quite clearly, goal-free evaluation (Scriven, 1972) seems to be an appropriate model for situations in which goals can change during implementation. Programs never will be deemed successful if evaluation begins with the assumption that originally perceived goals are the only legitimate ones, not only because they will change during implementation, but because there is a question about whose perception we are to use.

The distinction between programmed and adaptive implementation strategies (Berman, 1980) is a version of this problem. Programmed implementation involves

> a well-specified, perhaps completely specified plan that has clear and detailed objectives, clean lines of responsibility and limited participation in policy-making, anticipates various contingencies, and requires minimum discretion for all levels of implementors. (p. 210)

Adaptive implementation, on the other hand,

> allows policy to be modified, specified, and revised—in a word, adapted—according to the unfolding interaction of the policy with its institutional setting. Its outcomes would be neither automatic nor assured, and it would look more like a disorderly learning process than a predictable procedure. (p. 211)

If organizations are loosely coupled systems, then adaptive implementation seems to be not only the best but the only strategy. Berman suggests that most real-life situations require a mixed programmed and adaptive strategy rather than purely one or the other. This is resonant with the notion that organizations have stable, tightly coupled components within the larger, loosely coupled structure (Weick, this volume). For example, a policy concerned with a well-developed technology such as solar energy devices would be predominantly programmed, because the technology is relatively certain, a reasonable consensus exists on the policy's purposes, implementation takes place in a stable environment, and only minor changes are required for implementation. But because the existing users, distributors, and state agencies that regulate solar devices are loosely coupled, implementation of a solar policy would require adaptive strategies.

In an application of the Berman hypothesis to eleven case studies in England, Lewis and Wallace (1984) found that most situations called for an adaptive rather than a programmed implementation strategy. The only possible exception is the case of implementing food standards in the European Economic Community. Food standards, like solar energy devices, involve fairly clear technologies and can therefore be implemented without much change. However, according to Wallace (1984, p. 142), to be realistic in implementing food standards policy, the European Community's commission has

> to recognize that cherished policies need to be skewed and to some extent distorted to carry along different governments with diverse requirements and often contrary interests; this suggests that adaptiveness is the only sensible strategy to pursue.

There are areas that may seem appropriate for a programmed implementation approach: "The traditional comprehensive transportation study is programmed, focused on operations research and systems analysis" (Flyvbjerg, 1984, p. 296-297). However, even here,

> The assumption in the programmed paradigm of a controlled setting for evaluation and implementation does not fit the reality of the decision making environment, which is often turbulent and filled with conflict . . . when priorities have to be set between different transportation modes and when the relationships between transportation and other social

phenomena have to be considered, such a methodology is simply not adequate. (Flyvbjerg, 1984, p. 296-297)

The lessons that evaluation can learn from implementation research can be summarized in the form of nine general axioms:

(1) Government policies are bound to be general in character and tend to be incomprehensible except by reference to practice.
(2) In the world of politics, all policies (even those that involve hard technologies) have multiple objectives.
(3) Those who implement government policies have values of their own and will give meanings that they prefer to the policy.
(4) Conflict is an unavoidable part of policy formulation and implementation.
(5) Implementation is intrinsically an interactive process based on give and take and on trial and error.
(6) Any policymaker, including an implementor, is influenced by the pressures brought to bear on him or her.
(7) The cognitive structure of different levels of the organization is different, and thus the top-level commands must be translated into the cognitive structure of the street level; in the process, meanings get changed.
(8) Ambiguity is a necessity in policymaking, otherwise agreement is not possible. Because implementors are policymakers, ambiguity in implementation also is a necessity.
(9) Because of the ambiguous nature of political language, it is often difficult or impossible to fulfill everyone's expectations simultaneously.

CHANGES IN RESEARCH METHODS

Attempting to apply a programmed implementation strategy in a situation that clearly calls for an adaptive one is as bad as trying to study a complicated implementation process in complex organizations by using cross-sectional, quantitative analysis at one single instant in time. Obviously, only an extremely small portion of reality would be captured through this form of research and, if the research is conducted at the wrong point in the convoluted implementation process, its conclusions will be wrong and misleading. There is no doubt that there must be some resonance between the world being studied and the methods being used to study it. For example, most evaluations are based on the assumption that decision makers analyze the situation first, then act. The assumption is that decision makers, *before they act,* identify goals, specify alternative ways of getting there, assess the alternatives against a standard such as costs and benefits, and then select the best alternative (the rational model). But if organizations in fact do the opposite—if they act first and then analyze what they did—then evaluations based on the rational paradigm will be out of resonance. (Palumbo & Nachmias, 1983, pp. 9-11)

To be effective, evaluations must be based on realistic assumptions about the nature of organizations and the implementation process. Research methods, likewise, must be congruent with the multiple realities of organizations and implementation. This realization is leading to changes in the research paradigms that we use to study and evaluate organizations.

The assumptions underlying the traditional research paradigm have been clearly stated by Przeworski and Teune (1970, p. 4): "This assumption implies that human or social behavior can be explained in terms of general laws established by observations." In doing this, any specific local or historical circumstances in which particular observations are made would be ignored, as they are assumed to have no significance. Przeworski and Teune assert that there can be no bridge between theoretical and historical social science: "Theoretical statements would be formulated in terms devoid of proper names of social systems, whereas historical statements would include such names" (p. 7). The goal of comparative research, they believe, is to substitute names of variables for the names of social systems such as Ghana, the United States, Africa, or Asia. Their reponse to the argument that location is unique is "Social phenomena do not have the property of 'being comparable' or 'not comparable.' Comparability depends upon the level of generality of the language that is applied to express observations" (p. 10). For example, apples and oranges are fruits.

I take the position that this view is not tenable in evaluation and, perhaps, in social science research as well. Trudi Miller (1984) points out that most empirically established relations among variables such as political preference, citizen participation, political party, institutional function, and implementation do hold up over space (across jurisdictions or nations) or over time (across historical stages). She argues that we need models that represent these changes, not ones that try to reach generalizations or "laws" that are immutable. As Miller states,

If, as the literature reviews indicate, cases are diverse and social, and reality is to a large degree constructed by free-thinking humans, then no amount of methodological fussiness can make the old-fashioned natural science approach reflect social reality. (p. 253)

Lee Cronbach (1982) agrees with this position:

All this begins to suggest that general, lasting, definite "laws" are in principle beyond the reach of social science, that sheer empirical generalization is doomed as a research strategy. Extrapolation to new circumstances apparently has to rest on a theoretical argument, one that relies on *qualitative* beliefs about the processes at work in the old and new situations (p. 127).

And the authors in this book agree; Guba writes,

The aim of inquiry is to develop an idiographic body of knowledge. This knowledge is best encapsulated in a series of "working hypotheses" that describe the individual case; differences are as inherently interesting as (and at times more so than) similarities.

If generalizations about "laws" are not possible, what is the alternative? Miller (1984) offers design science as an alternative, which borrows from those fields of science that to some degree create the objects that they study. Computer science is one of these. Owing to science and technology, less of what we observe is controlled by natural law and more is controlled by human law and manipulation of nature. In addition, scientific work is increasingly driven by performance objectives. As a result, the distinction between pure and applied science is a tenuous one at best. Thus, creation of data is a better term than observation for the design sciences. Miller (1984, p. 254) writes,

It follows that the hypotheses of design science are not generalizations or predictions about current behavior, but are assertions that new levels of performance can be attained and diffused under the right conditions . . . the hypotheses of design science are empirical, but they can be supported only in the future.

The assumption underlying design science is that most regularities in attitudes and behavior are assumed to be the products of deliberate moral, intellectual, and political activities. "Being partly man-made," Miller continues, "they change over time, and given variations in conditions and values, they are different from place to place" (p. 254).

Whether it is in the direction of the design sciences approach or naturalistic inquiry as proposed in this book, it is apparent that research methods are, and should be, changing. As is the case with all innovations, there are likely to be a number of changes and reinventions as the new research paradigms are diffused among users. And, as is also the case with all implementation of complex programs, it is impossible to predict all of the consequences and outcomes in this specific innovation. But it is clear that the paradigm revolution has begun, and this book is a harbinger of its approach.

—*Dennis J. Palumbo*
Arizona State University

REFERENCES

Aaronson, D., Dienes, C. T., & Musheno, M. C. (1984). *Public policy and police discretion.* New York: Clark Boardman.

Bardach, E. (1980). *The implementation game.* Cambridge, MA: MIT Press.

Berman, P. (1980). Thinking about programmed and adaptive implementation: Matching strategies to situations. In H. Ingram & D. Mann (Eds.), *Why policies succeed or fail.* Beverly Hills, CA: Sage.

Berry, J. (1984). *Feeding hungry people: Rulemaking in the food stamp program.* New Brunswick, NJ: Rutgers University Press.

Cronbach, L. J. (1982). Prudent aspirations for social inquiry. In W. Kruskal (Ed.), *The social sciences: Their nature and uses.* Chicago: University of Chicago Press.

Dimock, M. E., Dimock, G. O., & Koenig, L. W. (1961). *Public administration.* New York: Holt, Rinehart & Winston.

Doig, J. (1981). *Resources, strategies, and constraints of the policy entrepreneur: Lessons from the (somewhat peculiar) world of public authority.* Unpublished manuscript.

Dunsire, A. (1978). *Implementation in a bureaucracy.* New York: St. Martin's.

Elmore, R. (1982). Backward mapping: Implementation research and policy decisions. In W. Williams (Ed.), *Studying implementation.* Chatham, NJ: Chatham House.

Emery, F., Marek, J., & Trist, E. L. (1965, February). The causal texture of organizational environments. *Human Relations, 18,* 21-32.

Flyvbjerg, B. (1984). Implementation and the choice of evaluation methods. *Transportation Policy Decision Making, 2,* 291-314.

Guba, E. (1985, August). What can happen as a result of a policy? *Policy Studies Review,* 5.

Guba, E., & Lincoln, Y. (1981). *Effective evaluation.* San Francisco: Jossey-Bass.

Hage, J. (1980). *Theories of organizations: Form, process, and transformation.* New York: John Wiley.

Hickson, D. J., Hinings, C. R., Lee, C. A., Schneck, R. E., & Pennings, J. M. (1971, June). A strategic contingencies theory of intraorganization power. *Administrative Science Quarterly, 16,* 216-229.

Kress, G., Koehler, G., & Springer, J. F. (1981). Policy drift: An evaluation of the California business enterprise program. In D. J. Palumbo & M. Harder (Eds.), *Implementing public policy.* Lexington, MA: Lexington Books.

Lewis, D., & Wallace, H. (Eds.). (1984). *Policies into practice.* London: Heinemann.

Lipsky, M. (1980). *Street level bureaucracy.* New York: Russell Sage Foundation.

McCain, L. J., & McCleary, R. (1979). The statistical analysis of the simple interrupted time-series quasi-experiment. In T. D. Cook & D. T. Campbell (Eds.), *Quasi-experimentation.* Chicago: Rand McNally.

McCleary, R., & Musheno, M. C. (1980). Floor effects in the time-series quasi-experiment. *Political Methodology, 7,* 181-203.

Meltsner, A. J., & Bellavita, C. (1983). *The policy organization.* Beverly Hills, CA: Sage.

Miller, T. (1984). Conclusion: A design science perspective. In T. Miller (Ed.), *Public sector performance: A conceptual turning point.* Baltimore: Johns Hopkins University Press.

Musheno, M. C. (1981). On the hazards of selecting intervention points: Time series analyses of mandated policies. In D. J. Palumbo & M. A. Harder (Eds.), *Implementing public policy.* Lexington, MA: Lexington Books.

Nathan, R. (1976, Winter). Food stamps and welfare reform. *Policy Analysis,* p. 64.

Palumbo, D., Maynard-Moody, S., & Wright, P. (1984, February). Measuring degrees of successful implementation: Achieving policy versus statutory goals. *Evaluation Review, 8.*

Palumbo, D., & Nachmias, D. (1983). The preconditions for successful evaluations: Is there an ideal paradigm? *Policy Sciences, 16,* 67-79.

Palumbo, D., & Sharp, E. (1980). Process versus impact evaluation of community corrections. In D. Nachmias (Ed.), *The practice of policy evaluation.* New York: St. Martin's.

Patton, M. Q. (1980). *Qualitative evaluation methods.* Beverly Hills, CA: Sage.

Pressman, J., & Wildavsky, A. (1981). *Implementation* (3rd. ed.). Berkeley: University of California Press.

Przeworski, A., & Teune, H. (1970). *The logic of comparative social inquiry.* New York: John Wiley.

Reichardt, C., & Cook, T. (1979). Beyond qualitative versus quantitative methods. In C. Reichardt & T. Cook (Eds.), *Qualitative and quantitative methods in evaluation research* (pp. 7-33). Beverly Hills, CA: Sage.

Rice, R. E., & Rogers, E. C. (1980). Re-invention and the innovation process. *Knowledge, 1,* 499-515.

Scriven, M. (1972). Pros and cons about goal-free evaluation. *Evaluation Comment, 3,* 1-4.

Siu, R.G.H. (1985). Chinese baseball and public administration. In E. Chelimsky (Ed.), *Program evaluation: Patterns and directions.* Washington, DC: American Society for Public Administration.

Wallace, H. (1984). Implementation across national boundaries. In D. Lewis & H.
    Wallace (Eds.), *Policy into practice* (pp. 129-144). London: Heinemann.
Wildavsky, A. (1980). *Speaking truth to power.* Boston: Little, Brown.
Yin, R. (1979). *Changing urban bureaucracies.* Lexington, MA: Lexington Books.

PREFACE

This book grew out of a conference jointly sponsored in November 1983, by the University Council for Educational Administration's Career Development Program, the Center for Public Affairs, a public policy research institute at the University of Kansas, and the University's School of Education and Department of Educational Policy and Administration. The virtually overwhelming requests for copies of the papers that each of the authors provided was a sound indicator that members of the administrative, managerial, and research communities wanted, desired, hoped that they might participate in creating and understanding the new world of organizational theory and new-paradigm inquiry.

The circumstances that led to the conference were remarkably simple, considering the subsequent desire of others to have been involved. An extended conversation between David L. Clark, Egon Guba, and myself about the resonances between the "new" organizational theory and emergent paradigm research prompted Dave to ask, "Why don't you front for a conference that'll explore those issues?" I rushed in where men and women of sterner stuff would have faltered, and a long series of conversations began which moved inexorably toward one of the most profitable symposia of our careers.

Major and abiding support came, of course, from Egon Guba, my husband and colleague. He not only suggested ways in which I might organize the original symposium (and saw me through the endless gritty details of such an enterprise), he also collaborated in the shaping of our two chapters and the extension of our earlier work. Each of those conference papers, now chapters, was the product of a mutual thought process which guided our development of those and later ideas. As each new period of growth in our ideas has arrived, the ideas have become inseparable in the sense that neither of us remembers where the original ideas were born.

The symposium would have been impossible, of course, without the aid and abettance of Charles L. Willis, then Executive Director of the

University Council for Educational Administration (UCEA) and
Dennis Palumbo, then Director of the Center for Public Affairs (CPA).
Both these men believed that what was going to be said was powerful
and anticipatory of the new world of organizational theory and inquiry
paradigms.

But thanks are due to others, too, some of whom intuitively
understand their contributions and know how much I and the others
appreciate them, and others who have no idea of what their contributions might be. Among the colleagues who contributed were not only
our American counterparts and persons who attended the conference
(and asked hard and relentless questions), but also colleagues abroad, in
England and Scotland, many of whom are consciously or unconsciously
inventing new metaphors and similes for describing a world we think we
see but "through a glass darkly" still. These colleagues, both British and
and American, are not just academics inventing jargon; they are men
and women of intense purpose who are struggling to capture poetic,
emotive, expressive portrayals of the "future we are rehearsing," as
David Hamilton has termed it.

In fact, a semester's sabbatical in Great Britain afforded me the
opportunity to recreate for myself what this new world might look like.
The interactions and scholarly exchanges with my British colleagues—
among whom were Maureen Pope, John Nichols, Michael Watts,
Andrew McPherson, Peter Cuttance, Doug Wilms, Barry MacDonald,
David Reynolds, and David Hamilton—in fact, created new intellectual
discontinuities for me. Those discontinuities were to lead to some new
metaphors of my own. David Hamilton's comment that the new
organizational theory, and the new paradigm of inquiry to support
research into it, were a "whole new ball game" is instructive, although
only partially correct. It is not a whole new ball game in the same sense
that "Trivial Pursuit" is a new form of family or friendship parlor game.
It is, rather, a whole new ball game in the sense that *it is several ball
games at once, all of them on the same field.* To build on Karl Weick's
earlier metaphor of the soccer game, which reappears several times in
the chapters here, it is not that the field slopes, or even that it's the only
ball game in town, or that people enjoy their season's tickets for the right
to play or to cheer on the home team. It is the stunning recognition that
what is going on on that sloped field is not a whole new ball game, but
several ball games at once, each "team" playing by its own propositional
and tacit rules, occasionally switching when it appears that there is more
"action" in another game, or when the scoring is more favorable, with
players taking "time outs" at will to study the rules of the other games

(insofar as they can understand what is the guiding framework for the other game), and referees calling players in each of the games out-of-bounds at their discretion. For some of the players the object of the game is to have their team declared the only players on the field, the legitimate "team." For others the object is simply to be recognized as one of the competitors. For still others "winning" simply means not being called out-of-bounds by referees. But all teams compete for space on the playing field, which also has arbitrary boundaries, and the competition for space means that there are bumps and jolts at virtually every intersection. The game is the paradigmatic equivalent of an intellectual fender-bender.

The teams have names, although they do not wear uniforms, so unless you know the players, you don't know for which teams they might play. The teams have been named by Dave Clark: the orthodoxists or traditionalists, the neo-orthodoxists, and the nonorthodoxists. Furthermore, within these three teams there are further divisions, including cognitive psychologists, neo-Marxists, critical theorists, and post-positivists. The fan in the stands is hard pressed to know who is playing whom, or what the winning score might be.

And the point is not just that there is a new ball game, or too many games on the field. The point also is that metaphors that come from other arenas of our lives have power to suggest ways of talking about what it is we think we see. Hamilton's comment on hearing about this book fed into earlier readings of organizational theory, including the now-famous soccer metaphor of Weick's, and also into a more general cultural understanding: that of the role of sports in Western cultures in general. We often use team and game metaphors to explain what it is we think all human organizations do, or ought to do: "not a team player" (read: belongs in individual, i.e., nonteam, entrepreneurial—sports); "part of the game plan" (read: what it is we think we're doing); "dropped the ball" (read: didn't do his or her part of what it is we thought we were doing); "way off base" (read: you obviously misunderstood what it was we were supposed to be doing); "strictly left field" (read: still doesn't understand what it is we want him or her to do); and others.

So it is not inappropriate that we should sound like sports fans, although it will be clear that others throughout this book sound more like poets, or novelists (constructing stories out of intuitive understandings of human nature), or soldiers under fire (leap before you look). The particular metaphors and similes one uses grow as much from one's own cultural context as from a desire for intellectual precision. Some metaphors are more powerful than others because of their wide cultural sharing. The exploration of varying perspectives on organizational theory (e.g., the neo-Marxists, the radical feminists, and the constructivist psychologists) led to other metaphors, some more and some less powerful. As some of them are shared by the authors of chapters in this book, they will come clear to the reader. Others will appear in whatever follows this book. But for all their evocative metaphors, for all their willingness to search for new descriptors, my British colleagues are to be thanked.

But not all the persons who contributed to the writing of this book were academics. Some of them were working-class Scottish men and women who gave warm acceptance to this "American professor," whole, honest, and abiding friendship, and a particularly wry Scots humor as I shared their pub in my search for sea legs in another culture on another continent. Their pointed, plainspoken, "untutored" questions at my explanations of what I was doing there added clarity and direction to my work. There is no experience quite as humbling as "explaining" academic research to a group of working-class people who are nevertheless avid and discerning readers of good newspapers and even better literature. Their questions are as bracing as a slap, even while framed in a kinship circle of mutual regard and respect.

Their humor and jokes often took the edge off a frustrating search for new means of expressing what the new organizational theory and inquiry might look like. Shulamit Reinharz proposes that research should be "unalienated labor." By this, she (and I) means that it ought to be hard work, but hard work that has power to draw one back to it again and again. Framing the "takes" of this book, shooting scenes, and trying to edit them into a moving picture of the future was satisfying, although each of us must feel more like directors of home movies than full-fledged creators of enduring works of art. Our *leit-motifs* and symbols may not be "right" yet; they may not work after a few years or a decade. But together, we are creating the new world of research into administration, and the debt we owe to one another, and to others who did not get named here, is enormous, for their visions have enlarged and sharpened our own.

Other thanks, too, go to ever-patient and ever-cheerful Carlene Cobb and her staff in the word processing center of the School of Education at the University of Kansas. 1984 and 1985 have to have been her least favorite years in that job, as she prepared the papers for the original UCEA Career Development Symposium, the book before this one on emergent-paradigm (naturalistic) inquiry, and now this one. Never has her spirit or courtesy faltered, even though there must clearly have been days when she wished I would take a job elsewhere. In fact, she did one smiling day invite me to go back to Scotland, for which we both laughed wryly. Even though organizational theory is not what it used to be, there are still some eternal verities; among them, laughter is the best medicine.

No number of acknowledgments, however, can possibly repay the debts that go into a book like this. For those who have read parts of it and made comments, thanks. For those who have "written" parts of it—in conversations, in personal correspondence, sharing ideas—the world that's coming is your world, too. But it is finally to four people that the book is dedicated: to one who believed in me as a professional, and said so; to one who had an eerie vision of me that I did not at first recognize, but that has satisfyingly been realized; to one who believes I should have this on my own floppy disks; and to one who shares his own professional disasters and triumphs in a friendship of nearly a quarter of a century.

To

J.H.R.

J.D.R.

J.M.R. and

J.T.R.

Yvonna S. Lincoln
University of Kansas

GUINDON   BY RICHARD GUINDON

Vicki the chimp, using language cards, is telling
a researcher that she is an existentialist. But in
reality she is a logical positivist.

1

INTRODUCTION

Yvonna S. Lincoln

Paradigm. It is such a popular word that to ask what, exactly, it means has become rather *de trop*, as though one should know already.

Paradigms, as defined by Webster's New Collegiate Dictionary, Second Edition, are models or patterns. This is hardly an adequate definition, however, considering what meanings usually attach and what meanings we would like to attach in the following papers.

Michael Patton goes a bit farther. Patton (1975, p. 9) defines a paradigm as

> a world view, a general perspective, a way of breaking down the complexity of the real world. As such, paradigms are deeply embedded in the socialization of adherents and practitioners telling them what is important, what is legitimate, what is reasonable. Paradigms are normative; they tell the practitioner what to do without the necessity of long existential or epistemological considerations.

It is this pervasive, engaged quality that focuses more completely the meaning of paradigm. A paradigm is much more than a model or pattern; it is a view of the world—a *Weltanschauung*—that reflects our most basic beliefs and assumptions about the human condition, whether or not there is any such thing as "sin," what is real, what is true, what is beautiful, and what is the nature of things.

But the pervasiveness of paradigms also carries with it dangers, as Patton (1975, p. 9) also points out:

But it is this aspect of a paradigm that constitutes both its strength *and* its weakness—its strength in that it makes action possible, its weakness in that the very reason for action is hidden in the unquestioned assumptions of the paradigm.

Thomas Berry, approaching the problem from a cultural perspective, sees the world in a crisis at this point. In a 1978 volume of *Anima*, he observed:

It's all a question of story. We are in trouble just now because we do not have a good story. We are in between stories. The Old Story—the account of how the world came to be and how we fit into it—is not functioning properly, and we have not learned the New Story. The Old Story sustained us for a long period of time. It shaped our emotional attitudes, provided us with a life purpose, energized action. It consecrated suffering, integrated knowledge, guided education. We awoke in the morning and knew where we were. We could answer the questions of our children. We could identify crime, punish criminals. Everything was taken care of because the story was there. It did not make men good, it did not take away the pains and stupidities of life, or make for unfailing warmth in human association. But it did provide a context in which life could function in a meaningful manner.

Each of us lives with several paradigms at any given time. We share a legal or adversarial paradigm, whether we have actually ever been in the courts or not. We have consented to—or violently disagreed with—judgmental paradigms in everyday life: We do or do not like the Olympic winners last year; we do or do not believe that one boxer should have earned a middleweight championship title over a technical knock-out call; we savor wines that the connoisseurs have called "fruity," "complex," and "mellow"; and the like. In our own organizations—schools, for instance—we have tried to make sense of the population figures that represent a demographic paradigm, and we try to project what mobility might mean to school budgets. And we grapple with theological paradigms: What is the nature of God? Is there a God? And how does the Judeo-Christian heritage inform our moral and intimate relationships?

As it appears appropriate, each of us moves in and out of paradigms throughout any work day, and with scarcely a thought about the belief and value systems that undergird them.

So long as belief systems are widely shared in our culture, the culture appears to others as integrated, holistic, directed, and internally consistent. When belief systems begin to fall apart, however, cultures become fragmented, disintegrated, undirected, and at odds with themselves.

This book is about two vast—and still largely underground— paradigm shifts. It is an examination of the scope and sequence of a revolution, a disciplinary and epistemological falling away. It is a form of what Gregory Bateson called "deutero-learning," learning about how we believe we can learn. It is about the fragmentation and disintegration of faith in old assumptions and substantive constructs, and the exploration of new beliefs about what we can see (since seeing is believing and believing is seeing). It is also about dissatisfaction, a quiet unease with the old solutions, the old unanswered questions, and the old and largely incomplete pictures we have formed as a culture and within our respective disciplines.

The next chapters seek to draw links between substantive or disciplinary shifts, and shift in epistemological and methodological assumptions. Specifically, of the two forms of paradigm with which this book is concerned, one is a disciplinary paradigm, concerned with organizational theory and the alteration of fundamental beliefs about the nature of organizations. The other is a paradigm of disciplined inquiry, concerned with how we explore the world, how it is we come to systematize or order knowledge about the world, and what methods might be most appropriate for accomplishing that end.

THE NATURE OF PARADIGMATIC BELIEFS

Paradigms are shaped by sets of beliefs. When those beliefs exist in a public and formal (as opposed to personal and informal) set, they are called axioms and theorems. The more formal the system of beliefs, the more one is likely to call its set of assumptions axiomatic. Formal philosophy is ordered just this way. So is mathematics. So also are the principles of Newtonian physics.

The set of axioms one adopts at any given time depends on what one is inspecting. So, for instance, the principles of right reason from philosophy are virtually useless with quantum mechanics. Likewise, the principles of Olympic gymnastics competition judging inform criminal proceedings very little. An example often used is that of geometries, to which everyone has been exposed. The axioms that make up Euclidian geometry have served us well for several millenia here on earth—where it is useful to have triangles with interior angles of 180°, and where all lines are straight (or at least where we might pretend they are straight). Turn those axioms on their heads, however, and you have what appears to be nonsense. Who could use triangles whose interior angles only approached 180° as the triangles got smaller? What if the shortest distance between two points were not a straight line, but a curved one, or several thousand of them? What could one do with a geometry with such axioms?

The quick answer is this: You can put people on the moon with such a geometry—which is called Lobatchevskian—and you can bring them back home again. The point is *fit*. Euclid's is the axiomatic set of choice in some instances and other geometries are the sets of choice when you have other kinds of problems to solve.

There is another kind of world view that is undergoing change, and the following papers will argue that we need to move to some new geometries—geometries, if you will, of human organization and inquiries. We need new ways of seeing organizations and we need new ways of exploring what our new visions might be like.

In empirical terms, we are moving from a positivist era to a postpositivist era. This is an era of transition and transformation. The old stories of how we came to know are no longer serviceable, but we don't have the new story in place quite yet. The new stories, however, are evident in dozens of formal disciplines. Peter Schwartz and James Ogilvy at the Stanford Research Institute have tracked the emergence of a new paradigm through years of exploring how and in what ways formal disciplines are changing. These two men have provided an analysis of ideas that are receiving serious attention and that are changing such fields as physics and quantum mechanics, chemistry, brain theory, ecology, evolutionary theory, mathematics, philosophy, politics, psychology, linguistics, religion and religious studies, the study of consciousness, and the arts. Several examples that are diametrically opposed to the dominant paradigm should serve to demonstrate the kinds of changes Schwartz and Ogilvy are tracking.

physics: Heisenberg's Indeterminacy Principle is enough in itself to break down the idea of the neutral observer. This principle states that at the submicroscopic level any act of measurement disturbs the thing being studied. We now know that there are "particles that refuse to behave as simple particles, domains that refuse to be reduced into one another."

chemistry: Ilya Prigogine's theory of dissipative structures demonstrates that fluctuations in a system are not merely random errors or deviations from the significant average; instead, these disturbances or fluctuations are sometimes the source of a new order. To understand the importance of this Nobel prize-winning theory, it is necessary to know that in traditional and classical equilibrium theory, fluctuations are "deviations that become damped toward a statistical average." In Prigogine's theory, "fluctuations become the essential element leading to dynamics, change and evolution."

mathematics: Rene Thom's catastrophe theory is a good example of a paradigm shift, because it entertains not continuous but discontinuous phenomena, and because it has ability to describe not quantitative but qualitative change.

biology: The old Darwinian notions are giving way to more complex, interactive models of evolution that depend on mutually causal processes. Then, too, biology has added the concept—unknown in ecological biology prior to the 1950s—of resilience in ecosystems, as opposed to stability. Resilience turns out to be a more useful term in that it results from adequate diversity, mutually supportive relationships, and open systems. The implication, of course, is that a "survivable ecosystem is not necessarily one that is stable."

political theory: A shift can be noted between the ancient paradigm of down-from-the-top author. *j*—also once known as the divine right of kings (and such a model still prevails in totalitarian regimes)—to a new social contract. Today, "the sources of political legitimacy cannot be traced to any singular origin, whether a divine authority or a natural order. Instead, legitimacy derives from the tacit contracts forged in relationships among the governed."

linguistics: The radical work of Saussure is a good example. Saussure demonstrated that words did not derive their meaning from their sound (which is called atomism), but rather from their "relational context within an entire language," or their location within that context. This new linguistic paradigm we call structuralism (Schwartz & Ogilvy, 1979).

I hope this list of examples, although incomplete, will serve to help convince the reader that there is a revolution going on out there. By extension, we will argue there is another field undergoing a revolution, and that is organizational theory.

This paradigm shift to which Schwartz and Ogilvy refer involves seven radical moves in the "map" of realilty with which most of Western society operates.

In analyzing the paradigm shifts in all of these disciplines, Schwartz and Ogilvy make clear that the paradigms are not inquiry paradigms (about which we will be talking later), but rather paradigms characterizing whole world views. In their analysis they have abstracted seven major characteristics of the new paradigm. These seven are important because they fly in the face of the dominant scientific paradigm, and they will appear in slightly different form again and again in the following chapters.

The first shift is from a simple and probabilistic world toward a view of reality that is *complex and diverse*. We have treated our world as a series of elements and processes that could be reduced to laws about their relationships and elements. We have behaved as if the world were simply additive; that is, complex elements were simply aggregations of much simpler entities.

We are now beginning to understand that systems are not merely the sum of more simple units; they are separate entities that possess idiosyncratic, dynamic, and unique properties all their own.

The second shift is from a hierarchically ordered world to a world ordered by *heterarchy*. Our belief that the old order was hierarchical, indeed pyramidal, and based on a "pecking order" of natural and social laws is rapidly giving way to a belief that there is not one set or order, but several or a plurality. The key words here are interactive influence, mutual constraints, simultaneous interests. Which order is dominant at any given time depends on a number of shifting and interactive factors.

The third shift is from the image of mechanistic and machine-like universe toward one that is *holographic*. The push-pull, single-action conception of the world is clearly more complex than levers and inclined planes could indicate. Moving toward the metaphor of the hologram, we begin to recognize a world—one that we already know is complex and heterarchic—that is the creation of constant differentiation and interaction. As Schwartz and Ogilvy (1979, p. 14) point out, "everything is interconnected like a vast network of interference patterns," each part containing information about the whole.

The holograph is important as a metaphor because of a unique property it possesses. If a normal recording or film has some part erased or clipped out, that portion of the film is gone forever. Not so with the holograph. In holography, even when large sections of the recorded laser interference patterns are lost, the remaining pieces contain complete information about the whole and can be used to reproduce the original image in its entirety and in three dimensions. The power of this metaphor is that every piece contains complete information about the whole. This is a particularly powerful concept when considering, for instance, genetic materials, in which a single cell is said to contain information about the entire organism, or in organizations, in which information about some subunit might provide information regarding the whole operation.

The fourth shift in world view is from the image of a determinate universe to that of an *indeterminate* one. The world as we know it, particularly the social world, is simply not predictable or controllable, even in the most sophisticated mathematical models. Witness the mess in attempting to predict economic behavior or money markets. The implication of such a shift is that future states of complex systems are not determinate or predictable. The future is ambiguous, and the condition or nature of things only in part knowable as a result of our choices.

The fifth shift is from an assumption of direct causality to the assumption of *mutual causality*. Most causal models proceeding from positivistic philosophies postulate some variety of an "if-then" notion of causal relationships. That is, the relationship between an action and an outcome is linear. Mutual causality implies that there is a symbiosis and a nonlinearity in systems such that A and B cannot be separated into simple cause and effect relationships. They grow, evolve, or otherwise change "in such a way as to make the distinction between cause and effect meaningless" (Schwartz & Ogilvy, 1979, p. 14).

The sixth shift in paradigms is reflected in the move away from the metaphor of assembly—that is, of construction of complex systems from a series of more simple units—toward the metaphor of *morphogenesis*. Morphogenesis describes the creation of a new form. The best example of morphogenesis in the physical sciences is the process of creation of planetary systems and stars from galactic garbage—elements that are in part identifiable, but whose identity give no clue as to what the new configuration will be like. They act mutually and symbiotically to constrain the makeup of the new form, but they do not allow us to predict what the new form will be. In order for morphogenesis to occur, we need most of the previous six elements: diversity, complexity, indeterminacy, openesss, and nonlinear causality.

Finally, the seventh shift is from one of pure objectivity—the posture that has been thought to characterize the scientist or researcher—to a posture that is *perspectival*. We finally have understood that it is impossible to be neutral—or objective—about our investigations, our experiments, our methods, or our rational processes. Objectivity as a pursuit in empirical investigations turns out to be a chimera, a Holy Grail, an illusion, and a snare. Subjectivity, however, is not the appropriate or only alternative. The concept of perspective may be more useful, as it implies multiple views of the same phenomenon, multiple foci that may be brought to bear, and multiple realities that are constructed of the same phenomenon. Schwartz and Ogilvy (1979, p. 16) link the term perspective with engagement:

> To know something requires engagement with it so that it is seen in the context of our concerns, and multiple perspectives so that we are not blinded by our own biases. This acknowledgement of the inescapability of perspective is very different from the attempt to gain objectivity by abstracting from all perspectives.

The six chapters that follow will argue that there is a new world. It has a story of its own, the New Story. But, in part, we are so blinded by the Old Story, by our attachment to it, and by the security it provides, that we are not hearing clearly the New Story. The authors argue that there is a paradigm shift occurring in two areas: the organizational theory paradigm and the inquiry or empirical paradigm—the one that tells us how to arrive at what we hope to be "truth." What the authors seek to demonstrate is that the two shifts are occurring alongside one another and that, furthermore, they are joined in such a way that the mutual shifting exhibits consonance, congruence, fit, sympathy, and power. We call this intellectual and methodological fit *value-resonance*. The structure of the chapters can best be shown by this "map" of the territory (see Table 1.1).

The rationale for the schematic is this:

(1) *Levels* represent the normal inductive/deductive pathway from paradigm through methods to application, and back again. As we learn from application we refine the methods and then the paradigm; and as we rethink the paradigm we tease out new implications for methods and operations.

(2) *Focus* represents the nature of the elements normally dealt with at each level. Paradigm sets the *context* of assumptions for the inquiry (these are often implicit; but as we think, so do we act); method describes the guiding operational *concepts*, and application delineates the actual activities in which researchers are engaged.

(3) *Areas* are the substantive arenas considered; for this volume, these are organizational theory and inquiry processes, but they could as well be any two others; for example, any one of the substantive or disciplinary arenas explored by Schwartz and Ogilvy.

TABLE 1.1
Schematic of the Arguments

Level	*The Six Thematic Chapters*		
	Focus	*Area*	
		Organizational Theory	*Inquiry Processes*
Paradigmatic	Context	Clark ⟷	Guba
Methodological	Concepts	Weick ⟷	Lincoln
Application	Practice	Huff ⟷	Skrtic
	Concluding Chapter		

(4) *Fit* is indicated by the arrows between rows and columns:
  (a) ⟷ = *congruence* (resonance) between organizational theory and inquiry processes at each level.
  (b) ↕ = *consistency* (logical) between levels in each area.

Part I, the context of the paradigm revolution, allows Clark and Guba to set the stage for the revolution. Clark's chapter traces the history of contemporary organizational theory from Weber to the present, tracing research on organizations as bureaucracies (largely ideal forms of organizations that Weber thought *ought to exist* more than he found existing) to accommodationist efforts that had as their basis the attempt to make sense of organizational forms that were not Weberian. Increased and increasing attempts to adapt the dominant paradigm and research on organizations that fit the two sets of constructs less and less comfortably, Clark argues, have led to the revolution in progress. The three sets of researchers, whose ideological positions are cast as orthodox (dominant-paradigm), neo-orthodox (transitional dominant paradigm), and nonorthodox (emergent-paradigm), exist in a state of polite but fierce competition, as they wage war for the axiomatic souls of their students, adherents, and journal space.

Guba undertakes a different task. His aim is a challenge to the philosophical underpinnings of the orthodox and neo-orthodox (or positivist) inquiry traditions. Utilizing both a dominant-paradigm construction of inquiry axioms and the Schwartz and Ogilvy research (to which this chapter has alluded), he argues for a rejection of conventional scientific inquiry's axioms and an acceptance of inquiry axioms (emergent postpositivistic or "naturalistic" paradigm) that both exhibit greater fit with the phenomena under investigation (which are largely, but not necessarily, social and behavioral) and under which most of social science is currently operating. For instance, in reviewing the Schwartz and Ogilvy characteristics of belief systems, he points out that both the natural (or "hard") sciences and the social sciences have experienced moves that are consonant with emergent-paradigm inquiry and that are rejecting of traditional and conventional scientific inquiry. Thus, the state of near-chaos in the inquiry world is due to shifts in both behaviors and assumptions, without the concomitant public recognition of shifts at the formal and epistemological level. The shift has been made already; what remains is the proposal of an alternative set of axioms that appear to have utility. That is what Guba undertakes, both here and elsewhere (Lincoln & Guba, 1985).

Part II revolves about the newest constructs and concepts, the terminology of the two revolutions. Karl Weick, in "Sources of Order in Underorganized Systems: Themes in Recent Organizational Theory," introduces the motifs of the paradigmatic shift. His introduction of the newer constructs by means of metaphor helps to capture the sense of a search that does not as yet have the descriptions of what it searches for in commonly agreed upon language. The search for order, the need for categorizing and assigning knowledge to some place in a system is present, too. How do we talk about what goes on in organizations—profit concerns or nonprofit organizations such as schools—without thinking of the activities in sets, in some kinds of clumps that make sense, in a language form in which we can agree on the rules? If we cannot attempt that activity yet with precise words and meanings, then it is possible to work around that issue with metaphors, for which the rules guiding their usage are freer, more poetic, and more visually oriented.

The second chapter, "The Substance of the Emergent Inquiry Paradigm: Implications for Researchers," takes up the question of what adopting a new axiomatic set for inquiry might mean in the actual performing of research tasks.

> Quantitative methodologies assume the possibility, desirability and even necessity of applying some underlying empirical standard to social phenomena . . . [and] there has arisen a concerted and widespread effort to formally test nomothetic propositions . . . [so] that theorizing on the basis of such data collection procedures becomes the principal duty of researchers. (Rist, 1977, p. 43)

In light of Rist's statement, what can it mean to discard the old axioms and their need for quantitative methodologies and embrace a new axiomatic set with their attendant reliance on (indeed, demand of) qualitative methodologies? It is argued that making certain epistemological choices (that is, buying into one set of beliefs or another) imposes certain other "postures" on researchers; that is, the set of beliefs itself prescribes that certain other choices be made in order for the inquiry to be internally consistent. Some of the implications of that choice process are laid out for inspection and discussion.

Part III treats the applications of such a set of beliefs to the results of inquiry. What might be the products of inquiry, and what is their utility, when conducted under a new set of beliefs? Anne Sigismund Huff, in the chapter entitled "Managerial Implications of the Emerging Paradigm," tries to demonstrate the kinds of knowledge and understandings toward which researchers aim in administrative inquiry. The richness and depth of case examples she provides, largely from the offices of big city superintendents, lends credence to the assertion that different paradigms and different methods evidence power in helping us to "see" what has always been there, but what we could not "see" with the old lenses.

Finally, Thomas Skrtic, in his chapter "Doing Naturalistic Research into Educational Organizations," illustrates how the axiological, epistemological, ontological, and methodological bases of naturalistic (emergent paradigm) inquiry came to be operationalized in a national, multisite, complex study of the implementation of the Education for All Handicapped Children Act (P.L. 94-142) in rural school districts and intermediate education agencies. This study, the first done using naturalistic inquiry as explicated by Guba and Lincoln (1981, 1982) and Lincoln and Guba (1985), adhered (insofar as was possible to test) to the axioms of naturalistic inquiry, and followed procedures for building and maintaining trustworthiness (a term analogous to the dominant paradigm usage of the term "rigor") and for negotiating the results of the study with stakeholding audiences and research respondents. Problems with conducting and interpreting the research are discussed in such a way that the reader can both understand policy implications and, at the same time, join the early debate regarding robustness of procedures.

REFERENCES

Berry, T. (1978). Comments on the origin, identification and transmission of values. *Anima* (Winter).

Guba, E. G., & Lincoln, Y. S. (1981). *Effective evaluation*. San Francisco: Jossey-Bass.

Guba, E. G., & Lincoln, Y. S. (1982). Epistemological and methodological bases of naturalistic inquiry. *Educational Communications and Technology Journal, 30*, 233-252.

Lincoln, Y. S., & Guba, E. G. (1985). *Naturalistic inquiry*. Beverly Hills, CA: Sage.

Patton, M. Q. (1975). *Alternative evaluation research paradigm*. Grand Forks: University of North Dakota Press.

Rist, R. C. (1977). On the relations among educational research paradigms: From disdain to detente. *Anthropology and Education Quarterly, 8*, 42-49.

Schwartz, P., & Ogilvy, J. (1979). *The emergent paradigm: Changing patterns of thought and belief* (Analytic Report 7, Values and Lifestyle Program). Menlo Park, CA: SRI International.

PART I

The Context of the Paradigmatic Shift

2

EMERGING PARADIGMS
IN ORGANIZATIONAL THEORY AND RESEARCH

David L. Clark

A colleague of mine once described the discipline of organizational behavior as "lay preaching." The phrase is particularly apt. The gospel that has been preached has been one of individual, proactive, foresightful choice. It is, indeed, a gospel that resonates nicely with many of the gospels espoused by the nonlay preachers. Most of its practitioners either do not recognize or do not acknowledge the extent to which values and ideas permeate their theory and empirical research. Thus, it is almost unintentional, accidental, and certainly not ordained preaching. The problem comes when we dress up lay preaching in scientific clothes, claiming for our theories and research an objectivity—and, hence, an unassailability—that simply belies the facts (Pfeffer, 1982, pp. 293-294).

INTRODUCTION

If ever a preacher fitted a time, Max Weber fit the search for order, rationality, and scientific legitimacy that characterized the post-World War II social and behavioral science community in the United States. The translation of his works into English in 1947 coincided with the emergence of an almost religious faith that the problems of humankind were susceptible to direct attack by social scientists; a faith supported for nearly twenty years by expanding federal investments in research and a growing body of empirical and theoretical research literature.

Contemporary, sophisticated treatises on organizational theory seldom refer to Weber or his propositions except by brief historical notation. The assumption seems to have been made that Weber's work has been rendered obsolete by the modifications, additions, and transpositions of the theorists that have followed him. That is an error, for the heritage of Weberian assumptions is an impediment burdening the field of organizational theory and practice just as surely as the heritage of the positivist paradigm is obstructing the creation of new paradigms for inquiry.

In this chapter I will revisit the original Weberian treatise; examine the inheritance from that paradigm; describe briefly how a new generation of researchers and theorists refined and expanded the paradigm; note some emerging perspectives that are anti-Weberian; and relate each of these topics to the emergent paradigm that Schwartz and Ogilvy (1979) argue is detectable in a variety of substantive disciplines.

WEBER: THE PARADIGM BUILDER

Max Weber was a social scientist with a broad brush stroke. He was a social historian who dealt with the decline of the Roman Empire, the sociology of religion, the Protestant ethic and the spirit of capitalism, and general economic history. Among his varied topical interests were types of authority and patterns of coordination. Within his interest in types of authority lay his special curiosity about bureaucracy, as its claim to legitimacy as a type of authority rested on rational grounds. This rational source of authority was critical to Weber as, as Parsons (1947, pp. 12-13) observed, Weber linked

> the methodological problems of science with the substantive problems of rationality of action. The rational ideal type thus probably appealed to him precisely because the normative patterns of rationality, since they were defined by the role of scientifically verifiable knowledge, directly embodied this element of generality in the determinants of action. . . . Thus it was that Weber, in his formulations of systematic theory, concentrated overwhelmingly on rational ideal types.

Interpreters of Weber's writings on bureaucratic theory have emphasized his position as a social historian. They note that his description
of bureaucratic organizations portrays an ideal type that he never
anticipated would be discovered in "pure" form. The type, in effect, was
a template for comparative analysis that allowed for the study of
individual cases. Although Weber did not expect to discover a pure
bureaucratic form in operation, he was, if not an open advocate of
bureaucracy, at least more than a disinterested social observer:

> Experience tends universally to show that the purely bureaucratic type of
> administrative organization—that is, the monocratic variety of bureau-
> cracy—is, from a purely technical point of view, capable of attaining the
> highest degree of efficiency and is in this sense formally the most rational
> known means of carrying out imperative control over human beings. It is
> superior to any other form in precision, in stability, in the stringency of its
> discipline, and in its reliability. (Parsons, 1947, p. 337)

Weber's enthusiasm for bureaucracy can be understood in the
context of his time. He was viewing its rationality, efficiency, and
reliability in contrast to feudalism, with its foundation in charismatic
authority. Weber did agonize over the potential negative effects of
bureaucratization, from its tendency to routinize activities to its
likelihood of depersonalization of the work force. Although Weber
seems at times to vacillate between the roles of advocate and prog-
nosticator, there is no doubt about his view of bureaucracy as inevitable,
pervasive, and the best available alternative. Is bureaucracy a major
development? "Its development is . . . the most crucial phenomenon of
the modern Western state." Are there alternatives? "However many
forms there may be which do not appear to fit this pattern . . . and
however much people may complain about the 'evils of bureaucracy,' it
would be sheer illusion to think for a moment that continuous
administrative work can be carried out in any field except by means of
officials working in offices." Is it the natural order of things? "The whole
pattern of everyday life is cut to fit this framework." Is it necessary? "The
choice is only that between bureaucracy and dilletantism in the field of
administration" (Parsons, 1947, p. 337).

Any world view possesses characteristics that believers cannot
ignore. It is omnipresent. No matter how narrow its intellectual origins,
the effect is "worldwide" (e.g., the most crucial phenomenon of the
Western state). Its assertions and consequences are aphoristic (e.g., it is

sheer illusion to conceive of administrative work being carried on outside the form). It is the "natural" order of things. There are no rational alternatives (e.g., the irrational alternative is dillentantism).

Weber did not expect to see historical instances of his monocratic bureaucracy in pure form, but he was committed personally to approach the ideal. While granting the difficulty of attaining excellence in bureaucratic performance, Weber viewed divergence from the ideal type as pathological, irrational, unnatural. Weber's language makes clear that he believes the burden of proof for deviation from the "pure" bureaucratic form lies on the head of the deviate.

Weber's disciples adopted his language, his portrayal of a well-functioning bureaucracy, and his world view. And his disciples ranged far and wide across the spectrum of practicing administrators, trainers of administrators, researchers, and theoreticians. The Weberian view was adopted less because of the writings of Weber than because it fit the predispositions of the adopters. Active inquirers and theorists in the United States and Great Britain were pursuing Weberian lines of inquiry in the 1920s and 1930s, when most of them were unfamiliar with his work. Weber's fascination with rationality fit the problem-solving model of the administrator and the positivist bent of the social scientist. His support of rational-legal authority, his linkage of capitalism and ascetic Protestantism, and the juxtaposition of his view against the Marxian view set the stage for the use of his ideas as a post hoc justification of a comfortable world view that has dominated administrative studies and practice in one form or another up to this date.

THE ELEMENTS OF THE PARADIGM

Weber's bureaucracy rested on rational grounds; that is, "a belief in the 'legality' of patterns of normative rules and the right of those elevated to authority under such rules to issue commands" (Parsons, 1947, p. 328). His "fundamental categories of rational legal authority" included the following:

(1) A continuous organization of official functions bound by rules.
(2) A specified sphere of competence, for example,
    (a) a systematic division of labor;
    (b) necessary authority to carry out functions;
    (c) definition of the necessary means of compulsion.

(3) The principle of hierarchy of offices.
(4) Rules regulating the conduct of offices.
(5) Separation of the administrative staff from ownership of the means of production.
(6) Absence of the appropriation of the official position by the incumbent.
(7) Decisions, rules, and administrative acts recorded in written form (Parsons, 1947, pp. 330-332).

His depiction of the exercise of this legal authority was as follows:

(1) Officials organized in a clearly defined hierarchy of offices.
(2) Officials subject to authority only with respect to official obligations.
(3) Each office with a clearly defined sphere of competence in a legal sense.
(4) Free selection of officials for offices.
(5) Candidates appointed on the basis of technical qualifications, by examination or diplomas certifying technical training.
(6) Remuneration by fixed salaries graded according to rank and a form of lifelong employment (N.B.: Weber noted, "Only under certain circumstances does the employing authority . . . have a right to terminate the employment, but the official is always free to resign" [Parsons, 1947, p. 334]).
(7) The office is a career. Promotion is based on seniority or achievement or both. Achievement is judged by superiors.
(8) The official is subject to strict and systematic discipline and control in the conduct of his or her office (Parsons, 1947, pp. 333-334).

Weber was a literal writer. He dealt in examples, not metaphors. In case the reader needed additional assistance in imagining a bureaucracy, he offered the following illustrations of organizations approaching the pure type, for example the modern army, the Catholic Church, private clinics, endowed hospitals, and hospitals maintained by religious orders.

Weber's reflections on the characteristics of an ideal bureaucratic administration display its essential qualities, for example:

—efficiency
—calculability
—substantive rationality
—technical competency
—knowledgeability

—formalistic impersonality
—universality

In a recent paper on coupling as an organizational variable, I inventoried the terms Weber employed when he was describing the relationship among elements in a bureaucratic organization. The tone of his words, as they are grouped roughly in categories, provides a feeling for an ideal bureaucracy in action: precisely, discretely, unambiguously, clearly; quickly, efficiently, rapidly; consistently, uninterruptedly; rationally, in a depersonalized way; obediently, harmoniously, conflict-free, shared from actor to actor; impactfully, significantly; and discreetly, i.e., out of the public view (Clark, Astuto, & Kuh, 1983).

DERIVATIVE LANGUAGE, APHORISMS, AND TECHNOLOGIES

Language

Parsons (1947, p. 336) noted, "military organization . . . was a subject in which Weber was greatly interested and to which he attributed great importance for social phenomena generally." Whether or not you find military organization of particular interest, reflect for a moment on the extent to which you employ military terms in describing or perhaps thinking about your organization—line officers, staff officers, commands, chain of command, subordinates, superordinates, discipline, task forces, authority, unity of command, standard operating procedures, span of control, troops, tight ship. Educational administrators discuss fail-safe mechanisms, quick-strike capabilities, points of no return, strategic withdrawals, all-out attacks, stretched communication and supply lines, and scanning devices. Weber's military example has assumed strong linguistic and metaphorical overtones for organizations.

The language of bureaucracy has several nested layers. It is militaristic, mechanistic, sexist, capitalist, Western, and rationalistic. In a popularized discussion of changes in management perspectives, Peters and Waterman (1982, pp. 41-42) noted, "the attack [on the problems of American business] ran into a language problem. It wasn't seen as an attack on . . . the 'rational model.' . . . It was seen as an attack on rationality and logical thought per se, thus implicitly encouraging escape into irrationality and mysticism." When even singular language blocks are difficult to surmount, the layered language that has grown up, around, and within bureaucratic organizations is very difficult to overcome. Thoughtful planning, data-based decision making, forceful leadership, responsible action, accountability, responsiveness, efficiency, and cost effectiveness sound so right and righteous that it is hard to entertain alternative perspectives to the images conveyed by these words. A widely accepted orthodox position, almost by definition, tends to hold the "high ground" with respect to language and values.

Aphorisms

An entrenched paradigm has a language base that is easily extended into aphorisms because the antonyms to the key words used to describe the concepts of the paradigm are unthinkable. What, for example, are the antonyms of Weber's characteristics of bureaucratic administration? They are inefficient, unpredictable, irrational, incompetent, ignorant, prejudicial! Such antonyms literally frighten practicing administrators, professors, and inquirers away from discussions about the logic-in-use in organizations; a logic that may encompass some or all of these characteristics some or all of the time. The frightening prospect is that one might conclude that such characteristics are descriptive of the way it is in human organizations and not a pathological condition to be remedied.

Dominant paradigms produce aphorisms that become over time comfortable, not frightening; for example,

—The buck stops here.
—Authority should be commensurate with responsibility.
—Look before you leap.

Let's try some counter-aphorisms. *The buck never stops in an organization.* There is always either someone else to blame or some set of uncontrollable circumstances that no reasonable observer would pin on a single administrator—not even a chief executive officer. For the buck to stop on an administrator's desk, it sometimes seems that one has to discover criminal action supported by a "smoking gun."

Authority and responsibility are almost never congruous in an organization. While some persons are squandering authority by avoiding responsibility, others are accumulating responsibility in the hope of increasing their authority. Individual authority and responsibility in organizations are variables governed jointly by the day-to-day sense-making activities of organizational participants and by designated organizational position. At any given time for any given task, congruity between these variables should be considered an aberration.

You should *leap for sure, look if you have time.* Peters and Waterman (1982, p. 141) contended that the most successful American companies have a bias for action; for example, "an analysis of Amoco, recently revitalized to become the top U.S. domestic oil finder, suggests just one success factor: Amoco simply drills more wells." Organizations and administrators that discover how they are doing by trying new things have inordinate success rates.

Now, let's put the two sets of aphorisms together so that we can compare jointly the impact of language and understandings on our view of organizations:

Aphorism	*Counter-Aphorism*
The buck stops here.	The buck never stops in an organization.
Authority must be commensurate with responsibility.	Authority and responsibility are almost never congruous in an organization.
Look before you leap.	Leap for sure; look if you have time.

If you have had any experience working in or studying organizations, the two lists have to make you feel uncomfortable. The aphorisms sound as if they are describing the way it ought to be—a responsible administrator with a charter to act employing a rational planning and behaving mode. The counter-aphorisms sound as if they reflect today's world of work but should not be tolerable—irresponsible leaders, jockeying for authority, stumbling into the future trying this and that.

Technology

Stable paradigms produce and are then supported by intricate technologies. The positivist paradigm of inquiry, for example, produced not only comprehensive, first-generation tactics of inquiry (e.g., experimental design), but second-generation modifications (e.g., quasi-experimental design) when the complexities of the real world were disparate from the assumptions of the model.

The Weberian paradigm is similarly replete with technologies that support its assumptions. Management information systems service management decisions. Program planning and budgeting systems link planning processes to resource allocations and, subsequently, to production. Management by objectives links planning and process and also integrates the expectations of employees with the assessment of their performance. Program evaluation and review techniques allow managers to monitor performance and progress. Future studies techniques provide tools to project organizational opportunities and obstacles. Marketing survey and needs assessment techniques match the organization's work with the preferences of its clients. Convergence techniques assist in goal formulation. Written policies, rules and regulations, organization charts, job descriptions, performance assessment tools, and supervisory techniques all form a part of the operating tools that are taught to and used by the practitioner.

Many of the same techniques are used by the researcher in studying organizations, and the output of the practitioner's technology is often viewed as input by the inquirer (e.g., the organization's formal goals statement, organization chart, plans and projections, personnel evaluations, program assessments, policy handbooks, and M.I.S. reports).

The point of this discussion of the language, aphorisms, and technologies that support the traditional bureaucratic paradigm in organizational theory is to forestall the argument of those who wish to brush the paradigm aside casually, as if it no longer holds primacy in the field. The Weberian structure has been built upon, rationalized, adjusted, twisted, and modified for the past forty years, but its essential assumptions still govern the popular conception of organizations and administrators, the training programs for administrators in our colleges and universities, the research that is undertaken in the field, the development activities that produce our most usable and used technologies, and the way we talk about our work places.

In Table 2.1 the Weberian view of the organizational world is depicted on the dimensions of the emergent paradigm that Schwartz and Ogilvy (1979) argue can now be seen across the social and physical sciences. Taking the characteristics of the "new paradigm" one by one, it seems clear that the traditional paradigm of organizational theory would be argued by Schwartz and Ogilvy to be a representative creature of its intellectual age. Taken collectively, the contrast between the

Weberian paradigm and Schwartz and Ogilvy's new paradigm is more startling. The characteristics are interactive and synergistic. The sum portrayed by the classical paradigm presents a view of organizational life that is so different from the logic-in-use in organizations that its utility as a reconstructed logic almost has to be challenged on grounds of simplism. The ease with which the Weberian view can be characterized at the extreme of each dimension also supports the argument that the classical paradigm of organizational theory is a cohesive world view. Furthermore, it is reasonable to argue that (1) such a view would constrain and determine thought, inquiry, training, and action in any field that subscribed to it; (2) organizational theory is currently dominated by this view; and (3) practice, training, and research in the field reflect that domination.

THE NEO-ORTHODOX RESEARCHERS AND THEORISTS

This chapter will not argue that the simplism of Max Weber's ideal bureaucratic structure has been lost on past generations of organizational theorists. A half-century ago Chester Barnard was describing the informal organization of bureaucracies and its significance for managers, and Mary Parker Follett was challenging both the centralized and mechanistic discharge of organizational authority. The Western Electric studies at the Hawthorne Plant in Cicero, Illinois, suggested that the human variable was a key determinant of industrial productivity. A vigorous decade of research and writing on human relations in business and industrial management was about to begin.

But there is an interesting characteristic of this work. Those inquirers who were discussing or describing empirically informal organization were not challenging the legitimacy of the constructs of formal organization. For example, a standard strategem suggested for managers in dealing with the informal organization was to attempt to negotiate the formal and informal structures of organizations so that they would be as nearly congruent as possible. The criterion for determining how the structure would be in its pure form was, of course, still the formal organizational structure as invented and recorded by the organization's chief executive officer. Informal organization was a real factor to be taken into account, but it was noise in the system.

The researchers of the human relations movement were intrigued initially by the search for more effective and efficient ways to harness

TABLE 2.1
Profile of the Classical Organizational Paradigm
on the Characteristics of the "New" Paradigm

Characterization of Classical Organizational Paradigm	Commentary
simple ———×——————— complex	Not a difficult call; the boundaries of a classical bureaucracy are clear; so in fact are the elements; operating efficiently and effectively a bureaucracy ought to be imagined as the sum of its parts; one of its charms is that it simplifies the operation of a large, complex organization; bureaucracy ideally achieves permanence and generality.
hierarchic ——————×——— heterarchic	This characteristic is asserted axiomatically in the Weberian paradigm; hierarchy is essential and unchanging; rules are written and binding; human action is oriented to a hierarchy of functions; there are commanders and commands, leaders and followers.
mechanical ———×——————— holographic	A less clear case; the inter-connectedness of the holographic metaphor suggests the tight coupling sought in the beaucratic paradigm; on the other hand, holography is employed as a counter-metaphor to a machine-like image which dominated the thinking of Taylor and the educationist efficiency movement; as an image of reality the mechanical metaphor better suits the classical paradigm.
determinate ———×——————— indeterminate	The Weberian adjectives noted earlier define the classical paradigm as determinate, e.g., precisely, unambiguously, clearly, shared. And Weber's reflections on the characteristics of a bureaucratic system included calculability; note from Weber, bureaucracy "is superior in precision, in stability, in the stringency of its discipline, and its reliability" (Parsons, 1947, p. 337).
linear causality ———×——————— mutual causality	The rational, sequential characteristic of the bureaucratic paradigm demands a distinction between cause and effect;

(continued)

TABLE 2.1 Continued

Characterization of Classical Organizational Paradigm		Commentary
		managers are instructed not to "think in circles"; mutual causality suggests that such circularity may be the only route to improvement; a bureaucratic paradigm is a rational sequential paradigm.
assembled ⊢—✗——————————⊣	morphogenic	A morphogenetic metaphor for organizational change was unimagined in the bureaucratic paradigm; the spontaneous, unpredictable, and discontinuous nature of the change process challenges the basic rational structure of bureaucratic functioning; again calculability is undermined, traditional organizational planning modes are useless.
objective ⊢—✗——————————⊣	perspectival	Weber believed that bureaucracy portrayed a natural order; such a belief assumes the notion that there is an objective reality to be discovered out there; as Parsons noted, Weber linked the methodology of science to the substantive problems of rational action—that linkage led him to both a positivist and bureaucratic position.

human potential in organizational settings. Their studies led to a modified set of tactics for leaders in organizations that placed emphasis on motivation and involvement of the workers (not the leaders, who were already assumed to be motivated and involved), physical conditions of employment, personnel relations, and styles of supervision. This line of inquiry qualified and added to some of the assumptions of the bureaucratic paradigm, but the studies were conducted within the framework of that paradigm.

These efforts to improve the adequacy of the bureaucratic paradigm seem to be best typified as a transitional neo-orthodoxy. The period gave rise to an abundance of alternative models, constructs, and theories for viewing and understanding organizations. However, the Weberian paradigm was the progenitor of the alternatives and remained unchallenged in its basic assumptions and elements. In the remainder of this section I propose to discuss two alternative models that gained particular popularity in the study of educational organizations, and several seminal constructs that affected the broad field of organizational theory.

ORGANIZATION AS A SOCIAL SYSTEM

In the late 1950s Jacob Getzels and Egon Guba introduced a model designed to increase the understanding of the behavior of people in organizations. The model proposed that a social system consists of two dimensions: the institution with its roles and role expectations (which they termed the organizational or nomothetic dimension) and the individual with his or her personality and need dispositions (which they termed the personal or idiographic dimension). Social behavior in an organization derives from the interaction of the two dimensions.

The Getzels-Guba model is a particularly interesting example because it illustrates so perfectly the lineage to the root paradigm and the link between the bureaucratic paradigm and the methodological concerns which, as Parsons noted, fascinated Weber. The concept of a formal bureaucratic structure with specified offices, job descriptions, and goals was not challenged. They were the nomothetic variables that determined institutional roles and expectations. The idiographic dimension added variables to account for the individual's personality characteristics and need dispositions. A given organizational act derived from the transaction of these dimensions. The methodological genesis of the work was noted recently by Daniel Griffiths (1983, p. 204), who commented, "Getzels and Guba were heavily influenced by the logical positivist movement." In identifying their intentions, Getzels stated the following:

> The model was constructed with three specific criteria in mind: (1) the model must provide a set of integrated concepts and relations capable not only of answering questions already asked in administration, but of posing questions that still need to be asked; (2) the concepts and relations must be operational in that they not only give direction to our understanding, but simultaneously provide blueprints for investigation; (3) the model must be able to handle as many of the commonplace or familiar issues in administration as possible within a single set of concepts and relations. In short, we sought a model that was at once heuristic, operational, and that had the elegance and power of parsimony. (Getzels, 1958, pp. 150-151)

This model received widespread attention and use in research in educational administration during the 1960s and 1970s. The conceptualization strengthened the bureaucratic paradigm by integrating idiographic variables into the study of organizational behavior. It provided a description of social behavior in organizations that conformed more nearly to individuals' experiences in organizational settings. In combination with the psychological instruments used to test the model, this effort achieved the intentions of the coauthors; that is, it was rooted in the past, it provided a way to deal with as yet unexplored questions, it was operational, and charmingly simple.

SITUATIONAL LEADERSHIP

A field of study dominated by a hierarchical, authority-heavy conceptual structure should produce a plethora of leadership studies; organizational behavior does just that. In 1974, Ralph Stogdill reviewed over 3000 studies in the *Handbook of Leadership*. Early leadership studies illustrated the dominance of the bureaucratic paradigm. Authority was vested in designated positions. Failure to use authority effectively was a flaw in the leader's behavior. Some leaders were more successful than others. As the formal organizational structure was a given, the most obvious place to look for the cause of the failure was in the individual. Leadership research emphasized initially the relationship between personal traits of the leader and her or his success or failure.

The field then moved from trait studies to style to behavior and, finally, to situational factors as inquirers confronted failure in establishing significant relationships between an array of independent, personal variables and either perceived success as a leader or organizational outcomes. To account for the ambiguous relationship between a variety of personal variables and success as a leader, Fred Fiedler (1967) added another contaminating variable to the field's understanding of leadership. Perhaps the low correlation between leader variables and success was accounted for by differences in the situations in which leaders found themselves. Fiedler identified three factors that might vary from organization to organization or among leader-positions in a single organization to reduce or increase the effectiveness of leaders with different traits, styles, and leadership behaviors. The three additions are revealing: (1) leader-member relations, (2) the level of task structure in the situation, and (3) the power of the leader's position. Each of the variables argues a deviation from the ideal bureaucratic form. The variables highlight the truism that the elements of apparently similar bureaucracies will vary. In one instance a leader may have the power to grant pay increases; in another he or she may not. In one instance the task structure may be technically simple and clear; in another ambiguous. In one instance the leader may be trusted; in another the same leader exhibiting the same behavior may be suspect.

The Fiedler example illustrates again how a generation of inquirers can add sophistication, clarity, comprehensiveness, and validity to a basic construct without abandoning or replacing the construct itself. The field continues to operate under the basic assumptions of its dominant paradigm, but it learns more and more about the paradigm. Simultaneously, of course, it adjusts the most troublesome instances of incongruity between the paradigm as a reconstructed logic and evidence about logic-in-use in the field.

A POTPOURRI OF PERSPECTIVES

Individual cases of inquirers who have attempted to reconcile the dominant paradigm of organizational theory to increasingly trouble-some attacks on its validity and utility could be extended by hundreds of pages. The intent here is only to illustrate briefly the pervasive effect of a dominant paradigm on inquirers and to point out the extended transitional period of intellectual struggle required to set the stage for the invention, construction, and acceptance of a new paradigm.

Bounded Rationality

As the limitation of rational choice in organizations seemed to be one obvious shortcoming of the dominant paradigm, Simon (1957) intro-duced the concept of bounded rationality to portray the limits of rationality while holding to its primacy. Organizational researchers accepted the fabricated word "satisficing" to describe the selection of the first generally satisfactory choice. This necessary modification of the theoretical position supporting the key role of rationality in organiza-tional behavior provoked and provokes interesting responses. Some true believers chose to view the condition as transitory and, conse-quently, relatively unimportant from a theoretical point of view; for example, Charles Perrow (1982, p. 684), reflecting on his interpretation of bounded rationality a quarter-century ago, observed, "I was not much impressed by these arguments. Of course, there are limits on human rationality and problem solving... but social scientists are going to push them back." Social scientists, in general, have lost some of their currency in the intervening time period, but technologists, mathematicians, and computer scientists working together still hold the promise for many that the limits of bounded rationality will be expanded significantly and indefinitely.

Operational Goals

The role of goals in organizational theory and practice has been problematic for decades, as the concept of a priori goals lies so close to the heart of the notion of a rational organization. Pfeffer (1982, p. 7) noted, "The critical distinguishing feature of organization theories taking the rational perspective is the element of conscious, foresightful action reasonably autonomously constructed to achieve some goal or value." Many organizational theorists define an organization as a goal-attaining entity. But the issue arises—whose goals, which goals? That the publicly recorded goals of an organization were an adequate representation of the organization's goals was a construct so simple it had to give way to the notion that there were widely accepted operational goals in organizations that could be discovered, although they differed from the official goals. The utility of the concept of operational goals was increased for some researchers by modifying the unit of analysis; that is, by studying operational goals at the work group level rather than the organizational level.

Again, the reasonableness of the basic paradigm was extended as inquirers were able to infer unstated organizational goals by observing and interviewing institutional functionaries. Operational goals could then be compared to official goals to test, in effect, the alignment of organizational processes. Importantly, for a transition period, the central feature of the organization as a nomothetic, goal-attaining entity was not attacked.

Contingency Theory

The central argument of contingency theorists has been that there is no one best way to organize or manage. Different strategies and tactics will work better or worse if, for example, the goals of the organization are dissimilar, or if the technical task of the organization is simpler or more complex, or if the organization is more or less accessible to clients or other extraorganizational environmental factors. Contingency theorists added sophistication to the classical model. Their link to that paradigm was noted by Pfeffer (1982, p. 148) in his review of their research:

> The structural variables presumably affected by these context variables are those emerging from a Weberian (1947) conception of organizational structure: the size of the administrative component, the degree of centralization and formalization of the structure, and the amount of differentiation, or the extent of task specialization and vertical elaboration.

Individual Expectancy, Needs, Goals Theories

Whereas contingency theorists emphasized the nomothetic dimension of the Getzels-Guba model, several significant lines of inquiry arose that examined the idiographic dimension. The inquirers studying the individual in the organization, consistent with the Weberian view, were dominated by a rational man approach. Pfeffer (1982, p. 41) summarized these lines of inquiry this way:

> Expectancy theory . . . argues that people undertake actions according to the probability that these actions will lead to some instrumentally valued outcome; goal theory argues that people undertake actions to achieve their goals; needs theory argues that people act purposefully to fulfill their needs or to overcome need deficiencies.

Collectively these efforts modified and supplemented the classical theory in ways that retrospectively seem almost inevitable. Can a theory of rational choice be sustained in organization? Within bounds, perhaps. Are the goals of an organization reflected in publicly recorded statements? Perhaps, some and sometimes; but one could look for operational goals throughout the organization. Does the structural heterogeneity of organizations affect processes and outcomes? Surely, these contingencies need to be taken into account. Can we understand organizations without focusing on the individuals who populate them?

Surely not, and that focus can be sharpened by appropriating the most useful theory and research from psychology and sociology.

THE HERITAGE OF NEO-ORTHODOXY

Two recent efforts to rationalize and categorize organizational theory and research will be used to assess where we have been and where we are in our understanding of organizations.

Pfeffer Schema

In a comprehensive critical review of organizational theory and research, Pfeffer (1982) suggested that one can imagine a 3 × 2 framework that represents the field. One dimension depicts the *perspective on action* taken by the theory:

- action as rational or at least boundedly rational, purposive, and goal-directed;
- action as externally constrained or environmentally determined;
- action as emergent from, and embedded in, social processes.

The second dimension is the *level of analysis* reflected in the theory; i.e., theories that

- treat the organization primarily as a unit,
- deal with smaller social units within organizations, such as individuals, coalitions, and subunits (p. 3).

The structure that emerges from the intersection of these categories is displayed, with examples, in Table 2.2.

The content of this chapter to this point would fall almost exclusively in Column 1. Pfeffer intended this column to include those theories in which the distinguishing feature "is the element of conscious, foresightful action reasonably autonomously constructed to achieve some goal or value" (p. 7). The emphasis on this column in this chapter is explained simply—it is the dominant theoretical paradigm in organizational theory.

TABLE 2.2
Categorization of Theoretical Perspectives in Organization Theory

Level of Analysis	Perspectives on Action		
	Purposive, Intentional Goal-Directed, Rational	Externally Constrained and Controlled	Emergent, Almost-Random. Dependent on Process and Social Construction
Row 1 Individuals, Coalitions, or Subunits	Expectancy theory Goal setting Needs theories and job design Political theories	Operant conditioning Social learning theory Socialization Role theories Social context effects and groups Retrospective rationality Social information processing	Ethnomethodology Cognitive theories of organizations Language in organizations Affect-based processes
Row 2 Total Organization	Structural contingency theory Market failures/ transaction costs Marxist or class perspectives	Population ecology Resource dependence	Organizations as paradigms Decision process and administrative theories Institutionalization theory
	Column 1	Column 2	Column 3

NOTE: Reprinted by permission from J. Pfeffer (1982). *Organizations and Organization Theory*. Boston: Pitman Publishing, Inc.

Theories in Column 2, Pfeffer argued, are distinguished by the fact that the analysis and explanation of action uses variables of the social entity's environment rather than entity-specific variables (such as goals, values, needs, or personality) in the understanding of behavior. A key distinction from the rational view of foresightful action is that "the role of cognition is viewed as a mechanism for making sense of or rationalizing behavior that has already occurred . . . thus, the external control perspective . . . talks to the issue of retrospective rationality" (p. 8).

Pfeffer had difficulty in defining the third column, pointing out that it is less homogeneous than the first two. Its key characteristic in Pfeffer's view ends up being its denial of traditional assumptions about rationality in organizations: "This view of behavior fundamentally denies either an internally directed or an externally determined rationality of behavior" (p. 9).

Pfeffer was interested in the levels of analysis because they provided an important analytic screen against which to play off problems of the appropriateness of the unit of analysis to the theoretical propositions being examined. Row 1, for example, represents the individualist position; that is, organizations do not behave, people do (Weick, 1979). The rows do not provide the sharp break in emphasis and activity in organization theory and research provided by the columns. I would argue that this is due to the fact that the dominant paradigm bridged, to some extent, both of the levels of analysis while being exclusionary in asserting a perspective on action.

Burrell and Morgan Schema

Daniel Griffiths (1983), in his recent analysis of the evolution of research and theory in educational administration, employed a perspective on the current scene in organizational theory proposed by Burrell and Morgan (1980). This schema combined a subjective-objective dimension with a sociological paradigm. The subjective-objective dimension is determined on ontological, epistemological, human nature, and methodological continua:

Ontological: those who believe each person creates his or her own world - to - those who assert an objective world for all;

Epistemological: those who argue that no laws underlie the social world - to - those who assert and seek regularities and causal relationships;

Human nature: those who assert free will - to - those who believe in external environmental control of the individual;

Methodological: an idiographic view of social science - to - the use of systematic techniques and designs of inquiry (Griffiths, 1983, p. 209).

This dimension is intersected with a social perspective that places in opposition the *sociology of regulation* (emphasizing social order, consensus, social integration, solidarity, need satisfaction, and actuality) and the *sociology of radical change* (concerned with structural conflict, modes of domination, contradiction, emancipation, deprivation, and potentiality). These continua generate four cells within which Burrell and Morgan classify the theories and paradigms that have been used to study organizations:

(1) *Functionalist cell:* Combining an emphasis on the sociology of regulation and objectivity, this cell includes almost all the theoretical and empirical activity in organizational studies. It unites the dominant substantive paradigm on organizations (the sociology of Weber) with the dominant paradigm of social science inquiry (positivism).

(2) *Radical structuralist cell:* Combining an emphasis on the sociology of radical change with objectivity, this cell has generated the critique of structural functionalism. Although radical structuralism has received little attention in educational administration in the United States, it is being pursued vigorously in the British Commonwealth. Griffiths noted that a recent article by Bates (1982) listed 73 structuralist references, of which 40 were written by Commonwealth scholars (Griffiths, 1983, p. 208). In the more general field of organizational theory, the structuralists are represented by the Marxist critique of organizational theory.

(3) *Interpretive cell:* Combining an emphasis on the sociology of regulation and subjectivity, this cell is represented by ethnomethodological approaches and phenomenological interaction in the study of organizational functioning.

(4) *Radical humanist cell:* Representing the antithesis of the functionalist paradigm, Griffiths reported that Burrell and Morgan found no one using this paradigm in 1979, but that if anyone does, "the result will be 'anti-organization theory' " (Griffiths, 1983, p. 212).

These two classificatory structures are introduced because they both illustrate dramatically the result that is obtained by neo-orthodox researchers and theorists. In the Pfeffer categorization scheme, neo-orthodoxy added much to what we know about organizations, but it accepted some features that defined the limits of its search, for example:

Behaviors are constructed to be chosen . . . such choice is presumed to occur according to a set of consistent preferences. . . . behavior is determined by and presumably reflective of conscious, purposive action. . . . choice is presumed to occur prior to the action itself. . . . rationality is prospective rather than retrospective in that actions are consciously chosen in the light of some anticipated consequences . . . action is goal directed (Pfeffer, 1982, p. 6).

The broader schema of Burrell and Morgan argued that the neo-orthodox theorists and researchers have tended to

- accept the existence of an objective social world for all persons;
- look for the causal relationships and regularities of that objective world;
- accept the constraints of choice and rationality in the Pfeffer categories;
- pursue their search for truth using the tools of the positivist;
- hold to a "regulation of order" rather than a "radical change" view of society.

In both instances the conclusion of the authors was that the theoretical and empirical work in organizational theory has been governed by relatively narrow limits substantively and methodologically.

The conventional research and theory of the past 25-40 years has had several important effects:

(1) More variables have been subjected to study—the field has become *more comprehensive.*
(2) More interesting variables have been studied and have been studied more interestingly—the field has become *more conceptually sophisticated.*
(3) Movement has occurred to reconcile the reconstructed logic of the field to the logic-in-use—the inquiry has become *more valid.*
(4) The results of organizational inquiry, for good and bad, have generated more research and more interest on the part of practitioners—the field has become *more practically and scientifically heuristic.*

However, I would argue that within the last decade neo-orthodoxy has approached its limits of contribution. The limits are being pressed because the inquirers cannot proceed beyond certain critical bounds without denying the root paradigm. Thus, behavioral choice has been considered a doctrine, not an affirmable construct. Arational and irrational behavior have been defined, not as alternative behavioral forms, but as pathological. The assertion that rationality cannot be defined apart from the existence of goals represents a belief, not a theorem. As researchers and theorists work within a dominant paradigm and create alternatives based on that paradigm, they finally confront points of no return. As it turns out, the dimensions employed in Table 2.1 are theoretically continuous but practically discontinuous. The simplicity of form sought in the classical organizational paradigm becomes an inappropriate construct at some point on the road to complexity: For example, contingency theory and bounded rationality are tolerable, arationality is not. The adjustments of hierarchical order to informal organization and even to organizations as social systems is appropriate. The assumptions of heterarchy are absurb.

Table 2.3 depicts crudely this discontinuity while attempting to describe the movement in organizational theory provoked by the neo-orthodox researchers and theorists. The modifications can be summarized as follows:

(1) Current mainstream organizational theory is more complex, consequently more consistent with experiential and empirical observations of organizational behavior.

(2) Little or no change is observable in critical dimensions of the paradigm (e.g., hierarchic, linear causality, objective reality).

(3) The fragility and probably the limits of change in the mainstream paradigm are illustrated by the checkered history of the characteristics of determinability and mechanicalness. Contingency theory, situational leadership, and bounded rationality suggest indeterminateness. Such conditions, however, give immediate rise to a search for more precise mathematical models, management information systems, and decision-making technologies to increase the sought-after determinability. Human resource management encourages a less mechanistic view of organizational characteristics, but mechanistic devices to restore orderliness are introduced to temper the disruption.

(4) As was noted in Table 2.1, the impact of the profile is more dramatic when all seven characteristics are considered simultaneously. The overall picture indicates that the dominant view of organizational theory is consistent and has changed less than one would have imagined from the onslaught of the neo-orthodox researchers.

The distinctions in placing the symbols and lines across the seven characteristics noted in Table 2.3 are not critical to the central argument of this chapter. They are included to stimulate debate. From this vantage point the classical paradigm can tolerate the least deviation on

TABLE 2.3
Profile of the Neo-Orthodox Organizational Paradigm
on Characteristics of the "New" Paradigm

Characterization of Neo-Organizational Paradigm		Commentary
simple ⊢——✗——⊣ complex		Clearly the transitional paradigm has introduced greater complexity to the field of organizational studies. The boundaries of classical bureaucracies were opened by inquirers concerned with external constraints and influences. The theorists of the individual (expectancy, needs) introduced added critical personal variables. Contingency theory and bounded rationality strive to account for complexity not found in Weberian models but the limit has been nearly reached; the model cannot stand added weight.
hierarchic ⊢—✗——⊣ heterarchic		Little movement; the basic hierarchy is essential and unchanging. The modifications deal more with style than substance, e.g., recognition that slavish adherence to hierarchical imperatives is ineffective, emphasis on techniques of participatory decision making and decentralization. The bureaucratic paradigm can tolerate only minimal manipulation of its concepts of order.
mechanical ⊢——✗—⊣ holographic		There has been a mixed history of movement away from and back toward the mechanical image of organizational reality. The human resource management theorists attempted to soften Taylorism and imagine a humanized if not human-dominated workplace. The systems theorists, more particularly the technology that followed them, revived interest in the mechanical or machine metaphor for organizing.
determinate ⊢——✗—⊣ indeterminate		An interesting struggle has occurred on this characteristic within the dominant paradigm. Can one argue reasonably that no change is discernible and still recognize contingency theory, situational leadership, bounded rationality? I think not. However, the values held by those who work within that paradigm suggest that precision, clarity, calculability, reliability is still what the game is all about.

TABLE 2.3   Continued

Characterization of Neo-Organizational Paradigm		Commentary
linear causality	mutual causality	Guba (1983) commented in his paper that the movement in inquiry on this characteristic has been from a linear view to Cook and Campbell's "activity theory." That roughly matches the change in organizational theory. Contemporary theorists recognize multiple causality and mutual causality, discuss feedback and feed-forward loops but finally deal with the issue as a transitory limitation to our understanding of organizations—a form of "bounded" causality.
assembled	morphogenic	Natural selection and associated evolutionary models have received sufficient attention by organizational theorists to argue that the morphogenetic metaphor for organizational change is more tolerable than other characteristics of the "new paradigm." The stumbling block is the extent to which rational selection dominates the use of the metaphor. The conflict arises around the issue of calculability in planning for or anticipating organizational change.
objective	perspectival	Modifications in this characteristic are more apparent than real. No one denies the impact of human constructions of reality on organizational behavior, but the overwhelming majority of organizational theorists, researchers and practitioners are solid in their faith in a discoverable, objective reality out there.

an axiomatic characteristic (e.g., hierarchy, limited variance on simplicity, determinacy, and objectivity) and more extensive deviation on the remaining characteristics. Thus, I would predict that continued neo-orthodox inquiry will produce only modest modifications in concepts of order. However, there is every reason to expect that some additional levels of complexity will emerge and that even more substantial adjustments will be introduced in handling mutual causality.

THE NONORTHODOX RESEARCHERS AND THEORISTS

Suppose, for a moment, that you are sitting on a plane and overhear fragments of an apparently serious discussion among some fellow passengers. The first snippet of conversation is from Character A: "It's okay not to know where you're going as long as you're going somewhere. Sooner or later you'll know where that somewhere is" (Weick, 1979, p. 246).

Character B seems to be agreeing: "I now believe that the concept of organizational goals as a major influence upon organizational behavior is only a convenient fiction" (Perrow, 1982, p. 684).

Character C picks up on that point: "We need a modified view of planning. Planning in organizations has many virtues, but a plan can often be more effective as an interpretation of past decisions than as a program for future ones" (March, 1972, p. 427).

Character A is back again, "[That's right] how can I know what I think until I see what I say?" (Weick, 1979, p. 175).

A new voice suggests that organizations can be viewed as "choices looking for problems; issues and feelings looking for decision situations in which they might be aired; solutions looking for issues to which they might be the answer, and decision makers looking for work" (Cohen, March, & Olsen, 1972, p. 2).

Character A concludes, "Most managers get into trouble because they forget to think in circles" (Weick, 1979, p. 86).

Do you think you have been listening to (a) business consultants who have had too many cocktails; (b) Bob and Ray inventing a routine to use at a business convention; (c) a group who are planning to hijack the plane to Cuba; or (d) a group of nonorthodox organizational theorists whose work and thought is breaking down the dominant paradigm in organizational theory? If you guessed (d) you win the guessing contest and are left with only the task of wrestling with the ideas.

At the risk of simplism, I will argue that the nonorthodox theorists have denied five basic assumptions undergirding conventional organizational theory and research:

(1) goal-directed organizational behavior
(2) preference-directed individual behavior
(3) sequential linkages between individual and organizational processes, e.g., intent → action

(4) reliability bounded only by situational and contingent factors
(5) predictability bounded only by the limits of current knowledge and technology

In sum, the assumptions being attacked are those supporting the functionalist cell in Burrell and Morgan's classification scheme and the purposive, intentional, goal-directed, rational column in Pfeffer's categorization.

SIMPLICITY/COMPLEXITY

The neo-orthodox theorists knew they were delaying with an over-simplified structure and increased the complexity of the traditional paradigm by adding variables of significance and combining the effects of formerly discrete variables. But that is simply not enough. Understanding real world systems means understanding the essential integrity of the elements, as the system transcends the elements. Deal and Kennedy (1983, p. 16) argued this point in a recent paper:

> We believe that the character or culture of organizations is not unlike the character of wines. Attempts to quantify important variables produces more precision and greater "rigor." But while the tightness of the metric increases reliability and reduces noise, it moves further from the essence of the organizational "truth." That truth is embedded in the meaning that humans assign to important things and events inside their own reality.

The point of distinction between the transitional theorists and those who would disaffirm conventional theory is a matter of type, not degree. The neo-orthodox position introduced complexity to achieve ultimate simplicity. The nonorthodox position accepts the infinite variety that social constructionism imposes on organization. Nonorthodox inquirers do not aspire to simplicity because they accept the inevitability that a richer understanding of organizations and organizing mandates ever-increasingly complex views of these structures and processes. *The objective of the nonorthodox position is to nurture complexity and eschew simplicity.*

HIERARCHY/HETERARCHY

The concept of hierarchy provided the cornerstone of rational authority for the Weberian structure. But heterarchy captures the spirit of the arguments of those who challenge the utility of goals in organizations and who find richer organizational understanding through the negotiated cause maps of organizational participants than from the company's organizational chart. Schwartz and Ogilvy (1979) described heterarchical order in terms of a net of mutual constraints and influences. Perrow (1982, p. 687) chose the same term to describe the place, or nonplace, of goals in organizations:

> I still believed, as long as 10 years after I encountered the March and Simon notion of bounded rationality, that organizations had goals. Now I think they have only constraints. All sorts of people inside and outside of organizations use them for their own purposes, and each of these uses is a constraint upon other uses. None of the uses deserves the exalted designation of "goal."

Nonorthodox theorists have attacked the hierarchical assumption from a variety of directions because this assumption embodies the character of the rational organization. Weick (1980) has suggested that the stimulus-response patterns in organizations can be described better by such adjectives as gradual, eventual, occasional, indirect, or ceremonial than by the Weberian terms direct and immediate. Cohen et al. (1972) challenged the orderly problem-solving configuration of the classical bureaucratic hierarchy. They noted that decision situations in organizations that they described as organized anarchies were often "sets of procedures through which participants arrive at an interpretation of what they are doing and what they have done while in the process of doing it" (p. 2). *And this depiction captures another essential challenge to hierarchy; that is, the sequence of processes argued by the paradigm is illusory.* Goals are discovered by acting. Action precedes intent. Solutions search for problems. Subordinates specify spheres of work to superordinates.

Again, it is necessary to emphasize that the challenge of the nonorthodox theorist is one of type. The issue is not whether the classical paradigm can be adjusted to account for these deviations. The deviations are, from the point of view of the new perspective, the norm in organizational life. The formerly dominant paradigm describes deviations from the norm of the new paradigm.

MECHANICAL/HOLOGRAPHIC

In arguing for the use of the metaphor, "organizations as tribes," Deal and Kennedy (1983, pp. 18-19) noted,

> We are at a juncture in the theory of organizations where we know that existing metaphors leave too much uncovered and unexplained. We have yet to find metaphors that will help applied scientists, managers and consultants to understand and improve modern organization.

Perhaps a period of metaphor testing is characteristic of the interregnum between the death of a dominant paradigm and the emergence of successor(s). Weick (1979, p. 47) noted that within the last decade, "organizations have variously been portrayed as anarchies, seesaws, space stations, garbage cans, savage tribes, octopoid, market-places, and data processing schedules."

Whatever alternative metaphors may emerge, the mechanical metaphor is under deadly attack. Its survival rests on rationality, sequence, and calculability. On all of these counts it is fatally flawed. Futures research is under attack not because the techniques employed are crude or nascent, but because the future is imponderable; worth pondering, but imponderable. Planning in organizations is in the same state. The available tools may be improved but they will still deal with the imponderable. Management information systems can be improved technically, but they are askew because their relationship to the organization is misunderstood. They are serving administrative decision making in organizations in which, as Cohen et al. (1972, p. 2) have pointed out, the preferences are problematic, the technology is unclear, and the participation in decision situations is fluid, even capricious. No one would argue that organizational participants should have less information about their organization. Many would argue that MIS systems gather the wrong information, from the wrong sources, for the wrong users, at the wrong organizational level. And the reason for the "wrong" orientation is the agonizing death throes of the mechanical metaphor of organizational form.

DETERMINATE/INDETERMINATE

The questions that are being raised about determinateness have been noted in relation to preceding characteristics. That provides an opportunity to reflect instead on the distinction between the denial of determinateness and its accommodation. Contingency theory and bounded rationality suggested that organizational events could be "a little bit" indeterminate. The Schwartz and Ogilvy definition of indeterminateness argues that future states of systems are, in principle, unpredictable. If one assumes the Cohen et al. description of organizations, the question arises as to whether an organized anarchy is "a little bit" determinate. If the coupling in most organizations most of the time is occasional, indirect, eventual, gradual, and ceremonial, the issue is not whether it is predictable but whether there are patterns within a given organization; that is, is it other than random, a little bit patternlike.

Perrow (1982) argued that our search for order where there was no order was overwhelming us. He noted that "We convert micro-confusion into macro-order" (p. 686). *The nonorthodox theorists point us toward disorderliness in studying and understanding organizations.* The order is the illusion we bring to organizations to make our workaday life handlable. The disorder is the "live" variables of organizational life bumping against one another.

LINEAR CAUSALITY/MUTUALITY CAUSALITY

Weick (1979, p. 246) argued that the consequence to practicing administrators of imagining linear causality in organziations is pernicious as

> there are no simple answers and there is no simple finite set of causes for anything that happens in an organization. Furthermore, origins are often impossible to discover, because they usually lie at some distance from the symptom and they have usually grown all out of proportion to their beginnings through deviation-amplifying loops.

To imagine the acceptance of mutual causality as an ordinary condition requires a quantitative reassessment of organizational occurrences. Weick's use of the term "usually" is more difficult to accept when it is turned to the ordinary sequential relationships assumed in organizations. The point is not simply that goals are sometimes retrospective or that action may precede intent or that acquired responsibility may determine authority. It is that goals are usually retrospective, action usually precedes intent, social enactment ordinarily determines the scope of an individual's authority.

The difficulty of accepting mutual causality is because of its conflict with the view of (1) an organization as a goal-attaining entity, (2) administration as a problem-solving and decision-making process, and (3) the rational organization as populated by rational persons. However, the difficulty should lie in accepting linear causality. Empirical evidence about organizations and the experiential evidence most people accumulate in organizations fails to conform to the three simple views just noted. To the contrary, what we discover suggests complexity. *To continue to accept linear causality seems to many organizational theorists to be insisting upon unwarranted simplicity.* Weick (1979) advised administrators to "complicate yourself." He adds, "Whatever additional ways we can find to complicate observers should also be adopted because the primary thrust of organizations is toward simplification, homogeneity, and crude registering of consequential events" (p. 261).

ASSEMBLY/MORPHOGENESIS

The search for how change occurs within and among organizations has been a rich vein of exploration for organizational theorists. The Marxian perspective and the dialectical view, an extraction of Marxist analysis, have moved theorists from Burrell and Morgan's functionalist cell to radical structuralism. These theorists have adopted the sociological perspective of radical change which interprets organizational life in terms of conflict, contradiction, domination, power, and class. The dialectical view, although clinging tightly to reasoned analysis as the basis for the reconstruction of social arrangements, is "fundamentally committed to the concept of process . . . theoretical attention is focused upon the transformation through which one set of arrangements gives way to another" (Benson, 1977, p. 3).

Natural selection models or metaphors for organizational change have a long history in the field of organizational theory. For at least 25 years they have reflected a break with the rational, bureaucratic tradition. Gouldner (1959, p. 409) noted:

> In general . . . the natural systems model tends to induce neglect of the rational structures characterizing the modern organization . . . tends to focus the analyst's concern for the forces that undermine the organization's impersonal principles and subvert its formal ends to "narrower" interests rather than on those that sustain these and bolster the distinctively bureaucratic structures . . . tends to minimize the role of rationality in human affairs and to counter-stress the way in which organizational behavior is affected by non-rational norms.

More recently, Weick (1979) building on Campbell (1970), employed a sociocultural evolution model to describe the organizing process. Weick argued as follows:

(1) Evolution is the result of variation, selection, and retention.
(2) Variations that are unjustified, i.e., untested, are emphasized in evolutionary theory. After generation and testing they may be labeled justified or rational.
(3) Evaluation is essentially opportunistic.
(4) Selection criteria are numerous and vary from time to time, from organization to organization, from unit to unit within a single organization.
(5) Retention opposes variation. At any given time, in complex organizations, the majority of mechanisms curb variation, foster retention (pp. 122-129).

OBJECTIVE/PERSPECTIVAL

Weick (1979, p. 135) reminded his colleagues that "Beliefs are cause maps that people impose on the world after which they 'see' what they have already imposed. . . . Believing does control seeing, but . . . the seeing in turn conditions further beliefs, which in turn constrain seeing, and so on." Marxian analysis stands as testimony to the impact of the inquirer's view of reality on what is observed, recorded, and known; an interesting impact for a view that is itself unabashedly objective rather than perspectival. How is the field responding on this characteristic of the Schwartz and Ogilvy paradigm? First, the population of perspectives that are viewed seriously by theorists is increasing. Second, acceptance of the viewpoint that a perspective produces its own knowledge is becoming more widespread. Third, confidence that a comprehensive viewpoint is appropriate for inquiry in the field is diminishing. Fourth, a recognition that alternative views in the past tended to be adaptations of a single view is gaining acceptance. Finally, the appropriateness of diversity in inquiry methodology is more widely acknowledged as diverse perspectives demand distinctive tools.

I would argue that the major change that has occurred in the past decade in organizational theory has not been simply the proliferation of metaphors, models, and theories. Previous eras have provided us with alternative theories in great number. Rather, the competitive views have broken out of the Weberian paradigm so that the traditional perspective (a world view) has become one of many rather than the progenitor of the alternatives.

How might the nonorthodox theorists be profiled in terms of the Schwartz and Ogilvy paradigm? If one were to undertake that task hypothetically, they would be positioned past the point of discontinuity. If one had individual theorists in mind, they might be nonorthodox on some characteristics, neo-orthodox on others. This is the nascent period of nonorthodoxy. Denying one traditional axiom or challenging one aphorism at a time is enough for even the most adventuresome.

The important distinction to be made about the nonorthodox position and its predecessors is that the difference is one of type, not degree. The traditional and neo-orthodox theorists were and are working within the classical organizational paradigm. The neo-orthodox profile (Table 2.3) suggests that one can work profitably within a comprehensive view, and generate alternative perspectives that are of immense value to researchers and practitioners. However, the contrast between the classical and nonorthodox positions is a contrast between comprehensive views of social science, social science methodology, and organizational theory. They brook no compromise. Within each comprehensive view there is room for great diversity. The middle ground, however, is problematic. Rather than being a position of compromise, the middle ground becomes discontinuous and is occupied by ethnomethodologists, who accept the sociology of regulation, or Marxists, who believe in an objective world; that is, the middle ground spawns other comprehensive views. What the nonorthodox position lacks currently is the rich tradition of theory development, research, documentation, storytelling, and engineering that has grown up around the classical paradigm. But the new paradigm will have its day.

SUMMARY AND CONCLUSIONS

Let me summarize, then, the argument I have attempted to formulate and support in this chapter:

- The traditional or classical paradigm of organizational theory fitted the belief system of Western scholars and practitioners of management so well that its elements became aphorisms too powerful to contest openly for decades.
- The diversity of organizational perspectives that grew rapidly from 1950 to 1975 were modifications of the root paradigm, which remained essentially unchallenged.
- Contemporary theorists, supported in their efforts intellectually and psychologically by an emerging new paradigm in the social and behavioral sciences, have ventured to the aphoristic core of the classical view. Their challenges to goals, rationality, sequence, causality, and purposive behavior are beginning to provide alternative views that deny rather than modify the classical view.
- The period of denial is well advanced. The period of construction is just beginning. However, the burden of construction is not on those who deny. It is enough that they have provided us with ways to see that were previously closed.

All of this sounds as if we are in the midst of a new era in organizational studies. Before my enthusiasm drowns my common sense, let me emphasize some earlier observations. Griffiths (1983) placed the overwhelming percentage of empirical research in educational administration in the functionalist cell. Pfeffer (1982) left no doubt but that the bulk of organizational studies fell in the category he labeled as purposive, intentional, goal directed, rational. Griffiths (1983, p. 216) went on to note that "At the present time the writers of the popular textbooks in educational administration use a strictly positivist definition of theory." There are exceptions in the more general field of organizational studies, for example, Weick (1979) and Pfeffer (1982), but the bulk of the training materials for all administrators are built upon the traditional paradigm.

I have no illusion that this situation will change in the immediate future. The dominant Weberian paradigm is supported by psychological, linguistic, and political biases both blatant and subtle. I have no doubt that I have expressed some of this prejudice unwittingly here.

I do assume that the process of denial has proceeded past the point of no return. Slowly, but inexorably, our understanding of organizations and organizing will be illuminated by new perspectives. Cumulatively, these perspectives will define and refine an alternative paradigm that will become the progenitor of numerous competing theories and structures. The configuration of the new paradigm will resemble the characteristics of the Schwartz and Ogilvy paradigm. The traditional paradigm will atrophy along with its derivative schema because it differs too markedly from the logic-in-use in organizations.

REFERENCES

Benson, J. (1977). Organizations: A dialectical view. *Administrative Science Quarterly, 22* (1), 1-21.

Burrell, G., & Morgan, G. (1980). *Sociological paradigms and organizational analysis.* London: Heinemann Educational Books.

Campbell, D. (1970). Natural Selection as an epistemological model. In R. Naroll & R. Cohen (Eds.), *A handbook of method in cultural anthropology.* Garden City, NY: Natural History Press.

Clark, D., Astuto, T., & Kuh, G. (1983). *Strength of coupling in the organization and operation of colleges and universities.* Unpublished manuscript, Indiana University, School of Education.

Cohen, M., March, J., & Olsen, J. (1972). A garbage can model of organizational choice. *Administrative Science Quarterly, 17* (1), 1-25.

Deal, T., & Kennedy, A. (1983). *Culture: A new look through old lenses.* Paper presented at the American Educational Research Association, Montreal.

Fiedler, F. (1967). *A theory of leadership effectiveness.* New York: McGraw-Hill.

Getzels, J. (1958). Administration as a social process. In A. Halpin (Ed.), *Administrative theory in education.* Chicago: University of Chicago, Midwest Administration Center.

Gouldner, A. (1959). Organizational analysis. In R. Merton, L. Broom, & L. Cottrell (Eds.), *Sociology today.* New York: Basic Books.

Griffiths, D. (1983). Evolution in research and theory: A study of prominent researchers. *Educational Administration Quarterly, 19* (2), 201-221.

March, J. (1972). Model bias in social action. *Review of Educational Research, 42,* (4), 413-429.

Parsons, T. (Ed.). (1947). *Max Weber: The theory of social and economic organization* (A. Henderson & T. Parsons, trans.). New York: Free Press.

Perrow, C. (1982). Disintegrating social sciences. *Phi Delta Kappan, 63* (10), 684-688.

Peters, T., & Waterman, R. (1982). *In search of excellence: Lessons from America's best-run companies.* New York: Harper & Row.

Pfeffer, J. (1982). *Organizations and organization theory.* Boston: Pitman.

Schwartz, P., & Ogilvy, J. (1979). *The emergent paradigm: Changing patterns of thought and belief.* Menlo Park, CA: SRI International.

Simon, H. (1957). *Models of man.* New York: John Wiley.

Stogdill, R. (1974). *Handbook of leadership*. New York: Free Press.

Weick, K. (1979). *The social psychology of organizing*. Reading, MA: Addison-Wesley.

Weick, K. (1980). *Loosely coupled systems: Relaxed meanings and thick interpretations*. Unpublished manuscript.

3

THE CONTEXT OF EMERGENT PARADIGM RESEARCH

Egon G. Guba

The two preceding chapters have set the stage for these comments and have considerably reduced the scope of my task by defining and placing into context the key ideas upon which I will draw. We have seen that paradigms represent ways of looking at the world—they provide the orienting and interpreting principles that we employ in making sense of it. Yvonna Lincoln has shown that there are many possible paradigms, and that each is defined by a set of explicit or implicit assumptions or axioms. These axioms constitute the basic beliefs that we use as the final arbiter or touchstone in guiding our actions and decisions; they may be thought of as our most fundamental values. That they *are* basic beliefs is easily demonstrated, for they are the tenets or propostions beyond which there is no appeal. If there were something else to which to appeal, then that something else would be *the* basic belief. Basic beliefs can only be accepted or rejected; they can be neither proven nor falsified.

Lincoln's introduction together with Dr. Clark's contextual remarks about organizational theory have called our attention to the fact that there is a paradigm *shift*—to use the Kuhnian (1970) term—going on; that the conventional terms we have been accustomed to using to guide inquiry are giving way to new and dramatically different terms. The penetrating analysis of Schwartz and Ogilvy (1979), to which the introduction referred, suggests that this paradigm shift can be character-

Author's Note: *The ideas presented in this chapter are the fruits of my collaboration with Dr. Yvonna S. Lincoln. I am delighted to share with her both the credit and the blame for what I will say.*

ized along seven dimensions: complexity, heterarchy, holography, indeterminacy, mutual causality, morphogenesis, and perspective. It is my task to show that this emergent paradigm (which Schwartz and Ogilvy have detected, let me remind you, in a variety of *substantive* disciplines) also supports a new form of *disciplined inquiry,* the assumptions of which are polar opposites to the positivist ones with which most of us grew up.[1].

I shall first describe what I believe to be the salient basic beliefs that characterize positivism, and then delineate the axioms that undergird the emergent position, which I shall refer to as *naturalism.*[2] I will then undertake to demonstrate that the Schwartz and Ogilvy terms well support the basic beliefs of naturalism, authenticating and legitimating them as part of the new paradigm that is coming to characterize vanguard thinking in virtually all disciplines. I also will endeavor to refute the contention that positivism and naturalism can be compromised in some form of postpositivistic "grand synthesis" which realigns the basic beliefs of both systems into compatibility, and I come to the conclusion that in this case we *are* dealing with an either-or proposition, in which one must pledge allegiance to one paradigm or the other; there is no compromise.

AXIOMS OF THE POSITIVIST PARADIGM

The hold that positivism has had on our minds is well illustrated by the fact that we describe the emergent period as that of post-positivism; the new has insufficiently formed character to have a name of its own. It is only with reluctance that we give up our cherished former basic beliefs. I will return to the phenomenon of the "reluctant mind" later, but here I want to focus directly on those beliefs we are being persuaded to abandon. Just what is it that the positivist believes?

And there's the rub. You can find in the literature almost as many versions of the positivist "manifesto" as there are authors. (I might add that this does not surprise me or my fellow naturalists, as one of our tenets is that of multiple constructions of reality.) Reese (1980) in the *Dictionary of Philosophy and Religion* asserts that positivism is "a family of philosophies characterized by an extremely positive evaluation of science and the scientific method," hardly an operative formulation. Positivism might be thought of as the sum (the average?) of the positions held by the members of the renowned Vienna Circle of Logical Positivists, including such philosophers and scientists as Gustav Bergman, Rudolf Carnap, Philipp Frank, Hans Hahn, Otto Neurath, and Moritz Schlick, the latter being the group's founder and sometime guru. As a naturalist, however, I am skeptical of the possibility of arriving at a single set of basic beliefs that would adequately encompass their individual perspectives; the members of the group were as argumentative among themelves as with outsiders.

John Stuart Mill, an early advocate of what came to be called the positivist position, had his own list of assumptions, summarized by Hamilton (1976) as including the following: that science's aim is the discovery of general laws that serve for explanation and prediction; that concepts can be defined by direct reference to empirical categories—"objects in the concrete"; that there is a uniformity of nature in time and space; that the laws of nature can be inductively derived from data; and that large samples suppress idiosyncracies and reveal "general causes."

From a different perspective, Wolf (1981) suggests that the axioms of positivism can be inferred from Newtonian mechanics: that things move in a continuous manner; that things move for reasons that are themselves based on earlier causes for motion; that, as a result, all motion is determined and all things are predictable; that all motion can be analyzed and broken down into its component parts, so that the entire universe could be understood as the simple movement of its various parts (even those parts beyond our perception); and that the observer simply observed and never disturbed.

Mary Hesse (1980, p. vii), the British historian and philosopher of science, describes what she terms the "standard account" of scientific explanation within an empiricist philosophy as depending on these assumptions:

The most important are the assumptions of *naive realism,* of a *universal scientific language,* and of the *correspondence theory of truth.*

These three assumptions between them constitute a picture of science and the world somewhat as follows: there is an external world which can in principle be exhaustively described in scientific language. The scientist, as both observer and language-user, can capture the external facts of the world in propositions that are true if they correspond to the facts and false if they do not. Science is ideally a linguistic system in which true propositions are in one-to-one relation to facts, including facts that are not directly observed because they involve hidden entities or properties, or past events or far distant events. These hidden events are described as theories, and theories can be inferred from observations, that is, the hidden explanatory mechanism of the world can be discovered from what is open to observation. Man as scientist is regarded as standing apart from the world and able to experiment and theorize about it objectively and dispassionately.

Each of these formulations has something to recommend it; each contains kernels of insight into the positivist mind. But it is also the case that they (and others that could have been cited) differ in interesting ways; it is my own observation that analysts tend to select and emphasize those aspects of positivism that "set up" the objections they wish to mount against it. These objections usually include one or more of the following: that positivism confuses the contexts of discovery and justification, limiting science to the latter and relegating the former to playful imagination; that theory is underdetermined in the sense that there are always multiple theories that can be devised to account for the available "facts"—thus, there can be no certain conclusions and no certain prediction or control; that facts are always theory-laden in the sense that there cannot exist separate theoretical and observational languages; that positivism exhibits an overdependence on operationalism; that positivism displays two highly repugnant characteristics (determinism and reductionism); and/or that positivism fails to deal adequately with certain emergent empirical/conceptual formulations (a Kuhnian "crisis"). Of course my formulation of positivism is also selective; like other analysts, I will choose to emphasize those aspects that happen to be most vulnerable to the exceptions that I wish to take and open to the counterformulations I wish to propose. *Caveat emptor.*

Nevertheless, I hope you will agree that the axioms that I outline below do constitute a fair statement of the positivist position, understanding from the outset that there is no "real" or "ultimate" or "absolute" statement that could be made. All statements are constructions; the issue is whether my construction is fair. Here is my list:

Axiom 1: The nature of reality (ontology). There is a single, tangible reality "out there," fragmentable into independent variables and processes, any of which can be studied independently of the others; inquiry can converge on that reality until, finally, it can be predicted and controlled. (This axiom corresponds to Hesse's assumption of naive realism.)

Axiom 2: The inquirer-respondent relationship (subject-object dualism). The inquirer is able to maintain a discrete distance from the object of inquiry, neither disturbing it nor being disturbed by it.

Axiom 3: The purpose of inquiry (generalization). The aim of inquiry is to develop a nomothetic body of knowledge; this knowledge is best encapsulated in nomic (nomological) generalizations which are truth statements independent of both time and context (they will hold anywhere and at any time); the stuff of which generalizations are made is similarities among units.

Axiom 4: The nature of explanation (causality). Every action can be explained as the result (effect) of a cause that precedes the effect temporally (or is simultaneous with it).

Axiom 5: The role of values in inquiry (axiology). Inquiry is value free and can be guaranteed to be so by virtue of the methodology that is employed—the "facts speak for themselves."

It is beyond the scope here to provide the evidence necessary to challenge the adequacy of these axioms, although Yvonna Lincoln and I have addressed this matter in several other contexts (Guba, 1978, 1981; Guba & Lincoln, 1981, 1982; Lincoln & Guba, 1985). But I might in passing mention a few of the more salient counterindications:

Against naive realism: the futility and frustration that physicists have experienced in their efforts to locate those illusive "basic particles" whose motion makes the world predictable and controllable; the substitution for the concept of particles of the concept of standing quantum (electromagnetic) wave functions that are not "realized" except by the action of an observer, who thereby literally "creates" reality; the fact that in the social/behavioral sciences the reality that is being investigated consists of mental phenomena that exist only (and holistically) in the minds of individual people.

Against subject-object dualism: the recognition, first, that the "objects" of inquiry, when they are persons, exhibit reactivity; the fact that investigators are not only capable of disturbing the investigated phenomena but are in turn disturbed by them; the emergence of the Heisenberg Indeterminacy Principle in physics (which is now seen to have broad applicability in all fields), which asserts, in effect, that the mere act of observation alters what is being observed and makes portions of the phenomenological field inaccessible to the investigator.

Against generalizability: the observation that everything is interdependent (as corroborated in physics by Bell's Theorem, which asserts that no theory, if it is to be consistent with relativity theory, can declare two "pieces" of the universe to be independent, no matter how remote); Cronbach's (1975) observation that generalizations "decay" in the same way that radioactive materials do, so that after a period of time, a generalization is more history than science.

Against causality: the observation by Cook and Campbell (1979) that the epistemology of causality is "in a productive state of near chaos"; the fact that although there are many formulations of causality, the adherent of any one formulation are able to mount searching critiques of the others; the fact that the concept is being rejected in many areas as unworkable, including, for example, physics (if everything interacts all the time, how can one separate causes and effects?), medicine (the search for cancer's cause has been replaced by an effort to understand the variety of interactions between genes and environment that are implicated in development of cancer in any given individual), and even family therapy (coming to an understanding that the behavior of each family member influences all the others in a continuing round that makes the idea of cause-effect linkages untenable).

Against value independence: the fact that a variety of entries in the literature bear evidence against that assertion (see, for example, Bahm, 1971; Homans, 1978; Kelman, 1969; Krathwohl, 1980; Morgan & Smircich, 1980; Scriven, 1971); the wide variety of historical examples that demonstrate otherwise (for example, that Louis Pasteur altered his position against the possibility of spontaneous generation in order to accommodate the new Darwinian theory but continued to perform experiments consistent with his older belief because Darwinism was politically unacceptable in the New Empire of the 1860s in France; Farley & Geison, 1974); and because the claim of value-independence (note that it is itself a value claim!) has led to noticeably bad consequences, imposing a ritual of method, limiting the range of knowledge accessible to inquiry, eliminating moral decision making from the arena of science (which has on at least two occasions led to explosive results), investing findings with normative implications, forcing political decision making into a technical mode, and obscuring the problem of balance among views behind a facade of objectivity.

AXIOMS OF THE NATURALISTIC PARADIGM

There are many forms of what I have chosen to call the naturalistic paradigm, just as there are of the positivist. Various names—such as case study methodology, ethnographic method, anthropological method, qualitative method, and field method—are applied to it by different writers, often with the term "paradigm" substituted for method, as in "ethnographic paradigm" and "qualitative paradigm." Each of these formulations has its own distinct implications. Some of these forms I would find acceptable, as, for example, ethnographic paradigm, but others I would not, as, for example (and particularly), qualitative paradigm. I base my opposition on the fact that *the objectionable forms confuse paradigm—the overall model of how we come to know—with method—the particular means that we may use in implementing a paradigm.* If the distinctions are reduced simply to those of method, the basically incommensurable nature of these two sets of basic beliefs is obfuscated, leading to the delusion that some accommodation or rapprochement is possible between them, when, in fact, hard choices must be made. I shall return to this theme in some detail later, although I shall not find it possible, given present constraints of time and space, to make that argument as fully as I might like.

Let me move without further ado to a statement of the naturalistic axioms themselves, making the contrast between the new and the conventional paradigms as stark as possible:

Axiom 1: The nature of reality (ontology). There are multiple constructed realities that can be studied only holistically; inquiry into these multiple realities will inevitably diverge (each inquiry raises more questions than it answers), so that that prediction and control are unlikely outcomes, although some level of understanding *(verstehen)* can be achieved.

Axiom 2: The inquirer-respondent relationship (subject-object dualism). The inquirer and the "object" of inquiry interact to influence one another; especially is this mutual interaction present when the "object" of inquiry is another human being (respondent).

Axiom 3: The purpose of inquiry (generalization). The aim of inquiry is to develop an idiographic body of knowledge; this knowledge is best encapsulated in a series of "working hypotheses" that describe the individual case; differences are as inherently interesting as (and at times more so than) similarities.

Axiom 4: The nature of explanation (causality). An action may be explainable in terms of multiple interacting factors, events, and processes that shape it and are part of it; this interaction manifests itself as mutual and simultaneous shaping; inquirers can, at best, establish plausible inferences about the pattern of such shaping in a given case.

Axiom 5: The role of values in inquiry (axiology). Inquiry is value bound in at least five ways, captured in the corollaries that follow:

Corollary 1: inquiries are influenced by inquirer values as expressed in the *choice of the problem* and *in the framing, bounding, and focusing* of that problem.

Corollary 2: Inquiry is influenced by the choice of the *substantive paradigm* that guides the investigation into the problem (as Clark, Weick, and Huff demonstrate in their chapters).

Corollary 3: Inquiry is influenced by the choice of the *inquiry paradigm* that guides the investigation into the problem (as Guba, Lincoln, and Skrtic demonstrate in their chapters).

Corollary 4: Inquiry is influenced by the *values that inhere in the context:* social and cultural norms.

Corollary 5: With respect to Corollaries 1 through 4 above, inquiry is either *value-resonant* (reinforcing or congruent) or *value-dissonant* (conflicting). Problem, substantive, paradigm, inquiry paradigm, and context must exhibit congruence (value-resonance) if the inquiry is to product meaningful results. (The demonstration of this corollary is one of the major intentions of the authors in this book.)

As you will appreciate, the axioms of the naturalist paradigm are in direct opposition to those of the positivist. A summary of the two positions is displayed in Table 3.1 to make this point clear.

LEGITIMIZING THE NATURALIST POSITION

It is incumbent upon the proposer of a new position to argue for it; to suggest why, in his or her opinion, the new posture is warranted and on what basis it can be recommended. In the past, Yvonna Lincoln and I have undertaken this task largely by trying to show that the naturalist paradigm adequately fills the vacuum left by positivism's shortcomings. Anyone particularly interested in that line of argument is invited to consult our earlier writing, to which I have already alluded. Now, however, I wish to take a different tack by showing how the naturalistic paradigm of inquiry is authenticated and suported by the "new" paradigm of Schwartz and Ogilvy (1979).

In the Introduction Lincoln proposed that Schwartz and Ogilvy represent the new paradigm as based on seven concepts. It may be useful to comment on those further:

- *Movement from simple to complex realities:* The diversity and interactivity that characterize reality make it impossible to focus meaningfully on one or a few elements while holding everything else constant. It is in principle impossible to separate any phenomenon from its environment without losing crucial aspects of meaning. The whole *is* more than the sum of its parts.
- *Movement from hierarchic to heterarchic concepts of order:* There is no natural order; those orders that are identified are impositions of the human mind; orders exist side by side, and which order is predominant at any instant depends on a number of interacting and rapidly shifting factors.
- *Movement from a mechanical to a holographic metaphor:* The "real world" is not like a "grand machine" or a "clock," but like a holographic image in which every piece contains complete information about the

TABLE 3.1
Contrasting Positivist and Naturalist Axioms

Axioms About	Positivist Paradigm	Naturalist Paradigm
Ontology: the nature of reality	single, tangible, fragmentable, convergent	multiple, constructed, holistic, divergent
Objectivity: the inquirer-respondent relationship	independent	interrelated
Purpose: generalization	context and time-free generalizations; nomothetic statements; focus on similarities	context and time-bound working hypotheses; idiographic statements; focus on differences as much as on similarities
Explanation: causality	real causes, temporally precedent or simultaneous	interactive mutual shapers (feedback *and* feedforward)
Axiology: the role of values	value-free	value-bound

whole. While the whole is more than the sum of the parts, each part contains the whole within itself.

- *Movement from determinacy to indeterminacy:* The "real world" is not so determinate that if one only knew the position and velocity of all particles instantaneously, the future would be fully predictable; instead, ambiguity is the condition of nature.

- *Movement from linear to mutual causality:* The simple push-pull model of causality, even when aided by probabilistic formulations and buttressed by the notion of feedback, gives way to the notion of mutual causality, with feedback *and* feedforward, characterized by simultaneous influencing of factors over time.

- *Movement from assembly to morphogenesis:* As the metaphor for form is altered from a mechanical to a holographic image, the metaphor for change has moved from assembly (a "construction project") toward morphogenesis: dramatic and unpredictable change that operates to create higher-order forms from lower-order forms (in contrast to the concept of entropy).

- *Movement from objective to perspectival views:* Although objectivity is an illusion, the alternative is not subjectivity but perspective. No single viewpoint—even a discipline—provides more than a partial picture. Efforts to understand reality cannot be more than partial—and even the aggregate of "all" perspectives cannot yield a total picture.

TABLE 3.2
Basic Beliefs and Associated Principles
of the Schwartz and Ogilvy Paradigm

New Paradigm Basic Belief	Associated Principle
Complexity	Real-world entities are a diverse lot of complex systems and organisms.
Heterarchy	Systems and organisms experience many simultaneous and potentially equally dominant orderings—none of which is "naturally" ordained.
Holography	Images of systems and organisms are created by a dynamic process of interaction that is (metaphorically) similar to the hologram, whose three-dimensional images are stored and recreated by the interference patterns of a split laser beam.
Indeterminacy	Future states of systems and organisms are in principle unpredictable.
Mutual Causality	Systems and organisms evolve and change together in such a way (with feedback and feedforward) as to make the distinction between cause and effect meaningless.
Morphogenesis	New forms of systems and organisms unpredicted (and unpredictable) from any of their parts can arise spontaneously under conditions of diversity, openness, complexity, mutual causality, and indeterminacy.
Perspective	Mental processes, instruments, and even disciplines are not neutral.

These definitions are summarized in the form of "principles" in Table 3.2 for convenience.

The discussion of their "new paradigm" by Schwartz and Ogilvy provides a great deal of support for the proposition that the naturalistic paradigm can be seen as an overlapping case, in the same way that the emergent paradigms in physics, chemistry, mathematics, biology, and all of the other areas they examined also are seen as overlapping cases. Schwartz and Ogilvy use developments in these several fields inductively to support their delineation of the "universal" new paradigm; they could, had they thought about it, have used the developments regarding inquiry paradigms in the same way. But in turning the matter on its head, we can see how the Schwartz and Ogilvy paradigm *deductively* provides support for the naturalistic paradigm of inquiry.

An examination of their work led to the development of Table 3.3, which indicates the ways—primary, secondary, or not at all—that the seven Schwartz and Ogilvy terms are related to the five naturalistic axioms. The entries in the table represent my own judgment call, of course, the reader, and perhaps Schwartz and Ogilvy too, might quarrel with some of the calls made. Nevertheless, I believe the evidence in favor of some such representation as that of Table 3.3 is overwhelming. Let me see if I can make that case.

As I first read the Schwartz and Ogilvy monograph and began to appreciate its implications, I tried to achieve a higher level of understanding of each of their terms by abstracting their concepts and ideas into the form of "sentences" that I thought would add to my insight; thus, I had made up seven tables that contain sentences bearing on each of the seven basic beliefs. These "sentences" were sometimes literal quotations and sometimes paraphrases. Later, I realized that these collections of sentences could be "mined," as it were, in support of the naturalistic axioms; that is, it would be possible to pull out from the tables I had developed materials that would support the concepts reflected in the axioms. What Table 3.3 suggests, then, is that it was possible to pull out quite a few (or a few very telling) sentences from those cells in which the designation "primary" appears, at least some sentences from the cells in which the designation "secondary" appears, but little to nothing from the other cells. It will be seen that each of the axioms is supported (in my judgment) primarily or secondarily by at least two of the Schwartz and Ogilvy terms, whereas at the other extreme two of the axioms are supported by six of the seven Schwartz and Ogilvy terms. Let me now display the supporting sentences that I identified for each of the axioms; the reader should be aware that these sentences represent only a sampling. Some sentences appear in relation to more than one axiom.

(A) *For the axiom of multiple reality*
   (1) From "complexity" (primary support):
   - Systems and organisms cannot be separated from their environments because their meaning and even their existence depends on their interactions with other systems and organisms.
   - As systems and organisms become more complex, they develop unique properties (the whole is more than the sum of its parts).
   - Systems and organisms cannot be decomposed (fragmented) into individual elements (parts) because their unique systemic and organic properties transcend the elements (parts).
   - Meaning is not atomistic but contextual; to find meaning one needs to focus on the complex interrelationships that create a structure.
   - Inquiry must account for history and detail rather than permanence and generality.

TABLE 3.3
Support for the Naturalistic Axioms from the Schwartz and Ogilvy Terms

Schwartz and Ogilvy Terms	Axioms of the Naturalistic Paradigm				
	A: Multiple Constructed Reality	B: Inquirer-Respondent Interactivity	C: Time and Context Dependence	D: Mutual and Simultaneous Shaping	E: Value Dependence
1: Complexity	primary	—	primary	—	—
2: Heterarchy	secondary	—	secondary	secondary	secondary
3: Holographic	secondary	—	secondary	secondary	—
4: Indeterminacy	secondary	primary	primary	—	—
5: Mutual Causality	secondary	secondary	secondary	primary	—
6: Morphogenesis	—	—	secondary	primary	—
7: Perspective	primary	primary	—	—	primary

(2) From "heterarchy" (secondary support):
- The order we experience is a function of the activity of ordering performed by the mind; all apparently "real" orders are also determined by a mental ordering activity.
- Human action is oriented more toward pluralism than singularity (of values, political structures, etc.); it is mediated more by a heteracity of guiding principles than by hierarchy of functions.

(3) From "holographic" (secondary support):
- Everything is interconnected.

(4) From "indeterminacy" (secondary support):
- There is a reciprocal involvement between the knower and the known.

(5) From "mutual causality" (secondary support):
- The universe is an interconnected network, an indivisible whole.

(6) From "perspective" (primary support):
- Where and how one looks at systems and organisms affects what will be seen; the knower's perspective is crucial in determining what is known.
- What we believe about systems and organisms determines much of what we see (believing is seeing).
- One form of knowledge or method cannot be reduced into another.
- Reality is not something that remains, no matter what people think about it; reality is utterly dependent on human cognition.

(B) *For the axiom of inquirer-respondent interactivity*

(1) From "indeterminacy" (primary support):
- There is a reciprocal involvement between the knower and the known.
- The nature of the observation process affects the results; measurements are determined by the relationship between the observer and the observed.

(2) From "mutual causality" (secondary support):
- We are part of the net; what we do affects other parts, including what we wish to study; thus, any description of reality is always partial.

(3) From "perspective" (primary support):
- Where and how one looks at systems and organisms affects what will be seen; the knower's perspective is crucial in determining what is known.
- Knowledge is protected not by abstracting from all perspectives (the claim for objectivity) but by balancing multiple perspectives to constrain bias (the claim for fairness).
- Objectivity is an illusion.

(C) *For the axiom of time and context dependence*

(1) From "complexity" (primary support):

- Systems and organisms cannot be separated from their environments because their meaning and even their existence depends on their interactions with other systems and organisms.
- Knowledge requires engagement with a system or organism in its environment, so that it can be seen in a meaning-defining context.
- Inquiry must account for history and detail rather than permanence and generality.

(2) From "heterarchy" (secondary support):
- Which system(s) or organism(s) are dominant or superior at any given time depends on the total situation and is determined by system or organism interactions.

(3) From "holographic" (secondary support):
- Information is distributed throughout the system rather than being concentrated at specific points.

(4) From "indeterminacy" (primary support):
- In complex systems and organisms future possibilities can be known, but precise outcomes cannot be predicted; that is, predictability is replaced by probability.

(5) From "mutual causality" (secondary support):
- To understand a system or organism completely requires knowing its history, which cannot be completely known from its present condition.
- Mutual causality in complex systems and organisms tends to produce unpredictable results.

(6) From "morphogenesis" (secondary support):
- Change is not only continuous and quantitative but discontinuous and qualitative.

(D) *For the axiom of mutual and simultaneous shaping*

(1) From "heterarchy" (secondary support):
- Structures of systems and organisms operate heterarchically, creating a net of mutual constraints and influences.

(2) From "holographic" (secondary support):
- Everything is interconnected.

(3) From "mutual causality" (primary support):
- Strict deterministic causality is replaced by unpredictable innovation arising morphogenetically through mutually causal interactions and fluctuations.
- There is a complex of mutually interacting "causes" leading to a particular outcome.
- The universe is an interconnected network, an indivisible whole.
- In complex systems and organisms, mutual causality leads not to stability but to symbiotic change (positive feedback and feedforward) and evolution.
- Mutual causality in complex systems and organisms tends to produce unpredictable results.

(4) From "morphogenesis" (primary support):
- New and different systems and organisms arise out of old through a complex process that amplifies deviation through a reciprocal (mutual) causality (positive feedback and feedforward) and through interactions with the surrounding environment.
- Fluctuations in a system or organism interact, affecting each other and mutually causing whole new systems and organisms to arise.
- More highly ordered systems and organisms are produced from less highly ordered, simple systems and organisms; order can arise even from disorder.
- Components constrain but do not determine form in morphogenetic change.

(E) *For the axiom of value dependence*

   (1) From "heterarchy" (secondary support):
- Human action is oriented more toward pluralism than singularity (of values, political structures, and the like); it is mediated more by a heterarchy of guiding principles than by a hierarchy of functions.

   (2) From "perspective" (primary support):
- Where and how one looks at systems and organisms affects what will be seen; the knower's perspective is crucial in determining what is known.
- What we believe about systems and organisms determines much of what we see (believing is seeing).
- Knowledge is protected not by abstracting from all perspectives (the claim for objectivity) but by balancing multiple perspectives to constrain bias (the claim for fairness).
- All knowledge, far from being disinterested, is ultimately interested knowledge; an imperative for science is to conduct inquiry as if people really mattered.
- Publicly shared reality is not unchanging (objective); what counts as reality shifts as shared paradigms shift.
- The concept of paradigm shift (itself a kind of perspectival difference) opens the possibility of an almost limitless proliferation of research programs based on widely different assumptions.

It is hoped that this analysis is persuasive if not compelling, although it may require several readings and considerable meditation to achieve even the former. Nevertheless, one can find in Schwartz and Ogilvy ample evidence for the naturalistic axioms. Conversely, Schwartz and Ogilvy would likely find in the naturalistic axioms further evidence for their "new" paradigm. They are all of a piece; the naturalistic paradigm is a representation in the specific arena of inquiry of the "new" paradigm in the same way that representations can be found in physics (e.g., quantum standing waves), chemistry (e.g., dissipative structures), mathematics (e.g., catastrophe theory), evolution (e.g., mutual adaptation theory), politics (e.g., pluralism), and in many other fields.

THE CALL FOR COMPROMISE: DARE WE HEED IT?

To return now to the question of whether it is possible to effect a compromise between the positivist and the naturalist paradigms: Is it not the case, after all, that the older paradigm can be refined to accommodate the emergent ideas? Is it the case that we do not need a revolution so much as a reconstruction, not *detente* but *rapprochement,* not divorce but reconciliation?

Gareth Morgan (1983), in his stimulating volume *Beyond Method,* has taken up the question of the degree to which different formulations about inquiry can be accommodated. He outlined five possible approaches:

(1) Supremacy: One approach is to seek to establish one of the approaches as "best," as supreme over the others. But I agree with Morgan in finding this approach impossible in principle, because no criteria can be found that are not themselves in a one-to-one relationship with the assumptions of one of the paradigms under test. Relativism makes this test impossible.

(2) Synthesis: This approach attempts to find ways "of combining the strengths and minimizing the weaknesses" of the several paradigms—a kind of eclecticism. Morgan suggests that "attempts to find an all-embracing paradigm or metaphor for framing inquiry, to translate different strategies into a common language, or to find ways of overcoming traditional dichotomies, provide good examples of such integrative effort" (p. 378). Although Morgan does not comment on the adequacy of this approach, it can be rejected on the grounds that it is reductionist and that it is inconsistent with Gödel's theorem (Hofstadter, 1979), which asserts that no consistent set of statements can ever hope to deal with all decideable propositions.

(3) Contingency: This approach suggests that the inquirer examine the contingencies that exist in the context and phenomena under study and then to select that paradigm that provides the best "fit" to those contingencies. It stresses the practicality of assumptions for given purposes rather than their ability to disclose "truth." This approach is not useful in the present case (although it might be, should some other new paradigm of evident power emerge) because I believe (despite some

opinions that I expressed in earlier writing) that the naturalistic paradigm is the paradigm of choice on fittingness grounds whenever human/social/cultural inquiry is at issue. Readers may wish to test that assertion personally by considering the axioms outlined in Table 3.1 and asking which seem to them more reasonable to assume in that case.

(4) Dialectic: This approach "attempts to use the difference among competing perspectives as a means of constructing new modes of understanding" (Morgan, 1983, p. 379). It does not lead directly to a decision; rather, it suggests a process whereby the paradigmatic debate may be carried on, hopefully to some eventual resolution (but if that solution is synthesis, see objections to 2 above). As professionals are now debating paradigmatic issues, this dialectic process may already be under way. The process is not, however, one in which an individual inquirer can engage to come to some decision about how to proceed.

(5) Anything goes: Morgan describes this approach as the "radical epistemology" espoused by Paul Feyerabend. Morgan cites Feyerabend as asserting that "there is no idea, however ancient or absurd, that is not capable of improving our knowledge. Approaches to research that are complementary, contradictory, or proceed counterintuitively are all acceptable because they may generate some form of insight and understanding that cannot be achieved in any other way" (p. 380). Radical epistemology thus seems to offer the naturalist some legitimacy, urging, as it seems to do, a "hands-off" policy on the part of adherents of the conventional paradigm who might otherwise be uncharitable to the upstart, perhaps even intending to dismiss the new paradigm as profane and unregenerate. On the other hand, the naturalist is likely to be equally intolerant of the old, feeling that the philosophy of "anything goes" simply makes it possible for outmoded ideas to continue to hold sway and makes an attack on them appear fanatical.

Having drawn all of these distinctions, Morgan does not help us to choose. An answer to the questions posed by him, "Should we attempt to evaluate assumptions, search for common ground, adopt a criterion of usefulness, engage in dialectics, or decide that anything goes?" (p. 380) is dogged by relativism, he concludes, as much as is any other aspect of this problem.

Despite this dilemma, the current literature does not lack in hortatory pieces urging the profession to effect an accommodation. Virtually all of the arguments mounted under this banner are based at bottom on a fundamental confusion between paradigm and method (see, for instance, Miles & Huberman, 1984). The siren song sung by the protagonists has several verses, each of which makes a somewhat different method-for-paradigm substitution:

The "mix and match" ballad: This tune suggests that the two paradigms are complementary; that is, that they can be used side by side with synergistic effects. In 1973, Sam Sieber called for the integration of fieldwork and survey methods. More recently, Cook and Reichardt (1979) have urged us to look "beyond" qualitative and quantitative methods to achieve a dialectical synthesis. Trend (1979) offers us a case study in support of the Cook and Reichardt thesis. Patton (1982), writing about evaluation, relegates the distinctions to an epistemological oblivion because at the practical level (he asserts) mix and match strategies are essential to meet all of the demands that are likely to be made on the evaluator.

The "straw man" symphony: Advocates argue that the distinctions between paradigms amount to "nothing more" than, say, the distinctions between quantitative and qualitative methods (Gibbs, 1979) or between the contexts of discovery and justification (but see Hesse, 1980, for a strong counterargument). Once the discussion is reduced to a distinction between methods, or focuses on the question of whether or not the context of discovery is, properly speaking, within the domain of science (Ford, 1975, for example, argues that it is not, because it is only the empirical methodology of the context of verification that should be viewed as "real" science), it is easy to dispose of the conflict and achieve resolution.

The "fix to fit" fugue: Proponents of this strategy argue that the naturalist paradigm is a special case of the conventional paradigm, but needs "fixing up" to fit the parameters of the latter. So LeCompte and Goetz (1982) suggest that something needs to be done to shore up the reliability and validity of naturalistic data; Huberman and Miles (1982) propose techniques of data reduction and display for qualitative data that are remarkably similar (in format if not content) to old, tried-and-true quantitative approaches; and Herriott and Firestone (1982) propose techniques that would permit drawing generalizations across case studies.

There seems to be little doubt that anyone interested in forcing a fit between these two paradigms can find a way to appear to do so. The distinguished epistemologist Quine (1953) has noted that any proposition can be maintained to be "true" in the face of any opposition, "if we make drastic enough adjustments elsewhere in the system" (p. 43). It is as if, to coin a phrase, the paradigm were "loosely coupled." Along similar lines, Wimsatt (1981) notes what he terms the "robustness" of theories, a robustness, he claims, that derives from the fact that portions of theory are walled off from one another:

The thing that is remarkable about scientific theories is that the inconsistencies are walled off and do not appear to affect the theory other than very locally.... When an inconsistency occurs, results which depend on one or another of the contradictory assumptions are infirmed. This infection is transitive; it passes to things that depend on these results, and to their logical descendants, like a string of dominoes—until we reach something that has independent support. The independent support of an assumption sustains it, and the collapse propagates no further. If all deductive or inferential paths leading to a contradiction pass through robust results, the collapse is bounded within them, and the inconsistencies are walled off from the rest of the network. For each robust result, one of its modes of support is destroyed; but it has others, and therefore the collapse goes no further. (Wimsatt, 1981, p. 134)

How the "reluctant mind" (or, less pejoratively, the neo-orthodox, to borrow Dr. Clark's felicitous phrase) must revel in this robustness, for it furnishes both hope that the old can be retained (it is ultimately impervious to demolition) and license for deft alterations that seem to eliminate conflicts. We are reminded of other examples of conceptual reluctance, such as the refusal of the Paduan professors to look for themselves through Galileo's telescope (Harre, 1981), or the complaint of chemists that Lavoisier's theory of oxygen could not be finally accepted until it also explained what happened to the phlogiston (McCann, 1978)! Indeed, one might argue that there exist current efforts to "close the gap" between paradigms by just such adjustments and modifications, designed to accommodate the "paradigm crisis" so well-described by Kuhn (1970) that now appears to beset the conventional approach.

I have tried to illustrate some of these "adjustments" in Table 3.4. Rather than move directly from the naive realism of positivism to the multiple, constructed reality of naturalism, we are urged to accept the posture of the "critical realist" (Cook & Campbell, 1979). Thus, the

critical-realist mode enables us to recognize causal perceptions as "subjective" or "constructed by the mind"; but at the same time it stresses that many causal perceptions constitute assertions about the nature of the world which go beyond the immediate experience of perceivers and so have *objective contents which can be right or wrong* (albeit not always testable). The perspective is realist because it assumes that causal relationships *exist outside of the human mind,* and it is critical-realist because it assumes that these valid causal relationships cannot be perceived with total accuracy by our imperfect sensory and intellective capacities. (p. 29, emphases added)

TABLE 3.4
Transitional Postures:
Attempts at Paradigm Reconciliation

Axiom	Positivist View (Normal Orthodoxy)	Transitional View (Retrenchment Neo-Orthodoxy)	Postpositivist View (Emergent Nonorthodoxy)
Reality	naive realism	critical realism	constructionism
Dualism	objectivity	reactivity	interactivity
Time and context dependence	nomic generalization (freedom)	statistical abstraction: multiple regression; multivariate analysis; path analysis	dependence
Causality	linear	activity theory	mutual, simultaneous shaping
Values	value freedom	values influence selection of problem theory, method, and analysis	complete value boundedness

This sounds suspiciously like the tale of the blind men and the elephant in new guise. Although the authors here are discussing causality, it is clear that their statements were predicated on the assumption of a final, objective reality that exists "out there" and would be accessible were it not for our imperfect sensory apparatus!

With respect to the objectivity assumption—subject-object dualism—the conventional paradigm has already made some remarkable shifts by recognizing the phenomenon of reactivity and by constructing means for dealing with it, for example, the quasi-experimental designs of Campbell and Stanley (1966) and the unobtrusive measures of Webb and his associates (1966, 1981). But these formulations fall far short of dealing adequately with interactivity, still denounced as leading to "mere" subjectivity and resolutely to be guarded against by interpolating ever more layers of "objective" instrumentation between inquirer and phenomenon.

With respect to dependence on time and context, efforts to take these factors into account are also well advanced. Multiple regression, multivariate analysis (with its delineation of interactions to third, fourth, and even higher orders), path analysis, and other techniques of modern statistics seem, to the positivist mind, to be ideal means for handling the contextual complexities that plague the analyst: technical means for handling what are, at bottom, merely technical problems. The argument seems to be simply this: If inquiry is designed in such a way as to enlarge the scope of variables considered, thereby accounting for more and more contextual influences, then the newer statistics are quite competent to take context into account and yield conclusions that can be considered as general laws. But of course this approach ignores the fact that phenomena are not only *influenced* by the factors of time and context *but derive their very meaning from them*. It is this order of interdependence that statistics cannot now and never will be able to handle. As LaBarre (1980) has noted with respect to cultures, which he describes as molar complexes, "numbers here can operate only etically fragmented shards assembled from maimed wholes" (p. 15). His marvelous metaphor can easily be extended to every other holistic phenomenon studied by social and behavioral inquirers.

On the matter of causality, we are urged to replace the archaic notion of linear causality with an "activity theory" (Cook & Campbell, 1979) that eschews more fundamental discussion about agency, mechanism, asymmetry, simultaneity, and other bugaboos of causal epistemology in favor of a cookbook or instruction book approach that stresses manipulation (one cannot but suspect that the activity posture is favored because it endows experimentation with so much legitimation). Indeed, Cook and Campbell (1979, p. 28) comment:

> The image of a recipe brings to mind the current limitations of learning about manipulable causal forces in the social world. Recipes usually specify multiple ingredients and precise quantities from which only a small deviation is allowed. In addition, the ingredients often are mixed and prepared in a set order, with a precise oven temperature for cooking. When reliable knowledge of causal relationships in the social world also depends on multivariate causal interconnections, on the exact specifications of levels for each causal force, and on specific orders of combining variables, acquiring reliable causal knowledge will be difficult and causal connections will simply not repeat from one instance to the next. Since the causal manipulanda of social policy interest can rarely be finely adjusted, we may have to content ourselves at present in more complex setting with manipulanda that only sometimes bring about intended effects. With more research and other experiences, the contingency variables on which causal impact co-depends will probably be specified, the knowledge of causal relationships will then improve in reliability.

Cook and Campbell seem to admit the point (e.g., multivariate causal connections; manipulanda that only sometimes bring about the intend-

ed effects; codependence of causal effects on multiple contingency variables), but then urge us to stand fast in the true faith, waiting on "more
research and other experiences" to delineate the added variables needed
to improve reliability, presumably to a point acceptable by positivist
criteria!

Finally, with respect to values, a spate of articles currently fills the
literature pointing out how values impinge on inquiry by guiding the
selection of a problem, a theory, a method, and a means of analysis and
interpretation. We are thereby asked to believe that modern positivists
understand the role of values and take them into account. But it would
be naive to accept this explanation at face value. Empirically, there is
still no evidence that positivist inquirers do take them into account; we
see no reflexive accounts in their reports, and the reconstructed logic of
their inquiries, which they present in their methodological sections, still
hews the traditional line. Further, admitting to the penetration of values
to this level is superficial at best; it betrays no insight into the possibility
that the theory and the method may also be value-based, that contextual
values may impinge to prevent the facts from "speaking for themselves,"
and, worst of all, that there may be resonance or dissonance among all
these value positions.

Yet, despite these arguments against the wisdom of attempting a
reconciliation, we continue to hear calls for it. Indeed, Campbell goes so
far as to suggest that we are ready to enter a "post-post-positivist"
period.[3] In his William James Lecture 5, delivered in 1977, he describes
science as a social system with all the usual attributes of such a system:
norms, roles, communication channels, modes for recruiting and re-
warding members and keeping them loyal, and so on. He goes on to say,

> But I want to assert that among all these belief preserving mutual admira-
> tion societies, all of which share this common human tribalism, science is
> also different, with different specific values, myths, rituals, and command-
> ments, and that these different norms are related to what is presumed to
> be science's superiority in the improving validity of the model of the
> physical world which it carries. . . . In spite of the theory-ladenness and
> noisiness of unedited experimental evidence, it does provide a major
> source of discipline in science. . . . The experiment is meticulously de-
> signed to put questions to "Nature Itself" in such a way that neither the
> questioners, nor their colleagues, nor their superiors can affect the an-
> swer. . . . In our iterative oscillation of theoretical emphases, in our
> continual dialectic that never achieves a stable synthesis, we are now
> ready for a post-post-positivist theory of science that will integrate the
> epistemological relativism recently achieved with a new and more com-

plex understanding of the role of experimental evidence and predictive confirmation in science. (cited in Brewer & Collins, 1981, pp. 15-16)

It is my opinion, to the contrary, that what we are witnessing is much more than one of those "iterative oscillations" that now and then plague any field, one of those swings of the pendulum characteristic of every mode of thought. Gödel's theorem in mathematics (Hofstadter, 1979) well asserts that no comprehensive theory can also be entirely internally consistent. To understand the meaning of that theorem, Hofstadter suggests that we imagine a tree with its many branches starkly outlined against a background that represents "all" possible knowledge. The tree has its roots in its axioms, from which spring the trunk and all the many individual branches (which might, if one were interested solely in mathematics, be thought of as the theorems). Now the branches take us into many nooks and crannies of the background of reality; as we climb up and down the branches, we can reach out and touch large parts of it. But there are always parts of the background that cannot be reached from any vantage point on that particular tree; to reach these other places requires climbing a different tree whose branches do afford an appropriate platform. But that tree has its own roots, its own axioms, that need not be consistent with the first (indeed, the separate root systems may, to continue the metaphor, be in competition with one another, in actual conflict as they struggle to acquire for their tree the appropriate sustenance and water). Climbing a particular tree opens many options for the climber, but also closes off others. When we elect to climb a particular tree we ought first to be as sure as we can that its branches reach where we want to go.

I hope that readers will come to see the naturalist tree as the one to climb *if*—and I stress if—they wish to study organizations from the point of view of the "new" theory outlined in the chapters by Clark, Huff, and Weick. The consistent concentration on variables within organizations, to the exclusion of the interconnectedness of members' roles, has resulted in an unprofitable narrowing of the range of considerations of organizational lives. By turning the assumptions of the classical paradigm on their heads, we derive a new set that exhibits both better fit and resonance with emergent administrative constructs.

NOTES

1. I use the term "disciplined inquiry" in the sense defined by Cronbach and Suppes (1969, p. 16): "the report of a disciplined inquiry has a texture that displays the raw

materials entering into the argument and the logical processes by which they were compressed and rearranged to make the conclusion credible."

2. The term "naturalism" should not be interpreted as implying a claim that the new paradigm is somehow more natural than were previous ones. It derives from the fact that naturalistic inquiries tend to be carried out in natural settings, as opposed to contrived, laboratory, or experimental settings (a point to be made in more detail in a following chapter).

3. This and other references to Donald T. Campbell in this chapter are not intended to label him as a leader among the "reluctant mind" group. Campbell has consistently displayed an openness to new ideas throughout his career. He does, however, display a remarkable singlemindedness in his efforts to accommodate new ideas within the old paradigm rather than to use them as a wedge to break away from traditional constraints.

REFERENCES

Bahm, A. J. (1971). Science is not value-free. *Policy Sciences, 2,* 391-396.

Brewer, M. B., & Collins, B. E. (Eds.). (1981). *Scientific inquiry and the social sciences.* San Francisco: Jossey-Bass.

Campbell, D. T., & Stanley, J. C. (1966). Experimental and quasi-experimental designs for research on teaching. In N. L. Gage (Ed.), *Handbook of research on teaching.* Chicago: Rand McNally.

Cook, T. D., & Campbell, D. T. (1979). *Quasi-experimentation: Design and analysis issues for field settings.* Chicago: Rand McNally.

Cook, T. D., & Reichardt, C. S. (Eds.). (1979). *Qualitative and quantitative methods in evaluation research.* Beverly Hills, CA: Sage.

Cronbach, L. J. (1975). Beyond the two disciplines of scientific psychology. *American Psychologist, 30,* 116-127.

Cronbach, L. J., & Suppes, P. (1969). *Research for tomorrow's schools: Disciplined inquiry in education.* New York: Macmillan.

Farley, J., & Geison, G. (1974). Science, politics, and spontaneous generation in nineteenth century France: The Pasteur-Pouchet debate. *Bulletin of the History of Medicine, 48,* 161.

Ford, J. (1975). *Paradigms and fairy tales.* London: Routledge & Kegan Paul.

Gibbs, J. C. (1979). The meaning of ecologically oriented inquiry in contemporary psychology. *American Psychologist, 34,* 127-140.

Guba, E. G. (1978). *Toward a methodology of naturalistic inquiry in educational evaluation* (Monograph 8). Los Angeles: UCLA Center for the Study of Evaluation.

Guba, E. G. (1981). Criteria for assessing the trustworthiness of naturalistic inquiries. *Educational Communication and Technology Journal, 29,* 75-92.

Guba, E. G., & Lincoln, Y. S. (1981). *Effective evaluation.* San Francisco: Jossey-Bass.

Guba, E. G., & Lincoln, Y. S. (1982). Epistemological and methodological bases of naturalistic inquiry. *Educational Communication and Technology Journal, 30,* 233-252.

Hamilton, D. (1976). *A science of the singular* (Workshop Paper on Case-Study Research). Urbana: University of Illinois.

Harre, T. (1981). The positivist-empiricist approach and its alternative. In P. Reason & J. Rowan (Eds.), *Human inquiry: A sourcebook of new paradigm research.* New York: John Wiley.

Herriott, R. E., & Firestone, W. A. (1982). Multisite qualitative policy research: Optimizing description and generalizability. *Educational Researcher, 12,* 14-19.

Hesse, M. (1980). *Revolutions and reconstructions in the philosophy of science.* Bloomington: Indiana University Press.

Hofstadter, D. R. (1979). *Gödel, Escher, Bach.* New York: Basic Books.

Homans, G. A. (1978). What kind of a myth is the myth of value-free social science? *Social Science Quarterly, 58,* 530-541.

Huberman, A. M., & Miles, M. B. (1982). *Drawing valid meaning from qualitative data: Some techniques of data reduction and display.* Paper presented at the annual meeting of the American Educational Research Association, New York.

Kelman, H. C. (1969). *A time to speak: On human values and social research.* San Francisco: Jossey-Bass.

Krathwohl, D. R. (1980). The myth of value-free evaluation. *Educational Evaluation and Policy Analysis, 2,* 37-45.

Kuhn, T. S. (1970). *The structure of scientific revolutions* (2nd ed.). Chicago: University of Chicago Press.

LaBarre, W. (1980). *Culture in context: Selected writings of Weston LaBarre.* Durham, NC: Duke University Press.

LeCompte, M. D., & Goetz, J. P. (1982). Problems of reliability and validity in ethnographic research. *Review of Educational Research, 52,* 31-60.

Lincoln, Y. S., & Guba, E. G. (1985). *Naturalistic Inquiry.* Beverly Hills, CA: Sage.

McCann, H. G. (1978). *Chemistry transformed: The paradigmatic shift from phlogiston to oxygen.* Norwood, NJ: Ablex.

Miles, M. B., & Huberman, A. M. (1984). Drawing valid meaning from qualitative data: Toward a shared craft. *Educational Researcher, 13,* 20-30.

Morgan, G. (1983). *Beyond method.* Beverly Hills, CA: Sage.

Morgan, G., & Smircich, L. (1980). The case for qualitative research. *Academy of Management Review, 5,* 491-500.

Patton, M. Q. (1982). *Practical evaluation.* Beverly Hills, CA: Sage.

Quine, W. V. (1953). *From a logical point of view.* Cambridge, MA: Harvard University Press.

Reason, P., & Rowan, J. (Eds.). (1981). *Human inquiry: A sourcebook of new paradigm research.* New York: John Wiley.

Reese, W. L. (1980). *Dictionary of philosophy and religion.* Atlantic Highlands, NJ: Humanities Press.

Reichardt, C. S., & Cook, T. D. (1979). Beyond qualitative and quantitative methods. In T. D. Cook & C. S. Reichardt (Eds.), *Qualitative and quantitative methods in evaluation research.* Beverly Hills, CA: Sage.

Schwartz, P., & Ogilvy, J. (1979). *The emergent paradigm: Changing patterns of thought and belief* (Analytic Report 7, Values and Lifestyles Program). Menlo Park, CA: SRI International.

Scriven, M. (1971). Objectivity and subjectivity in educational research. In L. G. Thomas (Ed.), *Philosophical redirection of educational research.* Chicago: University of Chicago Press.

Sieber, S. D. (1973). The integration of fieldwork and survey methods. *American Journal of Sociology, 78,* 1335-1359.

Skrtic, T. M., Guba, E. G., & Knowlton, H. E. (1985). *Interorganizational special education programming in rural areas: Technical report on the multi-site naturalistic field study.* Washington, DC: National Institute of Education.

Trend, M. G. (1979). On the reconciliation of qualitative and quantitative analyses: A case study. In T. D. Cook & C. S. Reichardt (Eds.), *Qualitative and quantitative methods in evaluation research.* Beverly Hills, CA: Sage.

Webb, E. J., Campbell, D. T., Schwartz, R. D., & Sechrest, L. (1966). *Unobtrusive measures.* Chicago: Rand McNally.

Webb, E. J., Campbell, D. T., Schwartz, R. D., Sechrest, L., & Grove, J. B. (1981). *Nonreactive measures in the social sciences.* Boston: Houghton-Mifflin.

Wimsatt, W. C. (1981). Robustness, reliability, and overdetermination. In M. B. Brewer & B. E. Collins (Eds.), *Scientific inquiry and the social sciences.* San Francisco: Jossey-Bass.

Wolf, F. A. (1981). *Taking the quantum leap.* New York: Harper & Row.

PART II

The Concepts of the Paradigmatic Shift

4

SOURCES OF ORDER IN UNDERORGANIZED SYSTEMS: THEMES IN RECENT ORGANIZATIONAL THEORY

Karl E. Weick

Because new ideas are often hard to grasp, authors sometimes use metaphors to introduce them. One recurring metaphor that has been used to suggest an alternative view of organizations portrays an unconventional soccer game played on an unconventional soccer field. There are at least two versions of this metaphor in the published literature. Although both versions suggest a new way of thinking, they differ in significant ways.

Version 1 of the soccer metaphor appears on page 1 of my 1976 article in *Administrative Science Quarterly* entitled "Educational Organizations as Loosely Coupled Systems." Version 1 read as follows:

> Imagine that you're either the referee, coach, player or spectator at an unconventional soccer match: the field for the game is round; there are several goals scattered haphazardly around the circular field, people can enter and leave the game whenever they want; they can say "that's my goal" whenever they want to, as many times as they want to, and for as many goals as they want to; the entire game takes place on a sloped field, and the game is played as if it makes sense.

Author's Note: *This chapter was written while I held the Thomas F. Gleed Chair of Business and Finance at Seattle University, and this support is gratefully acknowledged. Portions of this chapter were presented at a career development seminar entitled, "Linking New Concepts of Organizations to New Paradigms for Inquiry," Overland Park, Kansas, November 4-5, 1983.*

Version 2 of the soccer metaphor appears on page 276 of the March and Olson book titled *Ambiguity and Choice in Organizations* (1976) in a chapter that March coauthored with Pierre Romelaer. The second version reads as follows:

> Consider a round, sloped, multi-goal soccer field on which individuals play soccer. Many different people (but not everyone) can join the game (or leave it) at different times. Some people can throw balls into the game or remove them. Individuals while they are in the game try to kick whatever ball comes near them in the direction of the goals they like and away from the goals that they wish to avoid. The slope of the field produces a bias in how the balls fall and what goals are reached, but the course of a specific decision and the actual outcomes are not equally anticipated. After the fact, they may look rather obvious; and usually normatively reassuring.

The difference between the two versions can be understood by focusing on the second version. In it

(1) many people can join the game, but not everyone;
(2) people can either leave the game or join it;
(3) some people can throw balls into the game, but others can't;
(4) some people can remove balls from the game, but others can't;
(5) players do not kick the ball in just any old direction; they kick it in the direction of goals they like and away from goals they wish to avoid;
(6) there is just one slope to the field, not many slopes, and this slope produces a consistent bias in which goals are reached easily; but some goals are usually reached.

Goal setting is more haphazard in version 1, in which people lay claim to whatever goals they wish, whenever they wish. In version 2 goal setting is more stable and is defined in terms of things people like and things they wish to avoid.

Version 2 states that the course of decisions and the nature of actual outcomes are not easily anticipated, whereas version 1 makes no mention at all of decisions, outcomes, or anticipations.

Both versions state that people try to make sense of this confusing world. Version 1 states that people play the game "as if it makes sense." Version 2 states that decisions and outcomes may look "obvious" and "reassuring," but only after the fact (retrospectively). In both versions any sense that people make of these events is contained in their heads rather than in events and is superimposed on the events. The subtle difference is that in version 1 active efforts to make sense of the confusion occur while the game is being played (the presumption of logic), whereas in version 2 sense is superimposed after the game concludes and the outcome is known.

Version 2 states explicitly that people understand that they are playing soccer (see sentence 1). This constraint is not explicitly stated in version 1, which says only that people play some game as if it makes sense, although it's not clear that all participants have soccer in mind as the game they are playing.

Goals are "multiple" in version 2, but are scattered haphazardly in version 1. In version 2 there might or might not be some order in the way the goals are arranged.

The slope of the field in version 1 essentially adds one more complication for the confused player, whereas in version 2 the slope of the field seems to influence which balls reach which goals, a consistent influence that introduces some order.

In each of these comparisons version 1 contains less order than version 2. It's as if the author of version 1 thought that the key point about organizations is that they contain no order at all. Others have made the same mistake. Starbuck (1982, p. 16), for example, observed that "although the garbage-can model (which is the theoretical context within which March originated his version of the soccer metaphor), captures some aspects of real life, it puts too much emphasis on randomness."

The soccer game portrayed in version 2 is far from random. Small, subtle pockets of order occur in several places. Order resides in timing, participation, ideology, language, shared images, overlapping individual goals, stable a priori preferences, a consistent environment for the game itself (imparted by the slope of the field). Less prominent as sources of order in the soccer games are the usual trappings of administration such as rules, regulations, standard operating procedures, constant surveillance, lines of authority, clear narrow job descriptions, detailed specifications of desired outcomes, official goals, and organizational charts. Not only is order present in unexpected places, but the small amount of order that does exist seems to be sufficient.

There is room in the soccer game for improvisation, change, redefinition, new goals, experimentation, even as there is also an elementary structure within which people get their bearings. Any temptation to "tighten up" the soccer game would not be an obvious improvement and could, in fact, undo the structure that is there.

The point in dissecting the two versions of the soccer game is that the newer models of organization suggest that order occurs in unexpected places and spans fewer people for shorter periods than we thought. These newer proposals, however, do not claim that order is completely absent. Organizations may be anarchies, but they are *organized* anarchies. Organizations may be loosely coupled, but they are loosely coupled *systems*. Organizations may resort to garbage can decision making, but garbage cans have borders that impose some structure.

THEMES

Although there is enormous variation among newer proposals of what organizations are like, there are at least six themes that are found in most of them. I will describe these themes in an effort to give an overview of one alternative to the rational bureaucratic model of organizations that has been the prevailing paradigm up to now. The themes I will discuss include the following:

(1) There is less to rationality than meets the eye.
(2) Organizations are segmented rather than monolithic.
(3) Stable segments in organizations are quite small.
(4) Connections among segments have variable strength.
(5) Connections of variable strength produce ambiguity.
(6) Connections of constant strength reduce ambiguity.

THERE IS LESS TO RATIONALITY THAN MEETS THE EYE

There are growing doubts about the importance of formal rationality in organizations (see Anderson, 1983; Manning, 1983). The complaint is not that rationality is ill-conceived but, rather, that the conditions under which it works best are relatively rare in organizations. Starbuck (1982, p. 16) is representative when he notes that "very rarely, if ever, does an organization begin action be perceiving a problem, then define this problem carefully, next generate possible actions solely because they might solve the stated problem, and finally, select a single course of action solely on the ground that it ought to be the best way to solve the problem."

Adherence to the prescriptions of a rational model can improve decision making if the environment changes slowly (Starbuck, 1982, p. 5), if there are few social groups, and if the situation is reasonably well controlled by agents with centralized authority (Kling, 1980, pp. 90, 100). Rational procedures work where stable means can be identified that are instrumental to stable ends in an environment in which these stable means-ends linkages will not be disrupted by unexpected events.

Rationality in newer formulations is still discussed, but in the context of a narrower set of issues. Rationality is viewed (1) as a set of prescriptions that change as the issue changes, (2) as a facade created to attract resources and legitimacy, and (3) as a postaction process used retrospectively to invent reasons for the action.

The suggestion that rationality is issue-specific is made concrete in Westerlund and Sjöstrand's (1979, p. 91) observation that rationality is an honorific label "given to the individual or group acting in the manner the evaluator wishes." Rational decisions typically mean "managerially rational," which means rational in they eyes of the people on top, the owners, the current dominant coalition. When these stakeholders change, the definition of rational conduct also changes.

As a rule, many theorists now try to preface all generic references to rationality with a qualifier (see March, 1978, pp. 591-593 for an example). It is no longer acceptable to state that an action is rational or nonrational. Instead, an adjective is used to qualify the sense in which the action is judged rational. Thus, actions are described as class-rational, gender-rational, resource-rational, value-rational, labor-rational, decision-rational, and action-rational. There are forms of rationality such as contextual-rationality, process-rationality, or calculational-rationality (Dyckman, 1981).

To describe some action as rational within a specific context is to suggest that it may be seen as less rational in a different context. To specify rationality in this narrower sense is to strip it of some of its inflated value as the major criterion of effective performance and to suggest that it is sometimes a rhetorical claim buttressed by little more than brashness on the part of the claimant and inattentiveness on the part of the target.

Organizations use rationality as a facade when they talk about goals, planning, intentions, and analysis, not because these practices necessarily work, but because people who supply resources believe that such practices work and indicate sound management (Pfeffer, 1981, pp. 194-196). The appearance of rational action legitimates the organization in the environment it faces, deflects criticism, and ensures a steady flow of resources into the organization.

An educational organization, for example, must go through the rituals
approved in the environment for assuring legitimacy: hiring a ritually
approved staff, offering a conventionally established curriculum, and
granting the usual range of credentials, that is, degrees. None of these
performances assure that a meaningful or substantively integrated educational experience will ensue. In fact, the organization takes pains to
insulate its core teaching-learning activity from external evaluation or
accountability. (Benson, 1983, p. 47)

Organizations are often heavily invested in the dramatization of their
efficiency even though such displays often restrict actual efficiency.
Elaborate public efforts to make rational decisions can often undermine
the vigor and speed of subsequent action. However, if less deliberation
occurs, the firm runs the risk that it will be judged impulsive, erratic, or,
worst of all, unpredictable.

To meet the contradictory demands of deliberated decision and
decisive actions, organizations often decouple the outside from the
inside (Meyer & Rowan, 1977). The appearance of deliberation is fostered for public consumption while a different set of procedures is used
to get work done. Thus, every organization has a visible president,
hierarchy, and strategic plan; but internal functioning often ignores
these trappings.

The final sense in which rationality is used by newer theorists is as a
post hoc rationalizing device (Staw, 1980). "Societal ideologies insist
that actions ought to be responses—actions taken unreflectively without
specific reasons are irrational and irrationality is bad. . . . So organizations justify their actions with problems, threats, success or opportunities" (Starbuck, 1983, p. 94). The sequence in this quotation is the key
point. First action occurs, and then the "reasons" why the action
occurred are invented and inserted retrospectively into the organization's history. The action is reframed as a response to a threat, a solution
to a problem that becomes clear only after the action was finished, a
response to something that no one realized was a stimulus until the
outcome became evident.

Starbuck suggests that retrospective justification is done for external
consumption, but retrospective processes also serve important internal
needs for understanding and prediction. It is not just outsiders who live
by the theory that every action ought to be a response to some earlier
stimulus. Organizational members impose the same logic on themselves.
Insiders need reasonable reasons just as much as do outsiders. Insiders
use the existence of action and an outcome as the occasion to initiate
their own search for reasons. As the search backward for explanations

of the action occurs in a very different context than when the action was first initiated (e.g., the outcome is known), the reasons singled out retrospectively are likely to be of less help for the next prospective action because they underestimate the vast amount of uncertainty that was present during the early stages of acting.

ORGANIZATIONS ARE SEGMENTED
RATHER THAN MONOLITHIC

Not only do theorists qualify any reference they make to rationality, they also avoid the define article "a" or "the" when referring to an organization. No organization is monolithic, yet continued references in the literature to "the organization" often suggest otherwise. People persist in referring to *the* organization due to a combination of failure to discount for hindsight bias, casual sorting of organizations into undifferentiated categories, routine aggregation of individual survey responses to create nominal organizations, and preoccupation with central tendencies (the mean) rather than dispersion (variation).

These tendencies have introduced inaccuracy into most analyses of organizations. Organizations are seen as more unified actors than they are, operating in more homogeneous environments than exist, and capable of longer lines of uninterrupted action than in fact they can mobilize.

The impression that organizations are orderly is fostered in part by hindsight bias. Experiments show that people consistently overestimate the predictability of past events, once they know how they turned out (Fischoff, 1975; Fischoff & Beyth, 1975; Slovic & Fischoff, 1977). Once a person knows the outcome, the reasons for that outcome seem obvious and the person cannot imagine any other outcome (hindsight bias).

Second guessing of warnings about the imminence of Pearl Harbor represents one example in which such biases are especially evident (Fischoff & Beyeth-Marom, 1976; Chan, 1979). When people look back at prior events once they know the outcomes of those events, they "see" an orderliness and inevitability that suggests that the events unfolded in a rational manner and could be managed by a simple application of rationality. Observers come away from their analysis with a strong impression that there is sufficient order to sustain rational analysis and rational management.

But hindsight is not the only bias that tempts us to view organizations as monolithic. March and Olson (1976, p. 19) identify an even more generic bias that leads people to exaggerate the orderliness in organizations. The bias involves assumptions about reality, intention, and necessity.

(1) The reality assumption is that what appeared to happen did happen.
(2) The intention assumption is that what happened was intended to happen.
(3) The necessity assumption is that what happened had to happen.

The assumption that what appeared to happen did happen neglects the importance of interpretation in organizational perception. What appears to happen happens as a function of the different a priori beliefs that members impose on basically ambiguous data (believing is seeing). Given that interpretations tend to emphasize order rather than disorder, the reality assumption favors the impression that organizations are unified, predictable actors.

We have already seen an example of the second assumption (what happened was intended to happen) in the earlier discussion that people feel pressure to invent retrospectively, the stimuli to which their actions are a "response." It is usually assumed that action occurs when people translate the stimulus of an intention into actions. Different intentions produce different outcomes, better intentions produce better outcomes.

March and Olson argue that there are at least three reasons why intentions alone seldom control action. First, action often produces decisions that are intended by no one and desired by no one. Second, action often occurs in response to duty and obligation rather than in response to intention. Third, intention is often overwhelmed by exogenous factors such as when firms become bankrupt even though top management had no intention of folding the firm.

The third assumption (what happened had to happen) essentially states that the observed outcome is inevitable and substantially different from other outcomes that might have occurred. The flaw in this assumption is that substantial "differences in final outcomes are sometimes produced by small (and essentially unpredictable) differences in intermediate events leading to the outcomes" (March & Olson, 1976, p. 20). Thus, alternative outcomes were highly probable and chance, rather than design, produced the actual outcome that was observed.

When people impose each of the preceding three assumptions, they fail to grasp the indeterminacy that inheres in adaptive action. Blind to the effects of these assumptions, observers conclude that rational models work and that organizations are tightly coupled systems. When asked to explain why organizations are effective, people identify rational designs, failing to realize that such designs are retrospective intentions that were not present while the action unfolded. The steps actually responsible for effectiveness seldom can be discovered after the event has occurred (an exception is the instant replay).

The perceptual distortions we have described have an effect on practice as well as research. Practitioners often conclude that effectiveness is the result of rational, orderly action. That conclusion is often an artifact of hindsight—we know what happened before we look back to discover why it happened. What we fail to see when we use hindsight are the experiments, false starts, and corrections that enabled people to learn and improve. It is the opportunity to learn from mistakes that we need to build in when we start our next novel action. But the necessity for those opportunities is the very thing we don't see when we reconstruct a smooth, defensible line of action after the fact. When we design our next action, we don't build in enough chances to learn, experiment, improvise, and be surprised. Furthermore, we start with unrealistically high expectations about how smoothly the activity will unfold. We are not prepared for all the disruption that occurs and often do a poor job rebounding from it.

When practitioners and researchers are better able to identify and compensate for some of the perceptual biases we have mentioned, they are more likely to see segments than unity. To understand more fully why unity is impossible, consider that top management in complex organizations does not design operating structures, it designs decision structures. Top management divides the organization into segmented subunits, which then design the operating structures. The importance of this distinction is that management does not actually manage the organization. Instead, it manages the process that manages the organization (Kuhn & Beam, 1982, pp. 325-326 refer to this as metamanagement).

To design a decision structure, top management selects the people who will be in the decision-making group. Even this is a tricky process. As top management doesn't know enough to make some decisions, which is why they formed the decision structure in the first place, they also probably do not know enough to say who the members of the decision-making group should be or who they might need for advice. If top management acknowledges this reality, they are forced to give up some of their control over the list of people who will be their agents.

Although top management is accustomed to saying, "Do what I tell you and I will reward you in proportion as you do it to my satisfaction," they adopt a different philosophy to manage segmented complexity. They now say essentially

Do what you collectively think best in light of the objectives I have stated. I will try to reward you collectively as I will have no real way of knowing which persons will have had what effect in your decisions. In fact, you are probably better judges than I of whether your methods were the most effective available and which of your members is the most effective. All I can do is to tell you whether your accomplishment as a group strikes me as reasonably satisfactory relative to my purposes. (Kuhn & Beam, 1982, p. 327)

This revised job description for the decision-making group essentially says, "see what you can do and do your best." The manager retains some control over the purse strings and over decisions to hire, fire, and promote people. However, as individual contributions are concealed within the group product, even personnel decisions are difficult to make.

The manager still exerts some influence by seeing that wider organizational considerations are kept in mind when decisions are made between units, keeping decision makers informed of relevant constraints, replacing agents, and handling situations that exceed the range for which the group was designed.

An unusual twist implicit in the description of segmented control is that the organizational form looks very much like the control structures found in universities (Bess, 1982). The president of a university is unable to evaluate whether the intellectual products of the faculty are worthwhile. The best research goes the way the researcher wants it to go, not the way the administrator wants it to go. Administrators cannot directly manage the pursuit of hunches, so they say, "keep busy and do research." Segments within the university decide key issues, such as teaching and admissions requirements, and the only control presidents have over these subgroups is money and final approval of personnel decisions.

Questions of authority, legitimacy, and insubordination are greatly attenuated in universities, but the same is true in other organizations in which the ties among subsystems are loose and responsibility is delegated to groups rather than to individuals. Although people often object that much organizational theory has been drafted to explain university organizations and therefore has limited generality, in fact the loosely coupled university structure is a prototype for all complex organizations in which lower-level segments act like top management. The structures that result from strong delegation resemble a federation, a market, a holding company, or a confederacy that tries to keep from getting overly organized.

A school, for example, can be understood as a federation of dissimilar segments. Schools have taken what is basically a two-person interaction between a teacher and a learner, and have added all kinds of tasks, responsibilities, and activities onto this basic core relationship. Each item that is added represents a segment rather than an integrated part. Thus, there is no such thing as *the* school or *a* school. What the additions do is loosen the basic teacher-learner relationship. This basic relationship becomes complicated to the point where segments have only modest dependence on one another. To treat the school as a single organization is to miss most of how it functions.

STABLE SEGMENTS IN ORGANIZATIONS ARE QUITE SMALL

New perspectives emphasize not only that organizations are segmented, but also that the segments are both small and stable. Whenever complex organizations unravel, they fall back into these small stable units.

The logic for predicting this outcome was captured by Simon in a fable about two watchmakers named Hora and Tempus, who were continually being interrupted while they assembled watches. Simon's original fable has been recast by Kuhn and Beam (1982, pp. 249-250) in a more accessible form that makes even more clearly the point that stability resides in small entities.

Your task is to count out a thousand sheets of paper, while you are subject to periodic interruptions. Each interruption causes you to lose track of the count and forces you to start over. If you count the thousand as a single sequence, then an interruption could cause you, at worst, to lose count of as many as 999. If the sheets are put into stacks of 100, however, and each stack remains undisturbed by interruptions, then the worst possible count loss from interruption is 108. That number represents the recounting of the nine stacks of 100 each plus the 99 single sheets. Futher, if sheets are first put into stacks of ten, which are then joined into stacks of 100, the worst possible loss from interruption would be 27. That number represents nine stacks of 100 plus nine stacks of ten plus nine single sheets. Not only is far less recounting time lost by putting the paper into "subsystems" of tens and hundreds, but the chances of completing the count are vastly higher.

The list of forces within organizations that can unravel large, complex entities is long. They include things like high mobility of people among positions, faulty memories, attempts to cope with overload by lowering the standards of acceptable performance, public compliance undercut by private deviation, sudden changes in authority or job descriptions, merging of odd product lines, and the like. All of these can interrupt complex interdependencies and cause the complex states to revert to simpler, more stable configurations.

The question then becomes, what are some of these small stable segments in organizations? Mintzberg (1973) and others have suggested that, on the average, managers can work for about nine minutes before they are interrupted. That finding can be interpreted as one instance of small segmented stability in organizations. Life in organizations is lived in nine-minute bursts. Activities lasting less than nine minutes are relatively free from disruption, whereas activities that last longer are more vulnerable to interruption.

It is difficult for people to maintain more than ten strong pairwise relationships. The instability of a three-person group in which two can pair against the third makes the point that stable social relations inhere in small entities, often involving only two or three people. When a large group is under pressure, stable pairwise interactions will become the most common structure.

People have limited thinking capacity. They are described as serial information processors rather than parallel processors. They can do only one thing at a time. This means that on those rare occasions when a person is successful in doing several things simultaneously, this is an unstable condition and any interruption or sudden change will cause the person to drop all but one project.

Given that managers do little reading, people who talk about managerial writing emphasize the necessity for brevity, as in the one-page memo, the one-page executive summary, the one unshakeable fact. In each of these cases the stable segment is a very small number of words. Longer presentations often are ignored, misread, skimmed, or otherwise dismissed. Again, stability lies in small, short segments.

Other examples could be described, but the point is that small segments are not necessarily disorderly. Instead, what seems to be true within organizations is that coherence occurs in smaller sized entities than may be true in other settings. As an analogy, consider sentences and paragraphs. Individual sentences can be well crafted, clear, and self-explanatory. Sets of sentences, however, may be harder to assemble, less sensible when assembled, and confusing when read as if they were coherent paragraphs. If people work with individual sentences, there is no problem. Each sentence makes sense. When, however, people combine sentences to make longer, more complex arguments, the structures become more flimsy and often collapse back into separate assertions.

Organizations built of small stable segments make sense over shorter spans of time, involving fewer people than we thought. Once these temporal and spatial boundaries are exceeded, orderliness, predictability, and sensibleness decline. This outcome is the straightforward consequence of the basic instability of complex structures and the tendency for complex structures to change into simpler, more stable structures. Most of the time most segments of organizations will be found in these simpler states. It is these simpler structures that become linked and supply the basic orderliness found in organizations.

CONNECTIONS AMONG SEGMENTS
HAVE VARIABLE STRENGTH

Organizations often are described as systems, and the principal graphic used to portray this description is a set of boxes connected by arrows:

individual action   ←   individual beliefs
          ↓   ↑
organizational action   →   environmental response

This form of illustration is deceptive, because it suggests that the connections have constant strength and are tight. In most organizations, however, connections among segments are variable rather than constant.

The idea of variable strength can be illustrated in several ways. In a diagram such as the one àt the beginning of this section, if we estimate the probability that each variable will trigger the next variable within one day and multiply these values, we find that longer chains are looser than shorter chains.

In the same kind of diagram weak connections exist when the variables share few variables in common and when the variables they do share are themselves weak. If people express doubts about whether one variable has significant effect on another variable, this is an indication of weaker connections. If individual variables can vary over a large range, chains of these variables will be connected more tightly than is true in chains in which the range of a variable is small. Variables with little room to vary soon become frozen and fail to pass variation along to the other variables with which they are connected.

Loose coupling can be observed in many places. Connections among parts are loosened when solutions are inserted into organizations that have no problems requiring that solution. Computer purchases are a good example. Most computer sales are vendor-driven ("look what this will do for you"). The customer seldom asks, "Do I really need that capability?" Instead, in order to keep up with the competition, hardware is purchased and then employees are urged to use the hardware in order to justify the purchase.

Thus, the machine now becomes a required step in every process. Existing controls are disrupted and parts of the system that previously had been self-regulating are disconnected. No one knows what is occurring and everyone knows less about the organization than they did before, because interdependencies have been made more variable.

Variable connections come from managerial self-interest. People at the top of the organization frequently make decisions that maximize income to members in the dominant coalition (Kuhn & Beam, 1982, pp. 332-348), which means that there are tight ties among a handful of people, but looser ties between the managers and stockholders.

Loose coupling is evident in schools. Only a limited amount of inspection and evaluation occurs in schools. A principal who visits a classroom too frequently is accused of "harassment." Professionals are reluctant to give one another unsolicited feedback. As a result, poor performance persists in the name of professional autonomy.

The goals of education also are indeterminate, which makes them difficult to use as hard standards to evaluate individual performance. Administrators and instructors work on variable raw materials with little control over the supply; they have no firm standards by which to judge the impact of their work and no clear theory of causation that specifies the effects of the things they do.

Schools have large spans of control. There are few employees and many students. Teachers find it hard to keep track of the students, let alone of one another. Because the technology of education is not clear, educators try many different things and find it difficult to tell what works. Schools make extensive use of specialists; every time a specialist is inserted between a teacher and a student, the control over the student is loosened.

Some aspects of schools—the bus schedule, for example—are tightly coupled. Students and drivers know where people are supposed to be and whether buses are running late or early; principals know when to expect certain people for certain things. How people get paid is tightly coupled. When the payroll clerk fouls up, the system grinds to a halt. People raise their voices, and something gets done fast. Open classrooms are tightly coupled in the sense that one person's actions cannot easily be ignored by others; visual and aural dependencies exist whether or not people want them.

We have already mentioned some features of organizations that suggest why connections vary in strength (e.g., frequent changes in top management, ill-specified job descriptions, large spans of control), but there are at least four general features of organizations that directly affect the strength of connections:

(1) *Rules:* Rules vary in severity, number, latitude for deviations, and clarity. Connections become tighter and less variable as all four of these properties intensify.

(2) *Agreement on rules:* The more agreement there is on the content of rules, the nature of violations, and how violations will be handled, the tighter the coupling.

(3) *Feedback:* The sooner people learn about the effects of their actions, the tighter the coupling.

(4) *Attention:* As attention becomes more constant, connections become more stable (when attention shifts due to changes in salience or need, connections become more variable).

Obviously, these four characteristics are not the only sources of connections. Even if more items are added to the list, the point remains the same. An organization is neither entirely loose nor entirely tight. Most organizational segments contain a mixture of tightness and looseness (e.g., vague rules, minimal agreement, swift feedback, and highly focused attention). This combination means that although there is some order in the organization, it is less pervasive than rational bureaucratic models would suggest. Organizations are imperfect systems within which there is indeterminacy, but there is some order. In the language of systems theory, organizations are represented as

$$\text{input} \rightarrow \text{transformation} \rightarrow \text{output}$$
$$\uparrow \text{_____ feedback} \leftarrow \text{_____}\lrcorner$$

and this constitutes a rudimentary system. It is rudimentary because the connections among those four components may be activated "(1) suddenly (rather than continuously), (2) occasionally (rather than constantly), (3) negligibly (rather than significantly), (4) indirectly (rather than directly), and (5) eventually (rather than immediately)" (Weick, 1982, p. 380). Even though the connections are indeterminate, sooner or later the system completes a cycle and produces something approximating what it was designed to produce. If people watch the system long enough, they will see that the components are connected and that eventually everything gets processed.

The image of a loosely coupled system is important more as a summary description of a way to think about organizations than as a precise technical description of a specific quality of organizational structure. The phrase "loosely coupled system," in other words, is useful for what it connotes as well as for what it denotes. Diverse images that people associate with the phrase all include qualities that are visible when entities are less orderly, less predictable. Whatever people think of when they imagine a loosely coupled system is often what we actually see when we study the indeterminacies within an organization.

One set of connotations evoked by the label "loosely coupled system" is visible in the following description:

A loosely coupled system is a problem in causal inference. For actors and observers alike, the prediction and activation of cause-effect relations is made more difficult because relations are intermittent, lagged, dampened, slow, abrupt, and mediated.

Actors in a loosely coupled system rely on trust and presumptions, are often isolated, find social comparison difficult, have no one to borrow from, seldom imitate, suffer pluralistic ignorance, maintain discretion, improvise, and have less hubris because they know the universe is not sufficiently connected to make widespread change possible.

A loosely coupled system is not a flawed system. It is a social and cognitive solution to constant environmental change, to the impossibility of knowing another mind, and to limited information-processing capabilities. Loose coupling is to social systems as compartmentalization is to individuals, a means to achieve cognitive economy and a little peace (adapted from Weick, 1982, pp. 404-405).

CONNECTIONS OF VARIABLE STRENGTH
PRODUCE AMBIGUITY

The presence of variable connections means that ambiguity is likely to be high, superstitious learning is probable as it is more difficult to attach specific outcomes to specific prior causal actions, communications will be delayed and distorted, people may find it difficult to learn because feedback is delayed beyond the point at which someone is able to understand precisely what prior action is relevant to the feedback, and there may be a high incidence of giving up and resignation when systems are not responsive to demands.

Variability makes it difficult to anticipate, plan, implement, coordinate, and control. Even though variability makes it hard to be rational, it has the benefit of enabling people to stumble onto adaptive actions they had not thought of. Nevertheless, stumbling bothers most organizations. They dislike ambiguity even more than they like adaptation. If organizations dislike ambiguity, they will probably also dislike self-determination, delegation, and differentiation, because each one is associated with loose connections, and loose connections are a source of ambiguity.

McCaskey (1982) has identified twelve sources of ambiguity (see Table 4.1) and March and Olson (1976, p. 12) have identified four sources—intention: organizations have inconsistent and ill-defined objectives; understanding: unreliable connections between actions and their consequences; history: no single version of past events exists; and organization: participation and attention vary.

Ambiguity is found in all aspects of organizational activity. It can be found in changing and complex environments, nonroutine tasks, and networks that have dense interdependencies. Ambiguity is present when people cannot understand raw materials or do not know when a product or service is finished, and when people convert raw material into a finished product on the basis of intuition and chance rather than logic (Gerwin, 1981, p. 6).

Even though ambiguity is common, it is not sufficient to say simply that people try to reduce it. Because ambiguity is never fully removed, it is part of the normal context of orgnizational action. Ambiguity gives form to much of what occurs.

For example, individual actions often affect organizational actions, but organizational actions less often have a determinate effect on the environment. Nevertheless, individuals often believe that what they do brings about direct changes in the environment. This erroneous interpretation is called "superstitious learning." As Hedberg (1981, p. 11) describes it,

TABLE 4.1
Characteristics of Ambiguous, Changing Situations

Characteristic	Description and Comments
Nature of problem is itself in question	"What the problem is" is unclear and shifting. Managers have only vague or competing definitions of the problem. Often, any one "problem" is intertwined with other messy problems.
Information (amount and reliability) is problematical	Because the definition of the problem is in doubt, collecting and categorizing information becomes a problem. The information flow threatens either to become overwhelming or to be seriously insufficient. Data may be incomplete and of dubious reliability.
Multiple, conflicting interpretations	For those data that do exist, players develop multiple, and sometimes conflicting, interpretations. The facts and their significance can be read several different ways.
Different value orientations, political/emotional clashes	Without objective criteria, players rely more on personal and/or professional values to make sense of the situation. The clash of different values often politically and emotionally charges the situation.
Goals are unclear, or multiple and conflicting	Managers do not enjoy the guidance of clearly defined, coherent goals. Either the goals are vague, or they are clearly defined and contradictory.
Time, money, or attention are lacking	A difficult situation is made chaotic by severe shortages of one or more of these items.
Contradictions and paradoxes appear	Situation has seemingly inconsistent features, relationships, or demands.
Roles vague, responsibilities unclear	Players do not have a clearly defined set of activities they are expected to perform. On important issues, the locus of decision making and other responsibilities is vague or in dispute.
Success measures are lacking	People are unsure what success in resolving the situation would mean and/or they have no way of assessing the degree to which they have been successful.
Poor understanding of cause-effect relationships	Players do not understand what causes what in the situation. Even if sure of the effects they desire, they are uncertain how to obtain them.
Symbols and metaphors used	In place of precise definitions or logical arguments, players use symbols or metaphors to express their points of view.
Participation in decision-making fluid	Who the key decision makers and influence holders are changes as players enter and leave the decision arena.

complex interactions between organizations and their environments exceed people's cognitive capacities for mapping so that faulty inferences are drawn. Superstitious learning thus, in effect, separates one subsystem that produces actions from another subsystem that forms beliefs. Organizational learning proceeds but the coupling between actions and knowledge is weak.

Although it is tempting to say that superstitious learning is simply one more instance of organizational pathology, it seems more productive to ask, "How can organizational members continue to act and learn even though their descriptions of reality, causality, and the instrumentality of action have low validity?"

The concept of self-fulfilling prophecies contains a partial answer to the question. Members who mistakenly see a change in the environment as caused by their own action build into their causal theories the belief that they are able to change environments. This apparent efficacy is an error in the sense that it is an incorrect interpretation of what actually happened. What is more interesting, however, are those occasions when environments are sufficiently malleable that, acting on this mistaken belief, people can create a reality that makes the belief true. In changeable environments superstitious learning can set in motion a sequence of activities that transforms the superstitious conclusion into correct perception.

Self-fulfilling prophecies (Jones, 1977) tend not to be appreciated for the profound sense in which they provide insight into how organizations function. An original prophecy is incorrect and may result from a mistaken perception that an environmental outcome was caused by an individual action. Later, when the person acts as if the prophecy were correct, the prophecy can become correct and the environment becomes responsive to the individual action rather than to some other exogenous factor. Thus, the incorrect theory of action becomes self-correcting. It sets into motion a set of events that validate what was originally an invalid belief.

Notice that in the case of superstitious learning, ambiguity is partially dealt with when the person draws an inference about cause and effect and stores that inference in a cause map. That step represents an avoidance of uncertainty because no clarification actually occurs. But when that inference then becomes a constraint on subsequent action, uncertainty is actually reduced. When the person acts as if the stored inference is true, a previously loose relationship between cause and effect becomes tightened, and the uncertainty surrounding that effect becomes reduced.

Organizations can learn in the face of ambiguity because superstitious learning can be self-correcting in ways that are moderately adaptive.

To understand ambiguity, however, is not simply to become fascinated with the self-fulfilling properties of superstitious learning. Ambiguity also increases the extent to which action is guided by values and ideology. When ambiguity is present, people who can resolve it gain power. The values of these powerful people often affect what the organization becomes. When ambiguity increases, the person best able to resolve it gains power, as does that person's vision of the world and the organization. Ambiguity thus becomes the occasion when ideology may be shuffled. An organization may "reset" itself whenever there is an important, enduring ambiguity that is resolved by someone whose actions have surplus meaning. Those actions may implant a more pervasive set of values.

When new values are introduced into an organization, a new set of relevancies and competencies are created that can provide a badly needed source of innovation. An organization can learn new things about itself and about its environment when ambiguity is present. If an organization continues to act even though it does not know for certain what it is doing, there is a chance that the organization will emerge from its confrontation with ambiguity in slightly different shape than when it started to cope. In this way ambiguity can produce innovation and greater utilization of resources.

Continuous ambiguity also exerts continuous pressure on organizations to modify their structure so that coping is more successful. If Burns and Stalker's organic system is treated prescriptively as an arrangement capable of dealing with uncertainty, we would expect to see organizations pressured by ambiguity to demonstrate more use of specialized professional skills (high complexity), continual redefinition of individual tasks (low formalization), development of more ad hoc centers of authority located closer to the source of a problem (low centralization), and movement toward a network structure (this list is adapted from Gerwin, 1981, p. 6).

Although it is not new to argue that ambiguity determines structure, what is new is the suggestion that when organizations face chronic ambiguity, their ongoing activities can be interpreted as continuing efforts to move from a less appropriate mechanistic structure to a more appropriate organic structure. Thus, organizations may be responding not just to the substance of a particular ambiguity (e.g., a possible hint of a takeover), but to the more generic reality of ambiguity itself. Organizational action may be a partial attempt to deal with an immediate problem, but it may be better understood as a strong ongoing effort to redesign the organization so that it can handle whatever ambiguities occur in the future.

Thus, when members become more and more conscious of networks, this can be read as a specific attempt to reduce dependence on a single supplier of a scarce resource. But this same action can be interpreted more broadly as an effort to deal with the larger issue of interdependence as a continuing source of ambiguity. Efforts to enlarge a network reduce the power of specific interdependencies.

Again, what is happening can be understood as something more than simple effort to reduce uncertainty. The actions can be understood as attempts to accept ambiguity, live with it, and take advantage of some of the unique opportunities for change that occur when ambiguity increases.

All of these efforts are modestly patterned and can account for some regularities in organizational activity. To say that variable connections create ambiguity is to describe a prominent background characteristic to which organizations accommodate. As they accommodate, organizations assume predictable forms.

Ambiguity is prominent in organizations, but before organizations reduce it, ambiguity has already had some immediate impact on the processes and structures found in them. To understand ambiguity is to understand these immediate effects as well as the more active attempts to reduce ambiguity that are described in the next section.

CONNECTIONS OF CONSTANT STRENGTH
REDUCE AMBIGUITY

Given the existence of ambiguity produced by connections of variable strength, managers need to reduce ambiguity to tolerable levels. As Athos states, "good managers make meanings for people, as well as money" (Peters & Waterman, 1982, p. 29).

Whether one refers to organizations as garbage cans (Cohen, March, & Olson, 1972), anarchies (Cohen & March, 1974), loosely coupled systems (Glassman, 1973), negotiated realities (Hall, 1973), or arenas (Berg, 1979), the point remains that managers work amid a great deal of disorder.

One way managers cope with disorder is by presuming that there is a logic by which events cohere. These presumptions of logic are evident in the inferences about cause and effect that are assembled into cause maps (e.g., Ashton, 1976, Boughon, Weick, & Binkhorst, 1977; Goodman, 1968; Axelrod, 1977; Roos & Hall, 1980; Porac, 1981).

When managers then act as if loosely coupled events are tied together just as they are in a cause map, events often become more tightly coupled, more orderly, and less variable.

For example, the head of an extended care unit in a hospital (Roos & Hall, 1980) may believe that if he has more contact with influential outsiders, there will be less pressure on him from the chief administrator in the hospital to cut his budget. Having presumed that the world contains this causal connection, the head of extended care spends more time away from the hospital, which makes him more visible to outsiders. The outsiders pay more consistent attention to the hospital, which means that their actions become more predictable and focused.

Through the simple act of becoming visible, the head makes the "environment" with which the entire hospital must deal more homogeneous and more predictable.

The hospital becomes constrained by an environment that did not exist until the head of extended care changed the salience of events for significant others, who then intensified their demands on the hospital. Events became more orderly under the influence of interaction that itself was launched on the basis of presumptions that just such orderliness existed.

At the time the action was started, there was no guarantee that orderliness would be "there" to validate the initial presumption. Confident action addressed to a presumptively logical world gave it a tangible form that resembled the presumptions stored in the administrator's cause maps.

It is crucial to see that the issue here is *not* one of accuracy. Cause maps could be wrong and still be an important part of managerial action. The important feature of a cause map is that it leads people to anticipate some order "out there." It matters less what particular order is portrayed than that an order of *some* kind is portrayed. The crucial dynamic is that the prospect of order lures the manager into ill-formed situations that then accommodate to forceful actions and come to resemble the orderly relations contained in the cause map. The map animates managers, and the fact of animation, not the map itself, is what imposes order on the situation.

Thus, trappings of rationality such as strategic plans are important largely as binding mechanisms. They hold events together long enough and tight enough in people's heads so that they do something in the belief that their action will be influential. The importance of presumptions, expectations, justifications, and commitments is that they span the breaks in a loosely coupled system and encourage confident interactions that tighten settings. *The conditions of order and tightness in organizations exist as much in the mind as they do in the field of action.*

To review, there are several ways to regain constancy when it is lost through variable connections. Three that are of special interest are language, action, and interaction.

Organizations have been described as a "set of procedures for argumentation and interpretation" (March & Olson , 1976, p. 25). A significant portion of the environment consists of nothing more than talk, symbols, promises, lies, interest, attention, threats, agreements, expectations, memories, rumors, indicators, supporters, detractors, faith, suspicion, trust, appearances, loyalties, and commitments, all of which are more intangible and more influenceable than material goods (Peters, 1980; Gronn, 1983; Weick, 1980).

Words induce stable connections, establish stable entities to which people can orient (e.g., "gender gap"), bind people's time to projects ("Al, I'd like you to spend some time on this one"), and signify important information. Agreement on a label that sticks is as constant a connection as is likely to be found in organizations.

Labels carry their own implications for action, and that is why they are so successful in the management of ambiguity. Consider these labels: that is a cost (minimize it), that is spoilage (reduce it), that is overhead (allocate it), that is a transfer price (set it), that is a variance (investigate it), that is a surplus (distribute it), that is a need (fill it), that is a problem (solve it), that is a decision (make it), that is a bluff (challenge it), that is feather-bedding (remove it), that is stupidity (exploit it), and so forth. In each of these instances a label consolidates bits and pieces of data, gives them meaning, suggests appropriate action, implies a diagnosis, and removes ambiguity.

Much ambiguity occurs because there are events floating around that seem to bear no relation to one another. Because it is not clear what is going on, it is even less clear what ought to be done about it. Labels (sometimes any old label) serve to focus attention and shrink the number of possibilities as to what might be occurring. A mere hint as to what the connection might be may be all that is needed to connect diverse events, give them a theme, and allow them to be managed.

Given that so much of what happens in organizations can be understood as a self-fulfilling prophecy, labels often are sufficient to mobilize a response that fulfills the prophecy made by the label (e.g., they will be hostile). The reason prophecies fulfill themselves so often in organizations is that events are sufficiently disconnected and ambiguous that they can absorb quite different labels. People who find a vivid label and then push it persistently often are able to redirect organizational action, because they have gained control over how the organization defines itself and what it says it is up to.

Connections of variable strength can be stabilized by action as well as by language. Action can simplify environments, can make environments more orderly, can create linkages where none existed, and can construct feedback loops.

Action can stabilize a situation of high variability, if it is forceful, persistent, and confident. However, to develop a strong basis for action, people often need to sacrifice decision rationality. They need to analyze few alternatives, consider only the positive characteristics of the chosen actions, and choose as their objectives consequences that are likely to occur (Brunsson, 1982).

If people consider many alternatives, or both positive and negative alternatives, or argue over objectives, these all raise uncertainty that can lower motivation, commitment, and impact.

Action rationality contains a dilemma for everyone who administers an organization. If the decision process is made more rational and alternatives are considered more carefully, people may discover a better alternative, but in doing so they dissipate some of the energy that could help implement the better alternative. Thus, a good idea gets carried out less forcefully than it might have, and fails to solve the problem as adequately as it seemed it would when it was discussed. The disappointing outcome occurs, not because of a defect in deliberation, but because of a defect in implementation. In trying to discover the good alternative, people lost some of the commitment that they needed to put it into action.

The potential contradiction between choosing the right thing and getting it done can be examined as a problem in requisite variety. The principle of requisite variety states that no sensing device can control input that is more complicated than the sensing device. Thus, in a landscape scene with numerous gradations in texture and color, fine-grain film has more variety than does coarse-grain fast film, and the more varied film will register more of the variety in the complicated scene.

The relationship between requisite variety and action rationality is that organizations can use two quite different strategies to reduce ambiguity in complicated environments. First, they can try to register the fine grain of the environment and then choose an action that is sensitive to subtle but potentially important regularities in that complicated environment. This path is the path of decision rationality.

But there is another way to deal with complicated environments. This alternative strategy is to wade in, take vigorous action, and simplify the environment so that relatively crude analyses are sufficient to keep track of the main things that are happening. In an environment made simple by action decision rationality is unnecessary. You don't have to worry about registering subtle nuances if your action simplifies that environment and removes the nuances.

The choice between action and deliberation often is irreversible. If you choose in favor of accurate sensing, you reduce your capability to take strong action. Therefore, the analysis must be accurate and identify some small action that can remedy the problem that is sensed (small actions can be executed with less commitment). It is often the case that the more fully a problem is understood, the smaller will be the change necessary to solve it. All solutions do not require massive action (Weick, 1984). However, if only a relatively small action is available to correct a problem, detail and accuracy are crucial.

If you decide to take strong action in order to simplify the situation, you forgo any chance of learning more about the situation as it originally existed and about small changes that could produce big effects.

It is relatively hard to gain the best of both worlds. Administrators run the risk of knowing their world well but being unable to do anything about it, or they run the opposite risk of making some decisive change in the world only to discover that they changed the wrong thing and the problem got worse. Both outcomes represent a decrease in ambiguity.

The third classic response to ambiguity is to turn to another person and, in common, build some idea of what is occurring (see Schachter, 1959). Larger entities act in an analogous manner. Divisions come to look like one another because they imitate one another and build consensual definitions (DiMaggio & Powell, 1983).

It may seem unusual that two groups, both equally in the dark, could get clarity by watching one another. Apparently, the observer assumes that the person being watched understands the situation more fully. Having made this assumption, the observer then imposes meaning on what is observed and attributes the meaning to the observed person rather than the observer.

A great deal of interactive ambiguity reduction takes place inside individual heads rather than between heads. Puzzles become resolved into sensible constructions when people elaborate a grain of truth into a full-blown explanation. And people often discover these grains of truth when they compare their views with those of other people who see things in a slightly different way.

Social interaction seems to reduce ambiguity in the following way:

variability $\pm$ ambiguity ⌐

  ↑   −   =

  └─────────────── discussion ←───────────────┘

Two things are interesting about this solution. First, ambiguity created by loose connections is managed by increased interdependence between people. As depicted, once the variability has been reduced, people will revert back to more solitary action, in which there is less discussion. That prediction may not be accurate, especially if ambiguity reduction is reinforcing and people become closer to those who satisfy important needs. Thus, persistent mutual ambiguity reduction could tighten a previously loose social system.

A second implication of the diagram is that people may perceive that whereas they don't know what is going on, everyone else does. Having made this assumption, confused people tell no one about their confusion. These assumptions would be represented by a negative relationship between ambiguity and discussion: The more ambiguity an individual perceives, the less that person talks to others in the belief that others would view him or her as inept, unperceptive, stupid. If a second negative relationship is introduced, the cycle becomes unstable and a vicious circle results.

To illustrate, variability increases, which increases ambiguity, which decreases the amount of discussion that occurs, which causes variability and ambiguity to intensify, until the reluctant talker will have generated a situation that he or she simply cannot tolerate any longer.

On rare occasions instability can move in the opposite direction. Suppose variability declines. In the microcosm that has been drawn ambiguity also would decline, the person responds to a reduction of ambiguity with an increase in discussion, which further reduces variability, until, theoretically, no variability or ambiguity would remain. Although that might seem desirable, the likelihood of that occurring in an organization with variability is quite low.

IMPLICATIONS FOR ADMINISTRATION

Several implications for practice flow from the preceding analysis, and they are summarized below. The flavor of these suggestions is anticipated by Padgett (1980, p. 602), who warned, "don't expect orthodoxy where ambiguity is salient."

(1) Look for small pockets of order and protect them, grow them, or diffuse them. A little order can go a long way, so don't overdo it.

(2) Assess when decision rationality works in your setting and when it doesn't. Build your own ad hoc contingency theory of decision rationality.

(3) Don't treat rationality as a universal prescription. If you live by rationality alone, you lose options (use of intuition, quick response, trial and error) and you lose nondeliberated sources of variety (hunches).

(4) Retrospective explanations are poor guides to prospective action. We know relatively little about how we actually get things done. We don't know what works, because we misremember the process of accomplishment. We will always underestimate the number of false starts that went into the outcome. Furthermore, even though there were dead ends, we probably did learn from them—we learned more about the environment and about our capabilities. Keep good records during process, because hindsight will gloss over most of the difficulties you had while striving for the outcome. Failure to see difficulties may result in unrealistic expectations about how fast and how easily the next goal can be achieved.

(5) Intention is neither a necessary nor a sufficient condition for action.

(6) Practice enlightened delegation through control of the staffing process.

(7) Don't dismiss universities as mere ivory towers, at least until you understand more about how they actually function. They resemble your organization more closely than does a military organization. Think of your organization as a federation, market, or holding company.

(8) Design around the stable subsystem. Assign critical tasks to small stable units. For any task ask, "Can this task be done in nine minutes by two people who attend to one thing at a time?" If the answer is yes, you have assigned critical tasks to a stable unit. If you can't embed critical assignments in small, stable entities, then shield people against interruptions, simplify their tasks so stress has less disruptive effects on performance, or help people increase their tolerance for stress.

(9) Don't expect long chains of events to make sense. Sense occurs only in small bursts in organizations.

(10) Be patient: Systems are sluggish and slightly disorderly, but they do eventually act in a systemlike manner. If you persist, you may create connections that are more continuous, constant, significant, direct, and immediate. If you persist, this "both increases the likelihood that a proposal will be current at an opportune time and creates a diffuse climate of availability and legitimacy for it" (March & Olson, 1982, pp. 25-26). A persistent recommendation will fit some situation sooner or later ("every rain dancer brings rain if he dances long enough"), the

recommendation remains salient ("well, we could always do x"), the recommendation may accrue legitimacy ("we always hear about x, so at least it must have a place in this organization in someone's view"), and persistence signifies that some people value whatever is affirmed repeatedly.

(11) View loose coupling descriptively before you view it evaluatively, in order to see the functions it plays (generates variation, preserves autonomy, localizes trouble, is understandable to fallible minds).

(12) Accuracy is less important than animation. Any old map or plan will do, if it gets you moving so that you learn more about what is actually in the environment. A map is not the territory; a plan is not the organization.

(13) Anticipations matter; don't adopt them casually. They tend to fulfill themselves.

(14) Labels are a powerful means to reduce ambiguity. Impose them with caution and deliberation because they can direct action.

(15) To manage meaning is to view your organization as a set of procedures for arguing and interpreting. In any organizational assessment, ask questions such as these: How do we declare winners of the argument? When do we interpret? What interpretations do we tend to favor (blind spots?)? Whose interpretations seem to stick?

(16) To get things done, it is more important to capture a person's attention than a person's intention. People act in response to salient concerns (e.g., deadlines). So to control action, you need to control salience.

(17) To learn about your goals, preferences, and capabilities, act and treat your actions as conjectures about what these goals, preferences, and capabilities are.

(18) Be willing to leap before you look. If you look before you leap, you may not see anything. Action generates outcomes that ultimately provide the raw material for seeing something. Before action takes place, the meaning of any situation is essentially limitless. The situation could become anything whatsoever and therefore it is everything and nothing. The situation takes on distinct form and meaning only when action is inserted into it. When people examine the action they took, they see more clearly what the situation was and what it meant. By acting, often without the safety of knowing what the action will look like or amount to or come to mean, people learn something meaningful, even though what they learn may not be what they expected.

(19) You can optimize either deliberation or action, but not both.

As this essay began with a metaphor, it seems appropriate to end with one. In the final analysis managing may be more like surfing on waves of events and decisions (Westerlund & Sjöstrand, 1979, p. 121) than like either of the two versions of soccer mentioned at the beginning. People who surf do not command the waves to appear, or to have a particular spacing, or to be of a special height. Instead, surfers do their best with what they get. They can control inputs to the process, but they can't control outcomes. To ride a wave as if one were in control is to act and have faith. The message of newer perspectives often boils down to that.

REFERENCES

Anderson, P. A. (1983). Decision making by objection and the Cuban missile crisis. *Administrative Science Quarterly, 28,* 201-222.
Aschton, R. (1976). Deviation-amplifying feedback and unintended consequences of management accounting systems. *Accounting, Organizations, and Society, 1,* 289-300.
Axelrod, R. (1977). Argumentation in foreign policy settings. *Journal of Conflict Resolution, 21,* 727-756.
Benson, J. K. (1983). Paradigm and praxis in organizational analysis. In L. L. Cummings & B. M. Staw (Eds.), *Research in organizational behavior* (Vol. 5). Greenwich, CT: JAI.
Berg, P. O. (1979). *Emotional structure in organizations.* Farnborough: Teakfield.
Bess, J. L. (1982). *University organization.* New York: Human Science Press.
Boughon, M., Weick, K. E., & Binkhorst, D. (1977). Cognition in organizations: An analysis of the Utrecht Jazz Orchestra. *Administrative Science Quarterly, 22,* 606-639.
Brunsson, N. (1982). The irrationality of action and action rationality: Decisions, ideologies, and organizational actions. *Journal of Management Studies, 19,* 29-44.
Chan, S. (1979). The intelligence of stupidity: Understanding failures in strategic warning. *American Political Science Review, 73,* 171-180.
Cohen, M. D., & March, J. G. (1974). *Leadership and ambiguity.* New York: McGraw-Hill.
Cohen, M. D., March, J. G., & Olsen, J. P. (1972). A garbage can model of organizational choice. *Administrative Science Quarterly, 17,* 1-25.
DiMaggio, P. J., & Powell, W. W. (1983). The iron cage revisited: Insitutional isomorphism and collective rationality in organizational fields. *American Sociological Review, 48,* 147-160.
Dyckman, T. R. (1981). The intelligence of ambiguity. *Accounting, Organizations, and Society, 6,* 291-300.
Fischoff, B. (1975). Hindsight and foresight: The effect of outcome knowledge on judgement under uncertainty. *Journal of Experimental Psychology: Human Perception and Performance, 1,* 288-299.
Fischoff, B., & Beyth, R. (1975). "I knew it would happen": Remembered probabilities on once-future things. *Organizational Behavior and Human Performance, 13,* 1-16.
Fischoff, B., & Beyeth-Marom, R. (1976). Failure has many fathers. *Policy Sciences, 7,* 388-393.
Gerwin, D. (1981). Relationships between structure and technology. In P. C. Nystrom & W. H. Starbuck (Eds.), *Handbook of organizational design* (Vol. 2). New York: Oxford University Press.

Glassman, R. B. (1973). Persistence and loose coupling in living systems. *Behavioral Sciences, 18,* 83-98.

Goodman, P. S. (1968). The measurement of an individual's organization map. *Administrative Science Quarterly, 13,* 246-265.

Gronn, P. C. (1983). Talk as the work: The accomplishment of school administration. *Administrative Science Quarterly, 28,* 1-21.

Hall, P. M. (1973). A symbolic interactionist analysis of politics. *Sociological Inquiry, 42,* (3-4), 35-75.

Hedberg, B. (1981). How organizations learn and unlearn. In P. C. Nystrom & W. H. Starbuck (Eds.), *Handbook of organizational design* (Vol. 1). New York: Oxford University Press.

Jones, R. A. (1977). *Self-fulfilling prophecies.* Hillsdale, NJ: Erlbaum.

Kling, R. (1980). Social analyses of computing: Theoretical perspectives in recent empirical research. *Computing Surveys, 12,* 61-110.

Kuhn, A., & Beam, R. D. (1982). *The logic of organization.* San Francisco: Jossey-Bass.

Manning, P. K. (1983). *Queries concerning the decision-making approach to police research.* Paper presented to the British Psychological Society.

March, J. G. (1978). Bounded rationality, ambiguity, and the engineering of choice. *Bell Journal of Economics, 9,* 587-608.

March, J. G., & Olsen, J. P. (1976). Organizational choice under ambiguity. In J. G. March & J. P. Olsen (Eds.), *Ambiguity and choice in organizations* (pp. 10-23). Bergen: Universitetsforlaget.

March, J. G., & Romelaer, P. J. (1976). Position and presence in the drift of decisions. In J. G. March & J. P. Olsen (Eds.), *Ambiguity and choice in organizations* (pp. 251-276). Bergen: Universitetsforlaget.

McCaskey, M. B. (1982). *The executive challenge: Managing change and ambiguity.* Marshfield, MA: Pitman.

Meyer, J. W., & Rowan, B. (1977). Institutionalized organizations: Formal structure as myth and ceremony. *American Journal of Sociology, 83,* 340-363.

Mintzberg, H. (1973). *The nature of managerial work.* New York: Harper & Row.

Padgett, J. F. (1980). Managing garbage can hierarchies. *Administrative Science Quarterly, 25,* 583-604.

Peters, T. J. (1980). Management systems: The language of organizational character and competence. *Organizational Dynamics, 9,*(1), 3-26.

Peters, T. J., & Waterman, R. H. (1982). *In search of excellence.* New York: Harper & Row.

Pfeffer, J. (1981). *Power in organizations.* Marshfield, MA: Pitman.

Porac, J. F. (1981). Causal loops and other intercausal perceptions in attributions for exam performance. *Journal of Educational Psychology, 73,* 587-601.

Roos, L. L., & Hall, R. I. (1980). Influence diagrams and organizational power. *Administrative Science Quarterly, 25,* 57-71.

Schachter, S. (1959). *The psychology of affiliation.* Stanford, CA: Stanford University Press.

Slovic, P., & Fischoff, B. (1977). On the psychology of experimental surprises. *Journal of Experimental Psychology: Human Perception and Performance, 3,* 544-551.

Starbuck, W. H. (1982). Congealing oil: Inventing ideologies to justify acting ideologies out. *Journal of Management Studies, 19,* 3-27.

Starbuck, W. H. (1983). Organizations as action generators. *American Sociological Review, 48,* 91-102.

Staw, B. M. (1980). Rationality and justification in organizational life. In B. M. Staw & L. L. Cummings (Eds.), *Research in organizational behavior* (Vol. 2). Greenwich, CT: JAI.

Weick, K. E. (1976). Educational organizations as loosely coupled systems. *Administrative Science Quarterly, 21,* 1-19.

Weick, K. E. (1980). The management of eloquence. *Executive, 6* (3), 18-21.

Weick, K. E. (1982). Management of organizational change among loosely coupled elements. In P. Goodman (Ed.), *Change in organizations* (pp. 375-408). San Francisco: Jossey-Bass.

Weick, K. E. (1984). Small wins: Redefining the scale of social problems. *American Psychologist, 39,* 40-49.

Westerlund, G., & Sjöstrand, S. E. (1979). *Organizational myths.* New York: Harper & Row.

5

THE SUBSTANCE OF THE EMERGENT
PARADIGM: IMPLICATIONS FOR RESEARCHERS

Yvonna S. Lincoln

One of the most reasonable and, indeed, pragmatic ways of thinking about what is in the previous chapters, particularly what Guba has proposed, is in terms of what one would do in performing research if one actually adopted this particular paradigm. In fact, the question of what one would do is the position of most of us, as most of us carry out our work, whatever that might be, without reflecting about the epistemological foundations (value assumptions) undergirding action. We have internalized a set of beliefs, and we act upon them without much thought. In most instances it is exactly the same with scientists and, indeed, all researchers. We do things as our mentors taught us to do them, without probing deeply into the whys. If our mentors did things in that manner—and they were honorable and truth-seeking men and women—why should we abjure their methods and wisdom? Indeed, it is only when a perfectly unconventional wisdom is proposed that we need to examine its implications for our own behavior. So it is at the level of behavior that the implications of the emergent inquiry paradigm become apparent.

Guba earlier asserted that the emergent paradigm—or naturalistic inquiry—is in some way superior to the more traditional, conventional form—called scientific or rationalistic inquiry—for certain kinds of research, particularly social and behavioral research. This argument is made, and supported, on the grounds that the "methodological assumptions undergirding the dominant paradigm of inquiry are more consistent, or *more resonant* with the older mode of thought than with the newer," and that the methodological assumptions undergirding the emergent paradigm are more consonant with the emergent context and axioms. The "so-called naturalistic paradigm provides a better fit—a higher degree of resonance" (Skrtic, Guba, & Knowlton, 1985) with a new order of thinking about the world and that assertion is demonstrable.

The statement of axioms that has just been presented is, in some respects, a formal recognition and a philosophical restatement of the everyday and ordinary language of experience. It is sensible to assert that because, in some respects, although Schwartz and Ogilvy (1979) have referred to disciplinary paradigmatic shifts, in fact, we are undergoing a fundamental altering of the way Western peoples see the world; that is, the man or woman on the street is subtly altering his or her thinking about the nature of the world. This is borne out in developments in psychology, in common citizens' involvement with environmental concerns such as the Sierra Club and Common Cause, and in religious movements sweeping the Western world (including borrowings and adaptations from Eastern religions).

These are the stirrings of alternative lifestyles that reflect in part the seven concepts of Schwartz and Ogilvy, as experienced and accepted by ordinary citizens. It is not difficult to trace a variety of outcroppings on the collective subconscious that reflect complexity, heterarchy, morphogenesis, indeterminacy, mutual causality, perspective, and holography. For example, everyday experience suggests the following are completely consistent with the emergence of a new world view:

- *From simplicity to complexity:* The shift in general understanding of the nature of world affairs and theories of economic interdependence would seem to suggest an acceptance and tolerance of complexity (Reich, 1983). George Will has pointed out, in regard to Kissinger's detente policies, "A flaw in his detente policy was misplaced confidence in the constancy of a public *condemned to live with ambiguities"* (1983, italics added).
- *From hierarchy to heterarchy:* The local citizens' action committees and their national counterparts are good examples of governance and influence which come not from a hierarchy of elected officials, but from a heterarchy of interest groups and the disenfranchised, all seeking—and getting—a voice.
- *From mechanical to holographic:* The shift of small groups of persons in the 1960s and 1970s away from urban, assembly-line jobs on to communes that were self-sufficient and "small earth" oriented, on the theory that such self-contained communities represented microcosms of what

life would and ought to be like around the world. Such communities of caring individuals were to fulfill both material and emotional/affiliational needs of all their members and were to be a model for society to follow in returning to neighborhoods and comprehensible living space.

A second example is the explosion of computers and the move allowed by the computer revolution back to workers living and working at home. The newest and next cottage industry will be the computer secretarial and word-processing industry.

- *From determinacy to indeterminacy:* The shift from Freudian, deterministic psychology to behavioral, reality-therapy, and Gestalt interventions in dealing with neurosis. The focus has shifted from laying blame at the door of Oedipus—or mother—to taking responsibility for one's own actions, whatever their origin, and changing behavior. The origins of actions are indeterminate; therefore, only the action itself counts.
- *From linearity to mutual causality:* The recent rejections of Darwin's theory of evolution, suggesting instead that alterations in species come about because the species may *select* certain survival mechanisms, suggests that causality is, at best, in traditional terms, a misleading and occasionally wrong-headed concept.

A second such example concerns the ongoing search for a cause—and therefore cures—for cancer and the recent phenomenon, AIDS. In the searches it has become clear that there is no single phenomenon known as cancer, but rather that cancer is many diseases, with multiple factors influencing and shaping its appearance and growth. Thus, the search for cures involves not the finding of the vaccine that addresses the single cause, but rather the tracing of the various biochemical, biological, environmental, and nutritional factors which form a web that prevents or fosters the development of one or the other of these diseases.

- *From assembly or construction to morphogenesis:* Shifts in organizational literature itself, such as the garbage-can model of March and Cohen. This model posits fluid participation, crystallizing around issues, solutions looking for problems, and the emergence of new coalitions and alliances based on attention to any given issue. This is in sharp contrast to notions of building an organization based on tasks and separation of powers.
- *From objectivity to perspectival orientation:* The shift in journalism from straight, factual, "objective" reportage to additional coverage of "point of view" articles, which have explicit value bases and revolve about value concerns that arouse or incite action in various interest groups. Such reportage, formerly the province of the editorial pages only, are now commonplace throughout newspaper and television media alike; they signal a shift away from the "Holy Grail" of objectivity.

The point of these examples is to suggest that on many levels the paradigm shift is with us, and people are living it in their daily lives. Schwartz and Ogilvy (1979) suggest this notion of paradigms infiltrating every level of society by positing three levels of shift: the world view; the disciplinary view, which we will deal with more formally here; and the everyday view. Examples given earlier by Guba apply more purely to the disciplinary view, but these examples ought to convince one that *Time* and *Newsweek* are quite correct in their periodic assertions that, to borrow the words of Bob Dylan, "The times, they are a-changin'!"

For a portion of readers, this shift in assumptions will have some powerful implications, for the shift means nothing less than a shift, at the practical level, in the means and ends of research. By means and ends I mean what researchers do to gather information and what formats they use to finally report what they found.

The argument can be mounted here that these means and ends are synergistic, that they are mutually reinforcing, and that they exhibit value resonance with the axioms. That, however, is a mid-range position, as I believe that they are means and ends dictated as a logical, deducible, and inescapable outgrowth of examination and adoption of the axioms. Some would and have suggested that one might change the axioms, but go on carrying out research (and evaluating its products) by the old mandates, but I do not believe that is possible. Just as the invasions of the Vandals and Goths altered forever the Roman *latifundia,* turning them from summer farming villas and resorts into armed camps for mutual protection, and just as the industrialization of England altered for all time both the urban landscape and the role of the manor and the gentry, even the consideration of a new paradigm brings about changes in the way in which serious researchers frame and attack problems. The sheer explosion of new journals decidedly dedicated to ethnographic approaches should be testimony to the fact that something is afoot in the social and behavioral sciences, even if people do not fully understand yet what it is.

Both *means*—ethnographic and qualitative approaches—and *ends*—case studies as opposed to technical reports—of the new paradigm are coming out of the closet. What is suggested is that means and ends, like the axioms that undergird them, have not been considered as a logical set. It is to the means and ends—for most inquirers, the substance of their activities—that this argument is directed.

There are fourteen logical derivatives of the five axioms presented. The fourteen are largely justified on two sound bases. First, they are logical derivatives of the axioms presented earlier and, second, they add structural coherence and congruence to the research enterprise, and to each other.

NATURAL SETTING

The first implication for researchers—and for those who would use the results of that research to alter organizations—is that they must move out of the laboratory and into the contexts in which the phenomena of interest are situated. Researchers do this for any or all of several reasons, but principally because they understand that they cannot comprehend an event, situation, or phenomenon removed from its natural context. The isolation from a context imposes subtle alterations on the phenomenon under investigation so that it becomes something other than what was being studied. Naturalists believe an event must be studied in its own context before it can be fully understood. Such inquirers also are curious about the environmental shapers that influence any given situation; this mutual shaping will exhibit patterns and webs of influence that in turn select and are selected by participants on the scene in mutually reinforcing ways. And the naturalist is equally interested in which values chosen for what reasons shape actors and events in specific configurations. For these reasons, inquirers cannot stay safe in their laboratories; they must be in constant interaction with the setting and its inhabitants in order to understand them.

Nor is it likely that, having spent a year on site, researchers will retire to their studies to spend their lives writing up the results of their research. They will have processed their notes so considerably, and would have completed a sufficient categorization of things and events and interactions that much of what they know would be ready for publication or presentation. Unbuffered by the laboratory, the naturalists have only one choice: immerse themselves totally in the learning, digesting while they go. If the latter course is chosen, many of the findings are ready to be presented once the researchers have taken leave of their hosts. (Indeed, most of the findings will have been discussed and negotiated with the hosts long before the leave-taking.)

EMERGENT DESIGN

The naturalists, much like old-line anthropologists, can rarely prespecify their designs in any great detail. They prefer rather to let it emerge, unroll, cascade, or unfold. Because naturalists are committed to the concept of multiple and constructed realities, they find it incomprehensible to project those possibilities ahead of time. As a result, they believe that "design" will emerge as they begin interaction with the setting and its denizens (and they with him or her), but the unpredictable nature of those interactions prevents laying out schema for deciding or pursuing what is interesting or important ahead of time. What is interesting and important will be revealed as the multiple realities of actors and members of the setting, and of their shaping and influence, are exerted on one another and on the researchers. The values that inhere in such a setting will likewise intervene and influence in such a way that a formal preordinate design will constrain more than enlighten. Thus, the outcomes in any given research situation are to large extent unpredictable and therefore unspecifiable prior to entry on a site.

THE HUMAN AS INSTRUMENT

Naturalists generally, although not always, elect to make themselves the primary data-collection instruments, for no other reason than that the human-as-instrument, although not perfect, is infinitely adaptable. Because naturalists know they will be dealing with multiple realities, they require, above all, an instrument capable of recognizing, sorting, and honoring those multiple realities, one that is capable not only of distinguishing those subtleties of meaning, but of assessing the role of that meaning in shaping human behavior. Naturalists further understand that all instrumentation has embedded in it some set of values, but it is the human instrument that is capable of identifying, taking into account, coping with, and learning from its own and others' expressed and unexpressed values. The human instrument—unlike computers and paper-and-pencil tests—is capable of understanding the role of the irrational as a powerful emotive device. Because human behavior is rarely rational, the perfect instrument is one that acts in sympathy with the emotional, nonrational, spiritual, and affiliational renderings of its repondents. Shulamit Reinharz's formulation of a "lover-model" of research fits well here, because what she postulates is an *exchange*, a communication, a sharing—so that researcher and respondent learn from and teach one another, rather than take and leave bereft. As Reinharz points out, "Personal knowledge requires emotional involvement, not merely logical and rational analysis" (1979, p. 34). The human instrument provides that involvement better than any survey.

QUALITATIVE METHODS

Having chosen an instrument, one normally chooses next a method of administration. The method of administration most often preferred by those who work with instruments is the paper-and-pencil test, but the methods preferred by naturalists are those most congenial to the human instrument. Such methods include interviewing, participant observation, the recording and analysis of nonverbal communication, and artifactual analysis, which generally includes content analysis, documentary analysis, records usage, and other forms of analytic observation (e.g., unobtrusive measures and the like). Qualitative methods, particularly interviewing and observation, are those that can accommodate and explicate multiple, conflicting, and often inherently unaggregatable realities, and they are sensitive to—and, indeed, depend on—the interaction or exchange between the researcher and the objects or respondents of the study. It is those methods, too, that allow for examination of the extent to which the phenomenon of interest is shaped—or resistant to shaping—by the inquirer's presence and biases; furthermore, they not only allow, they demand consideration and exploration of competing value perspectives that may reside in the setting. By so doing, qualitative methods engender larger holistic understandings and work to prevent uprooting phenomena from their native context.

Generally, incidentally, students—even students of research methods—whether in business, in political science, or in education, rarely encounter formal training in qualitative methods; at least, they do not receive the level of training offered in quantitative and inferential methodologies. When training in some qualitative method is given, it usually is with an eye toward training for survey research; that is, interviewing training will be given as a means of orally administering questionnaires, or acquiring normative or statistically generalizable data. As a result, not only are the axioms unfamiliar, save in their ordinary, everyday experience of them, but the data collection methods also are unfamiliar. Many times what people know of them they have acquired on their own steam, by reading, by practicing, and/or by small workshops that offer training.

However the skills have been acquired, or however they will need to be acquired, qualitative methods of inquiry are those that are best suited for garnering, analyzing, and making sense of multiple realities and multiple, competing value systems. They also are those methods most sensitive to and responsive toward new learnings, new understandings, and connections between meanings not previously discovered. Such methodologies allow for the human as instrument not only to "get smarter," but to make use of learning as the inquiry progresses. Qualitative methods are those that permit both teaching and learning to go on in increasingly sophisticated fashion, without sacrifice to a priori design and without sacrifice to imperfect and unchangeable instrumentation.

UTILIZATION OF TACIT KNOWLEDGE

Polanyi (1966) makes a distinction between propositional knowledge, that which can be stated in verbal (proposition) form, and tacit knowledge, that which is known but which cannot be stated at the present time in verbal form. In the prevailing counter-culture (which is rapidly becoming mainstream), tacit knowledge has been legitimated as "vibes," "hunches," or "gut reaction." This legitimation recognizes the inherent utility of knowledge that is somehow known but that cannot be put into words. The utilization of this form of knowledge takes into account the constant construction of environments by the actors in it, and the usefulness of cues that are not verbally located or even individually examined. Czelaw Milosz (1982, p. 7), the Nobel Prize-winning novelist and poet, says of this largely unverbalized territory:

> The human imagination is spatial and it is constantly constructing an architectonic whole from landscapes remembered or imagined; it progresses from what is closest to what is farther away, winding layers or strands around the single axis, which begins where the feet touch the ground.

Naturalists strongly support this reliance on these additional intuitive, felt, or tacit knowledges, as the layers of both realities and values can be known initially only in this manner. Furthermore, much of what occurs between inquirers and their respondents transpires in this mode. This, incidentally, was part of the utility of an informant for anthropologists; as persons marginal to their culture, they often were in a position to study and convey the larger meanings of tacit or unspoken messages and understandings.

For those scientists who feel that utilization of this form of knowing is somehow "unscientific," at best, uncharacteristic of good science, and at worst, unutilizable by inquirers, let me point out that awareness of tacit knowledge and the willingness to ask questions and observe around it greatly amplify the understandings of the serious inquirer. As Schutz (cited in Weick, 1979) has pointed out,

> Through a combination of selective attention, activity, consensual validation and luck, organizational actors are able to stride into the streams of experience where things are mixed together in random fashion and unravel those streams sufficiently so that some kind of sensemaking is possible.

It not only is possible to make sense of organizations and environments without heavily regimented "maps," it is occasionally desirable to do so, as tacit knowledge may frame designs as it emerges, shaping the questions of importance to researchers.

GROUNDED THEORY

There are two ways to think of theory. On one hand, theory can guide the collection of data, in which instance data are sought to support or falsify some hypothesis. On the other hand, theory may be derived from—follow from—data. In the latter instance we refer to theory as grounded. Typically, naturalists choose to work in the construction of theory from data, rather than beginning with theory that constrains the seeing process. Theory that grows out of context-embedded data is likely to reflect more vividly the multiple constructions of reality that permeate the context, and to explicate more subtly and take account of value systems that each set of actors—inquirers, respondents, and audiences—brings to the inquiry situation.

Naturalists know they will bring values to the situation—values expressed in terms of beliefs, attitudes, prejudices, biases, and the like—but also realize that grounded theory is the most likely avenue for exposing multiple strains of values, including the naturalists' own. As a result, grounded theory is less amenable to inquirer shaping, and more truly anchored in respondent reflections of value positions.

INDUCTIVE DATA ANALYSIS

Naturalists generally prefer to use inductive rather than deductive data analysis. The reasons for that choice are grounded again in the axioms that describe the emergent paradigm. First and foremost, inductive, rather than deductive, analysis is much more likely to be capable of reflecting multiple realities constructed out of environments. Second, an inductive analysis structure has the capability of subsuming and taking account of values that not only inhere in the context but that are part of the inquirer/respondent transactions. Thus, values become explicit and traceable, not only as part of the data that may be encountered, but as part of the analytic process itself. Third, inductive techniques are more likely to result in "thick description" (Geertz, 1973), which in turn allows for judgments to be made about the transferability of phenomena or the similarities between environments. With adequate description in hand, researchers using inductive analysis at later times and in other places may be persuaded to adopt or adapt problem-solving strategies that worked in the first context. Without adequate description, testing for similarity between contexts is impossible.

PURPOSIVE SAMPLING

Michael Patton has written a thumbnail treatment of sampling strategies that draws a clear distinction between the goals of random and purposeful sampling:

> Random sampling is the appropriate strategy when one wants . . . to increase the likelihood that the data collected are *representative* of the entire population of interest. . . . [On the other hand] purposeful sampling is used as a strategy when one *wants to learn something* and *come to understand* something about certain select cases without needing to generalize to all such cases. (1980, p. 107; former italics the author's, latter emphases added)

Patton suggests several strategies for carrying out purposeful (or purposive) sampling, including (1) sampling extreme or deviant cases, (2) sampling typical cases, (3) sampling for maximum variation (picking three or four cases that represent a range on some dimension), (4) sampling critical cases, and (5) sampling politically important or sensitive cases (1980, p. 105). Strategies 3 and 4 are probably most important for naturalistic inquirers, but in point of fact, each strategy enables inquirers to "get the most information of greatest utility from the limited number of cases" (Patton, 1980, p. 104).

The purpose of achieving the maximum scope and range of data collected is the practical goal of naturalists, and they accomplish this by casting the net for deliberately opposite, deviant, idiosyncratic, and atypical constructions of the world or immediate situation. This in turn enables naturalists to have confidence they are portraying as many of the individual and group realities as exist in any given context. This can be done, incidentally, rather easily; one simply asks, "Surely there must be someone who feels very differently about the situation from you. Who might that be?"

Purposive sampling, in addition, grants the naturalist the ability to take account of local context situations, as not everyone on a site will see, or be privy to, the same circumstances. Maximizing the range of perspectives concomitantly maximizes the ability to take account of local conditions, to take account of local influences, and to trace *in situ* value patterns from one respondent to the next. Naturalists who wish to represent the infinite realities will seek those out, wherever the perspectives are held, regardless of the social caste or class of the respondent.

PROBLEM-DETERMINED BOUNDARIES

Naturalists often are asked how they go about focusing and bounding their inquiries if they have no null hypotheses ahead of time, and if the supporting theory and design of a given study are not prespecified. The simple solution is to let time, energy, or logistical factors determine the boundaries and, in fact, that is often what happens, particularly in the case of disciplined inquiries that are evaluations or policy analyses. That is to say, when decisions await information or funds run out, the inquiries are over. This is probably not the wrong way to run a railroad, as the lengthiest study in the world cannot account for incremental change, decision creep, contextual change, participant changes, or perfect information (there is no such thing as perfect information in any event).

The more complex solution is to let the inquiry bound itself as the problem emerges from time on site, rather than to bound it by prior theoretical formulations. In this manner, the problem is defined by participants, actors, and respondents equally with the inquirer, a position supported in the interest of negotiated research. In that case respondent realities set the limits to, or expand the margins of, questions that the inquirers might have brought into the setting. Because problems are largely created in the minds of inquirers—they do not exist in nature—and because problems cannot be satisfactorily separated from the environments in which they are to be found, the bounding of a problem is less difficult than might be imagined. Bounding cannot take place without contextual data, and this demands that context and inhabitants both inform the inquiry about values, conditions, and shaping structures that are important. As inquirers come to know what is important to residents and actors, they will come equally to know when the inquiry should stop. At that point the inquiry is bounded, as it has been defined and identified, and data collected have become redundant and duplicative.

IDIOGRAPHIC INTERPRETATION

Idiographic interpretation is counterpoised to nomothetic interpretation as is the particular to the general. Naturalists are alike in assuming that the particulars of any given context or site shape their data interpretations and conclusions. This shaping happens for the simple reason that different interpretations of conclusions will be meaningful or telling as they express the experiences of those in any given place. This telling includes having the conclusions embedded in the realities of those who live them, having the conclusions mirror the value systems owned by respondents, echoing faithfully the nature of inquirer/respondent transactions, and clearly and forthrightly characterizing the environmental shapers that call forth action or inaction on the part of respondents.

Another word on idiographic interpretation: It should not be inferred from this discussion that it is solely participant/respondent interpretation that is important. One of the important tasks for inquirers working in a naturalistic mode is to teach as well as learn. That involves a critical meta-analysis of mutual shaping and influences that sometimes does, and often should, lead to understandings that will be new to respondents. In this arena the inquirer may be working with latent as well as manifest meanings. What is important, however, is that respondents *recognize* the data and reasoning process that pushed the naturalist toward such meta-understandings, and that understandings of how the interpretations were achieved are accepted and shared.

TENTATIVE APPLICATION

Naturalists tend to be much more modest and reluctant about making sweeping application of their findings, simply because they understand the extent to which local conditions shape and influence those findings. Generally tentative about both situation-specificity and their

own interactions, they hesitate to broadcast startling news of general
social laws because they know that similarities between contexts alone
determine whether findings appropriate in one context will be appropriate statements about another (receiving) context. The melange of
value structures inherent in one context may be seriously at variance
with those found in another, and the events, circumstances, or situations
of one context, although similar to another, may be construed, constructed, or made real by totally different sets of cognitions about
meaning among participants.

The best naturalists can do is caution about the acquisition of description sufficiently thick to enable similarity of judgments between
contexts. Bound by a value structure of their own that is not permissive
of making broad generalizations, naturalists are loathe to enter into the
fray of making policy or designing interventions that fail to take into
account local particularistic conditions.

CASE STUDY REPORTING MODE

Case studies are part of the products and/or ends of naturalistic
inquiries. Although for a time case studies generally fell into disfavor as
a reporting mode (save for anthropologists and some strains of sociolo-
gists), they are beginning to be sought by journals as the products of
ethnographic studies. They have a much larger utility, however, than
just as a nod to the savvy of younger editors.

Reinharz, vindicating the mode, underscored its utility:

> The case history can serve as a bridge between the humanities and
> sociology, since it provides an alternative to commonsense generalization
> on the one hand and isolated, distorted empiricism on the other. . . .
> Particular case histories are inevitably grounded in particular context . . .
> the case history instrumentalizes George Herbert Mead's social psychol-
> ogy: "To understand why someone behaves as he does you must under-
> stand how it looked to him, what he thought he had to contend with, what
> alternatives he saw open to him; you can only understand the effects of
> opportunity structures, delinquent subcultures, social norms, and other
> commonly invoked explanations of behavior by seeing them from the
> actor's point of view." The life history method *seeks interpretations that
> people impose on their own experiences.* . . . The case history . . . compels
> the researcher to utilize and analyze experience . . . [and it] possesses a
> dynamic dimension since it spans across time periods. Processes unfold
> and are explained or at least described. *Readers reach conclusions with*

the researcher as they accompany each other through the processes.
(Reinharz, 1979, pp. 40-43, emphasis added)

So, to paraphrase her defense, case reports are inevitably grounded in the particulars of a given context, because they focus on individual and therefore multiple realities (in seeking interpretations that people attach to their own experiences), because they force the inquirer to take account of and render experiences, because they focus on description and processes, and because they provide vicarious experience to readers. In addition, case studies are peculiarly suited to providing thick description, without which naturalistic generalizations (as Stake describes them) or judgments about transferability are not possible.

Case studies have an additional advantage: Because such works are in narrative form, they are more skillful weapons in the consideration of mutual shapers and webs of influence. Although a picture may be worth a thousand words, those thousand words are worth considerably more than a statistical table when the subject is *why*. Only good narrative can trace the roots of behavior, can recreate the compulsions and unravel the complex tangles of human interaction. It is essentially narrative, too, that exposes and articulates the values that lie hidden in the setting: those of the actors, and those that guide the inquirer and the substantive theory chosen to direct the inquiry, and the methodological theory chosen to execute it. Thus, the case study becomes the appropriate product of a naturalistic inquiry as its strengths are precisely those the naturalist needs in order to honor and depict the setting of the inquiry.

SPECIAL CRITERIA FOR TRUSTWORTHINESS

Naturalists are often assaulted with the accusation that such inquiries are not rigorous. Thoughtful critics may preface their concerns by pointing out that they know that such inquiries often are powerfully relevant, but they nevertheless forcefully maintain that rigor is important. How, they ask, can such inquiry claim to have external validity? Where is reliability in such a study? and what about the awesome subjectivity of such a study? But naturalists are not without an answer: There is nothing wrong with conventional criteria for rigor (or trustworthiness), but they must be applied to that for which they were devised—the conventional, or scientific, paradigm. Inconsistency, maladaptation, or value-dissonance is the result of their application to a wholly new set of axioms or procedures such as have been outlined.

Generally, traditional trustworthiness criteria include internal validity, external validity, reliability, and objectivity. Analogous criteria for naturalistic studies are credibility, transferability, dependability, and confirmability. As criteria for trustworthiness have been dealt with in other places (Guba, 1981; Guba & Lincoln, 1982; Skrtic et al., 1985; Lincoln & Guba, 1985), a brief discussion should suffice.

The naturalist, for example, cannot accept the formulation of internal validity because that criterion implies an isomorphism between research outcome(s) and a single, tangible reality onto which inquiry can converge. The naturalist rejects external validity as a criterion of rigor because it is inconsistent with the basic axiom concerning generalizability. Reliability, likewise, is found to be wanting because "it requires absolute stability and replicability, which are inappropriate, unimportant, and, in any event, totally unachievable by a paradigm that implies emergent design." Finally, the naturalist finds that the objectivity criterion is useless because the paradigm admits and attempts to take account of two already recognized problems in human and behavioral studies: the inquirer-respondent interaction and the role of values (Guba, 1981, Skrtic et al., 1985).

The substitute criterion already mentioned have been developed over several years. They are, of course, not as perfect as those developed over the past two hundred years for the conventional paradigm. But buttressed by a set of empirical procedures that are already well-recognized in the social sciences, they can adequately, if not absolutely, assure the consumers of naturalistic inquiries that such case studies or reports have authenticity and are trustworthy.

NEGOTIATED RESULTS

A perfectly reasonable group of social scientists are arguing currently that the most appropriate form of inquiry with human respondents is that which they call cooperative—or negotiated—inquiry (Heron, 1981). In cooperative inquiry respondents—ordinarily called the subjects of the inquiry—contribute directly to hypothesis making, to formulation of final conclusions, and to whatever interactions and processes go on in between. Heron advances six major arguments for using this "cooperative paradigm," wherein the results of research are shared, bartered, exchanged, or negotiated. The first is the argument from the *nature of research behavior.* Here, he argues that an inquirer cannot define one kind of model of behavior for him- or herself and a separate or different one for his or her subjects. If the basic model for research behavior is that of "intelligient self-direction," then the same model must, to be consistent, be applied to research respondents. "If the subjects are not privy to the research thinking," he argues, "they will not be fully functioning as intelligent agents" (p. 22).

Second, Heron argues from the question of *intentionality*. There is a profound necessity to check with the subjects whether their intentionality and the researcher's coincide. This was the point Mead made in the quotation by Reinharz earlier in this chapter. Until we know what the actor's frame(s) of reference might be, we cannot attribute intentions to him or her (Heron, 1981, p. 23).

The third argument is the argument from *language*. Language formation operates as a kind of archetype for inquiry itself. But when human beings communicate, they have to agree on the rules of the language they will use.[1] "The use of language itself, then, contains within it the paradigm of cooperative inquiry" (Heron, p. 26). Heron goes on to admit that one

> *can* use language to make statements about persons who have not contributed or assented to the formulation of those statements.... [But] to use language in this way is to cut it off from its validating base in the realities of human encounter.... The result is a set of alienated statements hanging in an interpersonal void: statements about persons not authorized by those persons in relation. *For a science of persons as agents my considered view of your reality without consulting you is a very different matter from our considered view of reality.* (pp. 26-27)

Fourth, there is the argument from *an extended epistemology*. This is basically a consideration of what might be the best way of knowing when studying human beings, and Heron argues that knowledge is best acquired by bringing to bear propositional, practical, and experiential components of research. All three of these types of knowing are enhanced by the cooperative paradigm.

Fifth, he argues from *axiology*, or the study of values. Heron asserts that the truth of propositions depends entirely on shared values. If truth in research is a function of shared values, then the cooperative paradigm must be utilized to determine the extent of sharing. This is another and slightly different argument, incidentally, for grounding inquiries in values that are made explicit and inspectable.

Sixth and last, Heron constructs a *moral and political argument*. This argument is shared wholly by Reinharz, incidentally, who would agree that research in the conventional sense usually exploits people, for knowledge is power that can be used against the very people from whom the knowledge was generated or acquired. Again, the argument might be advanced that results are negotiated as the cooperative paradigm

> honours the fulfillment of [the respondents'] need for autonomously acquired knowledge; 2) it protects them from becoming unwitting accessories to knowledge-claims that may be false and may be inappropriately or harmfully applied to others; 3) it protects them from being excluded from the formation of knowledge that purports to be about them and so from being managed and manipulated, both in the acquisition and in the application of the knowledge, in ways they (the respondents) do not understand and so cannot assent to or dissent from. (Heron, 1981, pp. 34-35)

The point of this somewhat extended argument is two-fold. On one hand, there are moral, practical, and methodologically sound reasons for engaging in a negotiation process with respondents about research results. On the other hand, the notion of negotiating results is complementary and perfectly consonant with naturalistic inquiry. Research results are not to be ripped off like priceless cultural artifacts from unsophisticated and primitive peoples. Like artifacts, they belong to those who made them and are to be shared, if at all, in some mutually agreeable fashion.

One way of handling this problem is a procedure borrowed from the trustworthiness arsenal: member checks. Member check is an old sociological term that refers to the process of checking findings with members of relevant groups of those who provided the original information. In naturalists' language, this member checking is utilized as part of determining credibility, but one function it additionally serves is the negotiation of understandings about what is meant by the information provided by respondents. The naturalist checks his or her construction of information and patterns against those that are held by respondents; if those perspectives are not in agreement, additional sharing is called for so that the meanings and values are understood, respected, and represented appropriately by the inquirer.

THE SYNERGISM
BETWEEN THE VARIOUS POSTURES

Earlier it was argued that these characteristics—or postures—of naturalistic inquiry were complementary to, and existed in logical dependence to, the five axioms Guba outlined earlier. The second argument for these particular fourteen characteristics is that they exist in a kind of synergism with one another. They form a coherent and interdependent set between and among themselves, and one cannot easily pick and choose from among them, substituting in their places characteristics of method and setting that fit within the conventional paradigm. To do so forces violence on the epistemological and methodological system, and creates value dissonance inside the inquiry. Together, they form a circular support system, and no matter where one begins, one is led inevitably to other choices from among the characteristics.

For example, the naturalist is more or less forced into contexts that are nonlaboratory settings, as that is where the realities in which he or she is interested reside and are constructed. To use the Schwartz and Ogilvy holographic argument, information that the naturalist needs is distributed throughout the system rather than being concentrated at specific points. Thus, it is absolutely necessary to know the system and the manner in which that system works. So the naturalist moves into the natural setting. In order to collect information from this natural context concerning the realities that abound there, he or she must utilize the best instrument for comprehending wholes that he or she has at disposal: the human instrument. If the choice is made of the human instrument—especially as the instrument of choice to deal with complexity—then secondary choices must be made as to methods for applying the instrument. Those methods typically are qualitative methods.

A second example: Naturalists do not know exactly what the problem is that might be studied; that is, they do not know what will finally emerge as the important and salient characteristics of the setting. They are in a state of indeterminacy, and there is no indication of what the mutual shapers in any given environment might be. As a result, they cannot initially bound the problem, nor can they prespecify a design, nor would they project what findings might emerge. As a result of facing such indeterminacy, naturalists opt for an open and emergent design and only tentative projection of what the problem might be. Because design and bounding are not accomplished at the start, inquiries are at the mercy of actors on their home turf to help identify the problem—and thus naturalists move to the context itself, because that is where the respondents will be found. Because they are in part groping for understanding, they will wish to utilize methods that extend understandings, and those tend to be methods that extend all human characteristics: looking, seeing, hearing, listening, utilizing nonverbal and tacit cues. Thus, naturalists choose qualitative methods to help cope with indeterminacy and heterarchy.

The examples could go on. Each choice dictates another consonant and resonant choice, without which the inquiry falters for lack of coherence. To borrow from a recent book:

> In doing research from a naturalistic perspective, N is forced into the natural setting because he or she cannot specify, without an *a priori* theory or hypothesis, what is important to control or even to study. Until N has spent some time in the setting he or she cannot specify the problem even in rudimentary form, or place boundaries on it. N could not design a contrived study (an experiment, say) because he or she would not know what to contrive. If theory is to be grounded in data, those data must first be located and analyzed inductively.
>
> Since N cannot specify the precise form of the data to be sought, he or she must fall back on an open-ended adaptive instrument; the human being, who, like the "smart bomb," can identify and wend its way to (purposefully sample) the target without having been precisely preprogrammed to strike it. Humans find certain data collection means more congenial than others; they tend toward the use of qualitative methods that "extend human senses; seeing, hearing, and tacit "sixth-sensing" that lead one to observation, interview, documentary analysis and the like. These methods result in insights and information about the sending context so that the extent of transferability and applicability in some other receiving context may be judged. No aggregations, no generalizations, no cause-effect statements can emerge, but only idiographic interpretations; hence an air of tentativeness surrounds any proposed application. (Furthermore, the statements which do emerge have been thoroughly tested and tried with respondents in the context, so that they understand and can assent to, or dissent from, what is being said about them, and what constructions are made about their various realities.) Finally, the case study mode lends itself well to the full description that will be required to encompass all of these facets and make possible understanding on the part of the reader (building on his or her own tacit knowledge and making "naturalistic generalizations" possible). Judgments about the trustworthiness of such a process cannot be made with conventional criteria (thus) criteria devised especially for and demonstrably appropriate to naturalistic inquiry are required. (Lincoln & Guba, 1985)

The point is that no matter where one begins with the characteristics, one is led back to others that bear a synergistic relationship to the first.

In some ways the implications of the axioms are as important as the axioms themselves. Although it is axiomatic that the unexamined life is not worth living—and likewise, the unexamined research not worth doing—the *hows* as much as the whys will occupy researchers, students training to be researchers, and those who read and use the results of research as much as the philosophical underpinnings ever will. With the emergence of a new paradigm for doing research, the hows will likewise emerge as a controversy for years to come. The adoption of some of the means and ends is already well under way. When inquirers are willing to consider the implications of all their choices, and not merely their methods, the revolution will be on in earnest.

NOTE

1. In traditional anthropological field study, of course, the inquirer might not have much to agree to. That is, he or she might be entering a situation in which respondents and informants did not know his or her language, had no wish to learn it, and the rules for communication (the use of language) were clear-cut: Learn ours. Indeed, specialists in language instruction insist this is a primary way to learn about culture—to understand the subtleties of linguistic expression of a people.

REFERENCES

Geertz, C. (1973). Thick descriptions: Toward an interpretive theory of culture. In C. Geertz (Ed.), *The interpretation of cultures*. New York: Basic Books.

Guba, E. G. (1981). Criteria for assessing the trustworthiness of naturalistic inquiries. *Educational Communications and Technology Journal, 29*, 75-92.

Guba, E. G., & Lincoln, Y. S. (1982). Epistemological and methodological bases of naturalistic inquiry. *Educational Communications and Technology Journal, 30*, 233-252.

Heron, J. (1981). Philosophical bases for a new paradigm. In P. Reason & J. Rowan (Eds.), *Human inquiry: A sourcebook of new paradigm research*. New York: John Wiley.

Lincoln, Y. S., & Guba, E. G. (1985). *Naturalistic inquiry*. Beverly Hills, CA: Sage.

Milosz, C. (1982). *Visions from San Francisco Bay*. New York: Farrar Straus Giroux.

Patton, M. Q. (1980). *Qualitative evaluation methods*. Beverly Hills, CA: Sage.

Polanyi, M. (1966). *The tacit dimension*. Garden City, NY: Doubleday.

Reich, R. B. (1983). *The next American frontier*. New York: Times Books.

Reinharz, S. (1979). *On becoming a social scientist*. San Francisco: Jossey-Bass.

Schwartz, P., & Ogilvy, J. (1979). *The emergent paradigm: Changing patterns of thought and belief* (Analytic Report 7, Values and Lifestyle Program). Menlo Park, CA: SRI International.

Skrtic, T. S., Guba, E. G., & Knowlton, H. E. (1985). *Interorganizational special education programming in rural areas: Technical report on the multisite naturalistic field study*. Washington, DC: National Institute of Education.

Weick, K. E. (1979). *The social psychology of organizing*. Reading, MA: Addison-Wesley.

Will, G. (1983). Was Kissinger devious? *Journal-World* (July 24).

PART III

Applications in the Practice of Research

6

MANAGERIAL IMPLICATIONS OF THE EMERGING PARADIGM

Anne Sigismund Huff

I begin this chapter with the assumption that the world can best be seen as a multifaceted and complicated place: that it exhibits all of the characteristics that Schwartz and Ogilvy (1980) describe (in Table 6.1) as characteristic of an "emergent paradigm" for describing nature. My task is to ask what implications this world has for top-level administrators in school systems.

To carry out this task I will draw on a study of three school systems that is now in its fourth year (the NIE project). Superintendents in each of the districts we are studying were asked to identify four or five key issues—issues that they felt would affect the long-run life of their district and that currently demanded their time. Some of these issues are identified below:

- reorganize administrative staff after unexpected retirement
- reinstitute foreign language curriculum in the lower elementary grades
- replace junior high principal
- cut educational budget in anticipation of lower revenues
- consolidate neighborhood elementary schools into a smaller number of buildings

Author's Note: *I would like to thank James A. Conway for helpful comments. The contents of this chapter were developed from material gathered under Grant G-80-0153, National Institute of Education, U.S. Department of Education. Louis R. Pondy is coinvestigator. Support by the NIE is gratefully acknowledged. However, the contents of this chapter do not necessarily represent the policy of the NIE and are not necessarily endorsed by the federal government.*

TABLE 6.1
The Shift in Qualities

Dominant Paradigm	Emergent Paradigm
From	Toward
simple/probabilistic	complex and diverse
hierarchy	heterarchy
mechanical	holographic
determinate	indeterminate
linearly causal	mutually causal
assembly	morphogenesis
objective	perspective

SOURCE: Schwartz and Ogilvy (1980).

- remove asbestos in two high schools
- increase requirements for high school graduation
- develop a comprehensive program for "computer literacy," beginning in kindergarten

During the most intensive year of the study we attempted to interview each of the superintendents every two or three weeks to discuss developments on each of the issues we were following in their district. We also attended key meetings and interviewed other members of the organization and community at each site. We subscribed to the local paper in each area, and coded educational and community articles. We obtained copies of many kinds of written material, including board minutes, administrative meeting agendas, and news sent to parents.

The interviews, however, form the core of the data base. These interviews, which lasted approximately two hours each, were transcribed verbatim and entered into the computer. The interviews then were coded according to each of the major issues we were studying. This data base is now at the point at which we can quickly review every conversation that we have had about each of the issues we followed, and we are in the process of trying to analyze and interpret what we have observed.

In almost all respects this study follows the "means and ends" that Lincoln ascribes to naturalistic studies in Chapter 5 of this volume. Table 6.2 summarizes these aspects of the study.

Although the study in general exemplifies Lincoln's observations, the philosophy that guided us did depart in two ways from her recommendations. First, we decided at the beginning of the study that we could not follow the ideals of grounded theory and inductive data analysis (Lin-

TABLE 6.2
Naturalistic Aspects of the NIE Study

Lincoln's Means and Ends of Naturalistic Research	NIE Study Characteristics
Natural setting	The researchers conducted interviews and attended meetings in three school districts over a four-year period.
Emergent design	The issues studied arose from the work of the organization. Opportunistic data collection, including the transcription of a long series of budget meetings, held in response to unanticipated tax cuts, occurred throughout the course of the study.
The human as instrument	The coinvestigators were the "instrument" of research. Two simultaneous observers, of opposite sex, different interests and background helped counter bias, inattention, and other limitations of the human collecting device. Most interviews and meetings were immediately "debriefed" by the two principal investigators in an attempt to reduce reliance on memory.
Qualitative methods	Methods included interviewing; participant observation; content analysis of newspaper articles, interviews, and speeches; tracking of issues through minutes of meeting.
Utilization of tacit knowledge	The ability to act on hunches was facilitated by the presence of two researchers. One person was often engaged in conversation and note-taking, freeing the other to think about more global patterns and plan the next series of questions. Our coding methods, which focus on language use, also attempt to uncover the tacit knowledge of study participants.
Purposive sampling	The three districts studied were chosen because they had the reputation for being well-managed. Of course, there are some problems in each district, but in the perception of the panel we asked to help identify study sites, and in our own perception, these districts merit study.
Problem-determined boundaries	The "issue" as defined by the administrator involved determined the boundaries of the study. We tried to follow the top four to six issues concerning the superintendent in each district.
Idiographic interpretation	The research design involved six stages of activites. We (1) collected raw data in the form of interviews and documents; (2) collected community level data from newspapers, community publications, and the census; and (3) constructed an "event history" of each issue studied before we began analysis. We then attempted to (4) analyze the course of each issue individually before making (5) districtwide generalizations or discussing (6) "issue management" as a general concept.
Special criteria for trustworthiness	Computerization assures complete review of all data collected on a given subject. Close attention is also being given to measures of intercoder agreement in coding interviews and documents. Throughout the study we checked our emerging analysis against the perception and interpretations of the superintendents.

coln's sixth and seventh means) in their pure form. Researchers, in our view, are always a product of their past experience—the things they have read and the work they themselves have done. This theoretic "contamination" does have its positive aspects, however, in the sense that a rich and varied past provides so many perspectives that one may hope to rise above the limitations of any one approach. We saw ourselves as beginning the project without a firm commitment to a particular theoretical perspective, but with a provisional "tool kit" of many theoretic possibilities. As we interacted with our informants, we hoped to use their experience and our rudimentary tools to develop on site theory that would fit our data.

Our second departure from Lincoln involved the increasing boldness with which we are discussing and disseminating our findings. We have found that practitioners, in particular, have not appreciated "modest" attempts to draw conclusions from our observations (Lincoln's eleventh end). Nor have we, or they, been totally satisfied with the case study as a means of capturing our observations (Lincoln's twelfth end). We have found in our interviews and in discussing the study with others that too much qualification hinders communication.

In the interest of clarifying our own ideas and getting a clear response to those ideas, we have begun to speak quite boldly. Although we were initially clear about the data base and experience upon which we draw, we sometimes generalize beyond that data. We have found that listeners are easily able to add their own grain of salt to our statements. Never in interviewing or speaking to other audiences have we found that people abandon their own experience in deference to ours. Speaking prescriptively and moving beyond the data, then, can be seen as a mode of conversation—a mode that facilitates debate and the development of new knowledge. It is in this spirit that the rest of this chapter is written.

FIRST-ORDER IMPLICATIONS
OF THE EMERGING PARADIGM

As the chapters in this volume indicate, much of the advice currently given to administrators assumes that the world is relatively well-ordered, logical, and predictable. The emerging paradigm, on the other hand, finds none of these characteristics to be accurate descriptors. If administrators begin to see the world in the ways Schwartz and Ogilvy describe as an emerging paradigm in many different disciplines, the advice handed out in most textbooks no longer makes sense.

I believe, as does Lincoln, that in many ways the emerging paradigm is already with us. What that means for administration is that we can find ideas for managing within the new paradigm from the current activities of successful administrators such as those studies in the NIE project. Many lessons for managing within the "new" world view can be drawn from good practice right now.

This conviction is strengthened by a review of a number of other recent studies of high-performing organizations. Peters and Waterman's book, *In Search of Excellence* (1982), is the most visible of these studies. Other work by Kotter (1982), Quinn (1980), Vaille (1982), and McCaskey (1982) also is highly relevant to the subject of this chapter. From these studies and the NIE study I have drawn seven suggestions for administrators who wish to respond to a world that is complex, heterarchical, organic, indeterminate, and mutually causitive.

MAINTAIN AN INFORMAL INFORMATION NETWORK

The world described by the emerging paradigm is too transitory and too complex to be captured by formal information systems or formal organization structures. This appears to be why the superintendents we studied, and the administrators studied by Kotter and Quinn, rely heavily on informal means of understanding their organization and its environments.

These administrators maintain a variety of contacts across a number of levels in the organization. They are also well-connected outside the organization. They rely on informal conversations with these contacts for much of their information about the world within which they act. The basic principle seems to be this: *In order to understand the complex, heterarchical, organic, mutually causitive aspects of the world, one must have complex, heterarchical, organic and mutually causitive sources of information.*

A disparate set of contacts is not just a *source* of information. Superintendents use these contacts to get an informal response to their developing ideas. (Quinn calls this "shopping" an idea.) The network also is useful as a broad forum within which superintendents can informally deliver early cues about changes in policy. (One superintendent we studied called this "creating a mind set.") The overall point is that the people in the information network shape one another; for, of course, members of the organization "shop" their ideas with the superintendent and try to create "a favorable mind set" at the top. And the informality of the network is essential. People need a way to send and receive information that is too tenuous, complex, or political to be "on the record."

PLAY "WHAT IF?"

Although it often is impossible to predict what will happen in a complicated world, something will happen. The superintendents we studied tended to think casually and informally through their responses to many possible events, even knowing that most of these possibilities were unlikely to occur. In one district, for example, we were surprised at how quickly the superintendent reorganized his staff after an unexpected retirement. Although the particular retirement was not anticipated, the superintendent indicated that he had "played with" the possibility of another staff member leaving for a job with a different district, and with the possibility that a third staff member might retire early. The advice to be drawn from this and other examples of an able reaction to a new situation is this: *Thinking through responses to events that may not occur helps the administrator be prepared for the unpreditable events that do occur.*

MANAGE PREMISES RATHER THAN OUTCOMES

Most books on management suggest that administrators should have specific goals and actively attempt to achieve them. A basic finding of our study was that the superintendents we observed often acted in much more general terms. Instead of aiming for a particular outcome, the superintendents usually tried to obtain a certain kind of outcome. For example, in one district the superintendent hoped to reinstitute foreign language instruction, which had been cut back in an earlier period of tight resources. In anticipation of this action, the superintendent did several things, including encourage a potentially sympathetic board member to run for a second term. He did not, however, form specific ideas about what kind of program the district might adopt. A separate committee considered the details several years after he first began taking steps toward the new curriculum.

Again and again the superintendents we studied exerted leadership in this way. They gave careful attention to committee membership, the timing of meetings, the content of agendas, and other devices that might shape the general nature of a decision. They did these things far more often than they tried to elicit a particular decision. Bower and Doz (1979) suggest the basic principle: *Top level managers shape the premises of other executives' decisions more often than they make decisions themselves.*

IMPROVISE

If the world is a complicated place and it is impossible to anticipate what will happen, it makes sense to develop dexterity in using the material the world provides. In the classroom I sometimes bemoan the tendency of managers to "shoot from the hip." In the field I have come to feel that shooting from the hip is an essential skill.

We often think of improvisation as an immediate response to a sudden opportunity—taking advantage of a fortuitous remark made during a meeting, for example. But improvisation can also operate in a much longer time frame. In one of our districts the superintendent hoped to replace the principal of a junior high. For various reasons this was difficult to do. It was not until several years later that a district committee recommended strengthening curriculum support, the board approved a districtwide curriculum coordinator, and the superintendent saw an opportunity to make the personal change he had been contemplating by putting the principal into the new job.

In general, it seems that *acting in a complicated world depends on improvising connections between different decision arenas.* This is March and Olsen's (1976) "garbage can" from the inside out. The streams of solutions, problems, decision opportunities, and participants that look chaotic from a distance are, in fact, a rich set of raw materials that increase the possibilities for successful action.

BE CONTENT WITH MULTIPLE, PARTIAL "SOLUTIONS"

The longer we interview in our study districts, the more complicated is our understanding of the issues we are following. The attempt to change the junior high principal, for example, is just one aspect of a larger effort to improve conditions in the junior high, which is just one aspect of an effort to better coordinate the elementary and junior high curriculum and staff.

However, *the administrator's ability to perceive issues is almost always bigger than the ability to act on issues. As a result, the administrator often must be content to work on a small part of the larger whole.* In

Quinn's eyes this is an essential feature of management. Different sub-units of complex organizations often are on different time lines, and one unit often is ready to act long before other units. A disjoint approach allows organization members to accept, adapt, and understand new ideas. It allows administrations to do the same. Furthermore, the demands made on managers are so varied, as Mintzberg (1973) reminded us some time ago, that "time sharing" is inevitable in any case.

An interesting corollary to these observations may be that *a specific action should rarely be taken unless it is compatible with several different issues* facing the administrator. Given the vagaries of a complicated world, causal connections often are too weak to be reliable. The sensible action has several different utilities.

LET POLITICS INFLUENCE THE SUBSTANCE OF POLICY

We set out to study "the way groups of individuals make groups of decisions." We were nevertheless surprised at how much the superintendents we studied, particularly in the two larger districts, relied on groups—their administrative staffs, faculty committees, board members, and knowledgeable outsiders. The ability of these administrators to involve others is connected to their willingness to formulate only general goals. It is also connected to their understanding that administrators "work on" rather than "solve" problems. Those who want specific or grand solutions have no choice but to try to control the decision process much more closely. The emerging paradigm suggests that *unilateral control is not just difficult, but frequently impossible. Administrators must share the construction of the future.*

In our study even when managers did not intend to involve others in determining a course of action, it often happened anyway. The decision to sell an old junior high building began to be reexamined in one district, for example, when parents began to pressure the school board on a quite unrelated issue—the size of classes in one elementary school. The superintendent collected data to show that current classes in the school were within the bounds of decisions made in the past. Politics made an unexpected impact on policy in the next meeting, however, when a parent reanalyzed this data to show that under conditions of declining enrollment, *differences* in class size among schools had in fact increased substantially. The board decided to reconsider their recent decision to maintain neighborhood schools and think instead of putting all elementary students in the old junior high and one other building. One positive aspect of this alternative was to divide students into classes of more equal size.

There are two important aspects of the advice to let politics influence policy. The first is that differences of opinions have the healthy effect of pushing administrators to reexamine their assumptions. In the process they are more likely to generate policies in keeping with the current shape of the environment.

The second observation is that if organization members and other constituents help detemine an action, they are more likely to adopt it as their own. Leaving the details open is also compatible with a view of the organization as complex, heterarchical, and mutually causitive.

THINK AND ACT IN CONTRADICTIONS

Although the fifth piece of advice ("be content with multiple, partial solutions") suggests that administrators know more than they can act, it is also true that they must sometimes act more than they know. This is because it is difficult to know what is "true" in the world we are outlining in this volume, much less what will be true. Sometimes the sensible response to these ambiguities is what McCaskey calls "Janusean thinking." Administrators face more than one direction at a time, even though it means they must think and act in ways that are not always consistent.

In one of the districts we studied, for example, there were several indicators that the district would have significantly less revenue than it had had in the past. Steps were taken to reduce staff and otherwise trim the budget. At the same time the superintendent also believed that the decrease in state aid, and other negative factors, might be less drastic than predicted. He therefore kept "on the back burner" several projects that assumed a brighter financial picture. Furthermore, he began to act in ways that would ultimately allow these new programs to be instituted, even while his primary posture was one of cutback.

This example of Janusean thinking is familiar to almost every administrator. Meyer and Rowan (1977) point out, however, that the contradictions that necessitate Janusean thinking go far deeper than unclear funding situations. One of the deeper contradictions involves the tension between actions that are professionally desirable and actions that the public finds desirable. The district trying to decide whether or not to consolidate neighborhood schools faced this dilemma. The most vocal parents strongly supported maintaining neighborhood schools. The superintendent also was able to articulate good arguments for maintaining neighborhood schools, although he came to feel that it was educationally desirable to centralize shrinking resources into a smaller number of buildings. Whatever his recommendation, he also knew the board might make either decision, and he began to act in ways that would allow him to implement whichever alternative they chose.

The word *act* is important here. Quinn points out that by the time a new direction is clearly articulated, the organization has already put parts of the plan into action. In fact, it is this experience that allows the new direction to be articulated clearly. Weick (1979) has said "How can I know what I think until I see what I say?" It is also true that organizations need to see what they do in order to know what they think. If one operates from the emergent paradigm, this means that *to build understanding of a complex and contradictory world, one must do complex and contradictory things.*

PITFALLS

Although these guidelines seemed to work for the superintendents we studied, they were not foolproof. We observed three problems in particular:

MISUNDERSTANDING AND INCOMPREHENSION

A key task of the superintendents, and all administrators, is to communicate with other people who have substantially less information about strategic issues than they do. The more complex the superintendent's understanding of the organization and its environments, the more difficult it is likely to be to communicate that complexity to others. The more varied the administrator's response to the world, the more likely it is that others will misunderstand the administrator's intent.

The leader's level of information, and the breadth of his or her activity, is at variance with the information and activity of other important actors in the organization. The school board, for example, has the problem of trying to understand and make critical decisions about a complicated organization they encounter for only a few hours every month. The teachers have the problem of trying to understand decisions that suboptimize conditions in the part of the organization they know best, in the name of improving systemwide operations with which they have little contact.

These realities were important in the decision to replace the junior high principal. The superintendent was attempting to bring to a close an issue that he had found problematic for over four years. When the decision to transfer the principal to another position was announced, however, the teachers were less sympathetic than he had anticipated. Because his involvement with the issue was more intense and spanned a longer period than many teachers, because he had a different relationship with the principal than the teachers, because they had information about day-to-day operations he did not have, and because his broad contacts generated some information he was unwilling to share with the teachers, it is not surprising that he and the teachers did not have the same interpretation of the principal issue. The disagreement that ensued made bringing the issue to a close difficult.

LIMITED PARTICIPATION

The teachers in this case also charged the superintendent with not allowing them sufficient voice in the replacement decision. This raises a second potential problem with responding in complex ways to a complex environment.

The human relations school of management has emphasized involvement and participation in decision making. However, the more complexly decision situations are framed, the more time and effort participation requires. Although we believe that the sites we studied are on balance well managed, we would acknowledge that some decisions did not include the level of participation held up as ideal by those concerned with industrial democracy.

In fact, some of the very practices that we count as sensitive and intelligent—because they acknowledge a complex world in keeping with the emerging paradigm—inherently limit the involvement of others. Using broad informal networks, for example, can mean a decision is made on the basis of some information that is best kept secret. Improvising a link between two different decision situations can introduce extraneous criteria into a decision in the eyes of a particular constituency. It would certainly have undermined the new curriculum coordinator, in the case discussed above, for example, to admit that her appointment also satisfied a problem in the junior high.

DOMINANCE OF NARROW INTERESTS

But the question of organizational involvement also has another twist. Some of our observations suggest that participation in decisions is uneven rather than absent. This raises a third problem with complex and multideterminant views of the organization.

Because of the superintendents' position and responsibility, their appreciation of the world should be especially complex. When new events occur, however, this complexity may make it difficult to assess quickly the new situation. Other actors in the system, with narrower responsibilities, are not called upon to construct such a complex view of the world. They are unlikely to have the information to do so. The implications of a new situation may be much easier for them to interpret than for the superintendent.

We saw a dramatic instance of this situation in the school closing case. For some parents understanding the possibility of closing neighborhood schools was easy. They felt strongly that their children should be close to home, and they quickly organized to bring their point of view to the board. The superintendent, with a broader responsibility and a longer time horizon, found it more difficult to balance different aspects of the situation. He saw educational advantages both for neighborhood and centralized configurations. At the same time the financial implications of each choice became more difficult to compare as the calculations became more sophisticated. In the interim period, while the administration shaped and weighed alternatives, several key board members appear to have been persuaded by the parent group to vote against consolidation. In the end, when the superintendent made a recommendation to close neighborhood schools, a slim majority of the school board voted against it.

This appears to be a general problem. The special interest group may be able to make a more coherent and initially compelling assessment of a situation than those who labor within the emerging paradigm (Huff, 1984). The superintendent felt that the neighborhood school issue was so important that the community should be broadly involved. But the very breadth of involvement made detailed transfer of information difficult. Various parents weighed the information that was available in different ways, but not all of these individuals were equally active in the decision process. Those who focused on the advantages of neighborhood schools had a compelling case to make. Their case was more straightforward than the case the superintendent tried to make as he struggled under the emerging paradigm and the presciptions for action it seemed to demand.

SECOND-ORDER IMPLICATIONS
OF THE NEW PARADIGM

The point to be made is that *each of the ways in which the administrator responds to an organic view of the world in turn helps creates the complexity that characterizes that world, and this complexity has its own problems.* The informal information network generates mutual causality, for example, and the improvisational linking of different decision areas vastly complicates interconnections between issues and people. Weick's (1979) observation that the environment is the creature of the organization rather than the reverse is very apt here, and it carries with it the necessity of looking further for appropriate managerial responses to the new paradigm.

When we began the school district study, we expected that theories compatible with the emerging paradigm would be most useful for describing and analyzing our observations. We saw many things consistent with loosely coupled systems, garbage can processes, and other models proposed by influential writers in this area. That did not surprise us. What surprised us was that we also saw many efforts to impose order and comprehension on the world. These observations have become, for us, the most interesting aspect of the study. I now feel that *first-order responses to the new paradigm,* such as those described in the first part of this chapter, *in themselves help create the need for second-order responses that control the complexity with which the world is understood.*

These second-order responses can be tentatively framed in terms of seven more pieces of advice.

DEVELOP THEMES AND AGENDAS

There is a surprising amount of consistency across four years of our interviews with a single superintendent. I attribute this consistency to two sources. On one hand, each superintendent we studied tended to stress a small set of "themes" in responding to many different issues. These themes are perhaps best described as a set of values or preoccupations. In one district, for example, the superintendent thought often about the future, and he worried about the educational implications of societal change. In another district the superintendent was concerned especially by the integrity of the district dealing with conflicting demands.

The second source of consistency is more action-oriented. We found, as did Kotter in his study, that the superintendents had a personal "agenda," which provided an important pattern to their thoughts and actions. This agenda, although rarely articulated formally, can be identified as a set of changes the superintendent hoped to address over time. The reinstitution of foreign language is one example of such an agenda. The attempt to improve coordination between the elementary schools and the junior high is another. After the study had been going on for several years we realized that the issues we observed, from the superintendents' perspective, were important not just in their own right. They also were potential opportunities to accomplish these broader objectives.

The advice that can be drawn from this observation has to do with the advantage of a consistent orientation in a world with many complexities and side paths. Administrative *consistency across various issues is created, in part, by themes and agendas. This consistency appears to help organization members predict and accommodate themselves to changing situations. Consistency also helps organizational teachers maintain their bearing in the complicated world that their own actions and perceptions help create.* The more complex and indeterminate we understand the world to be, the more problematic coordinated action becomes. Themes and agendas help the members of an organization create coordinated perceptions and activities.

LAY A BREAD CRUMB TRAIL

We saw other ways in which the superintendent tried to help make sense of the organization. For example, in taking the school board on the annual tour of the buildings, the superintendent might remark as they walked into Central Elementary, "You might look at the roof over the west wing. We think it will probably need replacing in three years or so." Six months later the superintendent might end a discussion of capital expenditures with the statement: "The next major expenditures we'll probably need at Central are a new compressor for the air conditioner and then a new roof over the west wing." And so on. By the time a new roof is needed, the board is familiar with the project. They feel it's an expenditure that has been carefully considered. Out of all the many details relevant to one building, a trail has been constructed that leads toward a major decision.

The superintendents we studied tried to create such patterns even when there was significant time pressure. The district that discovered asbestos in one of its major buildings, for example, still gave attention to the "controlled leaks" that let those less intimately involved with the district assimilate and make a pattern from new information. The basic idea seems to be this: *Coordinated action within organizations requires that any given member "edit" his or her concerns into a smaller number of items that can be comprehended by others. Repetition of these concerns is almost always necessary to gain the attention of others and convince them of serious intent.*

DRAMATIZE EVENTS

The superintendents that we studied also were adept at utilizing external events to draw attention to key issues. For example, recent reports on problems with secondary education are being widely quoted by a superintendent who over the last four years has strengthened standards for graduation requirements, and now is thinking of raising the standards for grading and participation in athletics. Highlighting and discussing recent reports critical of American education helped create a favorable environment for strengthened requirements. These benefits cannot be taken lightly in a world such as the one identified by the emerging paradigm. In Quinn's words, *organizations must sometimes wait for Pearl Harbor before they can enter the war.*

DEVELOP FAMILIAR ADMINISTRATIVE MECHANISMS

Lou Pondy became more and more impressed, during the course of our study, with the way in which the superintendents used committees, meetings, and agendas to establish a familiar pattern on new issues.

In the budget cutting case, for example, we were surprised by how smoothly the district faced the first need to reduce expenditures in over nine years. Part of the explanation appears to be that the superintendent adopted a familiar form of meeting with his administrative group to discuss possible cuts and he used established ways of communicating with the school board, teachers union, and other publics.

In another district the decision to implement a new computer curriculum also relied heavily on well-known administrative mechanisms. In this case the superintendent had a long-term interest in introducing computers for classroom use. When he decided the time was right, he quickly mobilized a number of different mechanisms with which the district had previous experience, such as a "blue ribbon" committee of community members. These familiar mechanisms helped channel consideration of the new program and speed its adoption (Pondy & Huff, in press).

We have gradually increased our attention to standing committees, budget forms, familiar report formats, and other "habits" of organizations. They appear to be an important aspect of successful administration. *The availability of a broad set of familiar mechanisms facilitates the consideration of new issues in at least two ways: Organization members are not distracted by the vehicle of discussion; and the ability to "package" a new issue into a familiar vehicle clarifies the way in which it might become a normal part of the organization.*

SEE THE SAME INDIVIDUALS IN MULTIPLE CONTEXTS

As we've begun to talk about the NIE study, people in education administration have wondered whether our districts are not extremely atypical, as the superintendent with the shortest tenure (four years) had already outlasted the national average at the beginning of the study. Knowing the histories of the three districts we studied, which in each case involved a prior period of "revolving superintendents" until a good match was found, we suggest in return that our districts may be characteristic of stable periods in many districts. Averages may obscure the juxtaposition of several short administrations with a longer one.

Even the short-term administrator, however, must try to make decisions that make sense to a large and varied group of people. *Repeated contact with at least a few individuals, even over a relatively short period, is one way in which the organization leader creates the familiarity that facilitates the sense-making process.* A key advantage of these contacts is that the superintendent has the opportunity to present a larger set of "cues" with which a complex, diverse, indeterminate perspective on the world can be interpreted. If the emerging paradigm is accepted, it must be accompanied by such mechanisms to reduce confusion and misunderstanding.

REHEARSE AND REPEAT EXPLANATIONS

Talk is an important medium for bringing order and pattern to a complex world. The superintendent interested in computers, for example, frequently mentioned their importance, for society as well as for schools, in his speeches to teachers and other groups. When I analyzed these speeches over a fifteen-year period, I found that computers were seen in different ways, reflecting both changing capabilities of computers and changing district experience with them.

Persistent exploration of the general subject is important in itself, however. I interpret these speeches as a stage on which the superintendent practiced a way of explaining the importance of what became a key item in his agenda. This rehearsal may well have had a great deal to do with the way in which the superintendent was ultimately able to introduce a strong computer curriculum in the elementary school. The basic idea is that *rehearsal helps the leader work out the ramifications of a new issue in his or her own mind. In addition, repeated explanation makes the ideas familiar to constituents,* including the board, teaching staff, and community.

SIMPLIFY AND RATIONALIZE

There was often a discontinuity between the way in which individuals talked about issues in private and the way in which they talked about them in public. Decision meetings of the school board, in particular, were often highly ritualized. Issues with many thorny aspects were presented and discussed as if they were much smoother. Administrators and members of the board withheld reservations and complications they had expressed privately and in nondecision-making meetings.

We have come to see the utility of this kind of rationality. As the number of individuals discussing an issue becomes broader and broader, the likelihood for derailment increases. There is a "conspiracy," if you will, to keep such issues from going down the many side paths that present themselves. In a district of relative harmony and good faith, the conspiracy is a product of all parties involved. Meyer and Rowan (1977) make this point as well. *Given the complexities and irresolvable contradictions inherent in the emerging paradigm, the assumption of good faith, and the simplifying assumptions of rationality, help action continue.* A further point is that *the ritual of rationality, with its appearances of order and harmony, helps create order and harmony.* The individual who presents an issue in outline comes to see the outline more clearly. The individual who suppresses reservations diminishes those reservations.

DO THESE PRESCRIPTIONS MATCH
THE IMPLICATIONS DRAWN BY WEICK?

In many ways the fourteen pieces of advice to practitioners developed in this chapter echo the implications for practice Weick drew at the end of Chapter 3. Table 6.3 highlights some of these similarities.

At the same time, there are several key areas in which I disagree with Professor Weick, and these areas are highlighted in Table 6.4.

First, there is the question of how administrators can do damage. Weick focuses on the problems of anticipation and labels. Although I agree that both can be problematic, I feel that in practice it can be difficult to make a label stick or create an anticipation that shapes future understanding. Managers should use some care, but bigger problems—problems of others not being able to make sense of intentions—arise if the manager does not anticipate and label. So, I would rewrite Weick in this way:

> Treat anticipations and labels with care; but use them as the main tool available to fight misunderstanding and incomprehension.

Second, although I accept hindsight bias, I feel that hindsight is critical in making sense of situations for oneself and others. The past, especially the shared past of a group of organizational participants, is critical raw material for making sense of the present. If our memories were *clear,* the past would rarely be of value in a world that is complex and changing. In fact, hindsight bias works to our advantage. It allows us to pick out of the past not what was actually most important for a situation that will never repeat itself, but what our understanding of today's situation now allows us to see as relevant to today. The virtues I attach to playing "what if" can also be attached to playing "what was." It is not important that the situations we remember with hindsight never existed; our interpretations of them help us fulfill the task of the moment, which is to find out what can be important about what is. I would say,

> Retrospection allows individuals and organizations to edit the past. In the process they select parts of long chains of events and give them meaning. Hindsight bias makes this possible. "Hindsight bias" is another name for the perspective one is trying to develop to understand today's situation.

TABLE 6.3
Basic Agreement Between Weick and Huff

Issue	Implication from Weick	Advice from Huff
The usefulness of rationality.	1. Look for small pockets of order and protect them, grow them or diffuse them. 10. If you persist, you may create connections that are more continuous, constant, significant, direct and immediate.	8. Develop themes and agendas. 9. Lay a bread crumb trail. 10. Dramatize events. 11. Develop familiar administration mechanisms. 12. See the same individuals in multiple contexts. 13. Rehearse and re-peat explanations. 14. Simplify and rationalize.
The importance of action; the drag created by analysis.	5. Intention is neither a necessary nor sufficient condition for action. 12. Accuracy is less impor-tant than animation. 17. Act and treat your actions as conjectures about goals, preferences and capabilities. 18. Be willing to leap before you look. 19. You can optimize either deliberation or action, but not both.	4. Improvise. p-3. Narrow interests can dominate the decision the leader tries to frame as complex heterarchical and indeterminate.
The difficulty of capturing others' attention.	16. It is more important to capture a person's attention than his intention.	9. Lay a bread crumb trail. 10. Dramatize events. 13. Rehearse and re-peat explanations.
Patience and approximation as administrative virtues.	10. Be patient. Systems are sluggish and slightly disorderly, but they do eventually act in a system-like manner.	3. Manage premises rather than outcomes. 5. Be content with multiple, partial solutions.
Inconsistency, argument and improvisation as organization attributes.	15. View your organization as a set of procedures for arguing and interpreting. 17. Act and treat your acts as conjectures.	2. Play "what if." 4. Improvise. 7. Think and act in contradictions.

TABLE 6.4
Areas of Disagreement

Issue	Weick	Huff
When should managers be careful?	13. Anticipations matter, don't adopt them casually; they tend to fulfill themselves. 14. Labels are powerful means to reduce ambiguity. Impose them with caution and deliberation because they can direct action.	P 1. Misunderstanding and incomprehension are linked to complex managerial action. 13. Rehearse and repeat explanations.
What is the virtue of hindsight? More broadly, what kind of understanding is possible?	4. Retrospective explanations are poor guides to prospective action. Hindsight will gloss over difficulties. 9. Don't expect long chains of events to make sense.	2. Play "what if." 9. Lay a bread crumb trail.
What is rationality? How should managers use it?	2. Assess when decision rationality works in your setting and when it doesn't. 3. Don't treat rationality as a universal prescription. 9. Don't expect long chains of events to make sense.	8. Develop themes and agendas. 14. Simplify and rationalize.

Finally, and perhaps most basically, Weick and I appear to disagree about the nature of rationality. Weick believes that rationality is achieved primarily in stable situations involving a small number of people. Even that rationality may be illusory. In his words, "there is less to rationality than meets the eye." One must be careful not to believe the illusions one has manufactured for external consumption.

The rationality I have been talking about in this chapter is of a different sort. It is order that also acknowledges disorder. I believe that one should take whatever one can for granted, until one gets bored or in trouble. That is because one often is "in trouble"—faced with situations that appear to have little order. And it is precisely here, in these unstable situations, with many participants, where "rationality isn't likely to work," that one must try to create rationality. The effort to do so will only be partially successful. But one risks creating cynical organizations if one allows oneself or others to view the order-creating effort as building a facade.

In the emerging paradigm the participants themselves are complex and capable of contradiction. We can see that our actions and the actions of others have both rational and irrational aspects. The organization leader can and should reinforce our ability to think in complex, heterarchic, indeterminate, mutually causitive ways. We can become better at seeing both the rational and irrational aspects of situations. If I had written Weick's chapter, then, I might have said:

> Delegate responsibility for the situations in which rationality can be easily achieved; take them for granted until they prove troublesome. Your efforts should focus on bringing partial order to those situations that resist rationality. To do so you must encourage yourself and others to have faith in the partial order you create.

CONCLUSION

At this point we must reconsider what rationality—the rationality usually linked to the dominant paradigm outlined in Table 6.1—can mean. I have always been perplexed by the strength of this paradigm, which assumes the world is well-ordered and mechanical in the face of circumstances that seem clearly to the contrary. I now feel that rationality has a continuing place in controlling the complexities of a complicated world.

It is true that the dominant paradigm is frustrating. I believe that the first-order responses we observed in our three study districts will come to characterize a greater proportion of all organizational leaders' time, as more and more individuals become comfortable with the less frustrating, more useful paradigm that is now emerging.

However, this responsiveness to the new paradigm has within it the ability to make the world yet more complex. At some point the mutual reinforcement becomes dysfunctional. The language of rationality, objectivity, and linearity, with its simplifying assumptions, offers a genuine aid. Viewed broadly, each of the second-order responses identified in the second half of this chapter is a rationalizing device that provides pattern and understanding in the midst of a complicated world. Each second-order response has its unrealistic simplifications, but each facilitates purposeful action.

The task, then, is to develop first-order responses that are congruent with the emerging paradigm. But these responses can never be enacted without some undesirable side effects. The leader's task is thus also to develop second-order responses to the new paradigm. The administrator must be responsive to the irrational, complex, mutually causitive aspects of the world. He or she must also be able to contain these aspects of the world by creating simplicity and order. But this rationality is not the rationality within which we operated before people like Weick and March helped articulate the emerging paradigm. It is rationality in the context of complexity, heterarchy, mutual causation, and all the rest.

The interaction between rationality and the emerging paradigm can perhaps be illustrated better by returning to the game of soccer that Weick and March have described. But this time one must not describe the game from the perspective of the fan in the stands who has seen many different games. One must think about the game as the players experience it.

Down on the field one of the first things one notices is that many of the players seem to like playing soccer. They apparently enjoy the exercise, the contact with a varied group of players, and their ability to occasionally hit a moving target. In general, they don't seem to think much about the conditions under which they play. They are far less worried than the fans in the stands about the vagarities of the field, the many balls in play, multiple and vague goals, or the inconsistent number of participants.

One of the advantages the players have is the ability to observe and label objects on the field. Players often hastily scribble notes, or quickly refer to past notes. If you are near a ball, player, or umpire who has been in the game for long, you will see that each bears the signs of play—some faint, some more recent. As a ball comes near, players look for these idiosyncratic marks to help them predict how it is likely to play. They can identify and make predictions about other players and umpires. The sign of players with experience is the bulge of memoranda in their pockets. They make sense of the game in the process of play, even though notes they work with are incomplete, idiosyncratic, easily erased, and often forgotten.

Then, too, you must listen. This is not a game played in silence. The players yell to one another all of the time. They yell "Hey, you fool, get off my toe!" They make points by throwing their hands up in the air and shouting, "I score!" They even create new ideas in the heat of the moment. "Nice deke," one player may call—and suddenly "the deke" is born; a word that for a time, to a small group of players, on one part of the sloping field, describes a particularly effective way of faking an opponent. This ability to talk and create shared interpretations is another way—although it too is incomplete and idiosyncratic—that the players make sense of what's happening on the field.

Finally, the game is easier to understand, from the player's perspective, if one remembers that no one on the field has ever played any other game. In school some have heard of a game called "realsoccer," but in fact the game on the field is the only game in town. The players are as good as they are because they don't have to try to play realsoccer. Realsoccer is a strange game. Those who have heard it described say it is played on an odd shaped field with almost no balls or goals and that the rules are extraordinarily fussy about the number of players and the way they must behave.

REFERENCES

Bower, J. L., & Doz, Y. (1979). Strategy formulation: A social and political process. In D. E. Schendel & C. W. Hofer (Eds.), *Strategic management*. Boston: Little, Brown.

Huff, A. S. (1981). Multilectic methods of inquiry. *Human Systems Management, 2,* 83-94.

Huff, A. S. (1984). Situation interpretation, leader behavior, and effectiveness. In J. G. Hunt et al. (Eds.), *Leaders and managers: International perspectives on managerial behavior and leadership*. New York: Pergamon Press.

Kotter, J. P. (1982). *The general managers*. New York: Free Press.

March, J. G., & Olsen, J. (1976). *Ambiguity and choice in organizations*. Bergen: Universitetsforlaget.

McCaskey, M. (1982). *The executive challenge*. Marshfield, MA: Pitman.

Meyer, J., & Rowan, B. (1977). Institutionalized organizations: Formalized structure as myth and ceremony. *American Journal of Sociology, 30,* 431-450.

Mintzberg, H. (1973). *The nature of managerial work*. New York: Harper & Row.

Peters, T. J., & Waterman, R. H. (1982). *In search of excellence*. New York: Harper & Row.

Pondy, L. K., & Huff, A. S. (in press). Achieving routine. *Journal of Management*.

Quinn, J. B. (1980). *Strategies for change*. Homewood, IL: Irwin.

Schwartz, P., & Ogilvy, J. (1980). *The emergent paradigm: Toward an aesthetic of life*. Paper presented at the ESOMAR meetings, Barcelona, Spain.

Vaille, P. B. (1982). The purpose of high performing systems. *Organizational Dynamics*.

Weick, K. E. (1979). *The social psychology of organizing* (rev. ed.). Reading, MA: Addison-Wesley.

7

DOING NATURALISTIC RESEARCH INTO EDUCATIONAL ORGANIZATIONS

Thomas M. Skrtic

This chapter describes a research project that was guided by a deliberate application of the naturalistic inquiry axioms and implications presented in the chapters by Guba and Lincoln. It attempts to give life to the axioms and implications by selectively illustrating how the ontological, epistemological, and methodological bases of naturalistic inquiry were operationalized in a study of complex educational organizations.[1] The project from which the illustrations are drawn investigated the impact of educational service agencies (ESAs) on rural school district implementation of the Education for All Handicapped Children Act (P.L. 94-142).[2]

This study is unique in at least two respects. From the perspective of emergent paradigm research, it represents the first national, multisite application of naturalistic inquiry as explicated by Guba (1978, 1981) and Guba and Lincoln (1981, 1982). Although much of the theoretical work had been completed prior to the study's inception, specific procedures to operationalize the axioms and implications—particularly various procedures subsumed under "special criteria for trustworthiness" and "negotiated results"—remained to be developed and tried. From the perspective of organizational analysis, the ESA represents a relatively unstudied entity. Its multidistrict nature creates a highly complex situation. As a single organization—with varying degrees of authority over and/or responsibility to member districts—it engages in transactions with an array of constituencies and organizations that vary considerably in terms of interests and characteristics. Using Weick's (1976) imagery, the ESA may be viewed as a loosely coupled alliance of loosely coupled systems. And within states ESAs themselves are coupled in varying degrees with one another and with the state education agency.

Although my intent is to translate the naturalistic paradigm's axioms and implications into the actual doing of naturalistic research, a comprehensive treatment of each axiom and implication is beyond the scope of this chapter. For ease of presentation, I have clustered the implications into five sets that correspond roughly to the sequence in which the research was conducted (Table 7.1). Because the axioms have been treated extensively in the chapters by Guba and Lincoln, I have not included separate sections on them here. Instead, I have addressed them, where appropriate, in relation to the various implications as well as in a concluding section on the fittingness of the naturalistic paradigm.

RESEARCH DESIGN: EMERGENT DESIGN, PROBLEM-DETERMINED BOUNDARIES, PURPOSIVE SAMPLING[3]

The previous chapters by Guba and Lincoln presented a justification for an emergent research design and its advantages, particularly with respect to inquiry into complex human organizations. In this section I will attempt to illustrate selected features of an emergent design in action.

Our design emerged in two distinct ways. The first coincides with the problem-determined boundaries implication and perhaps is best characterized as "new directions." Here, change occurred as the direct result of new insights that had developed from studying the problem at hand. In these instances the boundaries of the study were altered to allow us to pursue relevant lines of inquiry that were not part of our initial conceptualization.

One example of a new direction change in design is the instance in which, after studying our first site, we recognized the need to include an additional organization. Originally, we had decided to study the ESA; its member districts; school buildings within districts, which included teachers, administrators, and other staff; and parents. After our initial data analysis of the first site, it was apparent that to approach a comprehensive understanding of regionalized special education services, we must also include the state education agency (SEA).[4] Thus, the decision to change our design to include the SEA emerged as we became

TABLE 7.1
Clustering of Naturalistic Inquiry Implications

Aspect of Inquiry	Cluster
Research design	Emergent design
	Problem-determined boundaries
	Purposive sampling
Data collection	Qualitative methods
	Human instrument
	Tacit knowledge
Data analysis	Grounded theory
	Inductive data analysis
Reporting	Case study reporting mode
	Idiographic interpretation
	Tentative application
Trustworthiness	Special criteria for trustworthiness
	Negotiated results

NOTE: Because the implications are interactive and synergistic, this particular arrangement is somewhat arbitrary. It is intended only as a framework for providing the reader with a feel for doing naturalistic research. Also, I have not included the "natural setting" implication here, as it is so central to the naturalistic paradigm that it can be assumed to be a given.

"smarter" about the problem we were studying. The problem itself had alerted us to our initial shortcoming; our paradigmatic epistemology allowed and encouraged us to capitalize on emerging insights.

The second way our design emerged could be characterized as refinement or evolution. Unlike the direction changes that result from new insights, refinements occur as a planned process and represent expected changes. The best example would be the sampling plan we employed.

The naturalistic paradigm not only takes a disinterested posture with respect to representativeness, it also makes a strong case against generalization (in the usual sense). The sampling was to be purposeful, not statistical. Thus, our first task became to determine carefully just what the purpose of sampling was to be.

We found Michael Patton's (1980) six purposive sampling strategies useful not only for sampling respondents (as noted by Lincoln), but also for sampling sites (states and ESAs) and units within sites (districts, schools, communities). Moreover, it seemed apparent to us that the purpose of sampling would change as the research progressed. Thus, the six different sampling strategies might appropriately serve our purposes at different points in time. However, each strategy required that we know more about the topics under study than we actually did at the outset of the research. To accommodate this need, we elected to select sites serially. That is, we did not select later sites until earlier ones had been identified and at least preliminarily explored. When Site 1's characteristics were well-known, for example, Site 2 could be selected using one or more of the six purposive sampling strategies, and so on.[5] Under these conditions our sample emerged as we learned more about the key factors upon which to make sampling decisions.

Although this sampling plan served our purposes well once the study was under way, our initial task was to identify at least some of the important site selection factors to enable us to select the first site. The staff developed a preliminary list of factors by searching relevant literature and by involving a group of knowledgeable consultants. Although this preliminary list was adequate for selecting the first site, it became obsolete after our experiences at Site 1. Based on these experiences, factors were added, combined, eliminated, and reordered in importance. After spending time in one natural setting, we were able to identify the significant aspects that influenced its status with respect to implementation of P.L. 94-142. Selecting the second and third sites (and eventually the fourth and fifth sites) thus became a matter of using Patton's six strategies, individually or in combination, to characterize potential sites with respect to the reconstituted site selection factors.

Had we relied exclusively on available literature or expert advice to predetermine selection of all five sites before studying one or more of them, our findings would have been constrained by a priori decisions that were less informed than they could have been. Moreover, one should not interpret this assertion as somehow discrediting the literature or the wisdom of our consultants. Rather, it should serve as an illustration of the overly nomothetic nature of most literature sources and the multiple value positions of our consultants.

DATA COLLECTION: QUALITATIVE METHODS, HUMAN INSTRUMENT, AND UTILIZATION OF TACIT KNOWLEDGE

Guba and Lincoln have made the point that qualitative methods are preferable to quantitative methods when the phenomena to be studied are complex human and organizational interactions and therefore not easily translatable into numbers. Once one accepts this position—and understands that qualitative methods are techniques such as interview, observation, use of nonverbal cues and unobtrusive measures, and documentary and records analysis—the choice to the human instrument is obvious.[6] And when people use such methods, they use tacit as well as propositional knowledge to ascribe meaning to the verbal and non-verbal behavior that is uncovered. As such, data are analyzed as they are collected, and these preliminary analyses guide further data collection. Such a process requires an adaptable data-collection instrument that can ascribe meaning to data as they emerge. As Hofstadter (1979) has pointed out, adaptability and perfectability stand in close trade-off with one another. The more perfect an instrument is (as the reductionist might purport a paper and pencil one to be), the less adaptable it is. The human, far from perfect, is virtually infinitely adaptable.

FIRST SITE VISIT INTERVIEWS

Prior to the first site visit (SV-1) to a given site, project staff furnished the ESA director with a list of respondents whom they wished to interview. Key personnel such as the agency director, director of special education, psychologist, budget officer, board chairperson, and the like were scheduled by name when that was possible. This was done on the basis of preliminary documents (rosters, organizational charts, and so on) that had been requested after entrée to the site had been arranged. In other cases role types were specified and it was left to the director to choose the actual persons.

The same procedures were followed for sampling LEA respondents, except that LEA central office and/or building administrators typically chose the actual respondents in line with project staff's specifications of role types. In the case of LEA respondent sampling, however, project staff specified the districts and, in some cases, the communities and schools to be included. These specifications were accomplished using Patton's (1980) purposive sampling strategies in conjunction with a priori site selection factors (for the first site) and the refinement of those factors over time as subsequent sites were studied.

Room was left in the interview schedule for other respondents (or respondent types) who would be identified by the research team during the site visit. Once at the site, the team identified other persons who ought to be interviewed because of their special characteristics in relation to the most pervasive attributes and issues of the site, as the attributes and issues emerged from the site. For the first site visit, the intent in sampling respondents and districts within the sites was the same as the intent at the site level; that is, to maximize the information and perspectives obtained so as to develop as broad and deep an understanding of the ESA as possible.

Although it is an oversimplification, there are basically two types of interviews: those in which the interviewer *knows* what information he or she lacks and can therefore pose specific questions; and those in which the interviewer *does not know* what he or she lacks and therefore cannot be specific in the questioning process. In the latter case it is important to uncover informants who not only have the answers but also know what questions to ask. The interviewer must take the posture of learner; he or she says, in effect, "Tell me what questions I ought to ask, and then answer them for me." It was the latter situation in which we found ourselves during the first of our three visits to each site. During later site visits to the same site, the former situation was more closely approximated and questions became much more specific.

Accordingly, the protocol for the SV-1 interviews was open-ended. During the first visit it was more important to identify useful informants than to know specifically what to ask them. The first site visit interview proceeded through a number of phases.

Introduction and Warm-Up

During this phase the interviewer would remind the respondent of the purpose of the study, and, in order to get the respondent accustomed to speaking freely and warmed up, some personal "grand tour" questions were asked. Examples are, "How did you come to be a _____?" Or, "What's a typical day like for you around here?"

Delineation of Roles and Responsibilities

Because it was important to understand the informant's particular perspective, the next series of questions dealt with a description of the informant's role in the organization (ESA, LEA, or SEA) and his or her responsibilities. Typical questions were these: "Just what do you do here?" "For what are you responsible?"

Delineation of Relationships

At this point it was usually possible to explore the respondent's relationships with other persons in and out of the organization. A description of these relationships indicates how the various organizations operate, what channels of communication exist, how accountability works, and so on. Example questions were as follows: "For whom are you responsible?" "What expectations are held for you, and by whom?" "How do you communicate with these other people?" "How are disputes or conflicts settled?" "What is the nature of your interactions with parents?"

Delineation of Issues

By this time in the interview the informant was usually involved and ready to deal with more substantive issues. The point of this phase was to have the respondents identify as many issues (and how they personally felt about them) as possible. Some sample questions: "What do you think are the big problems that keep the [agency] from doing as well as it might?" "What are some of the factors that make it easy for you to do your job?" "Hard for you to do your job?"

Dealing With Issues

When the respondent had volunteered as many issues as he or she could think of, the interviewer moved on to explore each issue in detail. If, for example, the respondent had mentioned a lack of adequate diagnostic services, the interviewer might say, "Among the things you mentioned as troublesome is the lack of diagnostic services. How do you get around that problem? What do you do about it? What ought to be done about it?"

Certain issues had been identified previously by the research team from prior studies or, in the case of later side visits, from earlier ones. When all the interviewee-identified issues had been explored, the interviewer introduced those a priori issues (assuming they were not already included among those volunteered by the respondent) and sought an opinion. After a few interviews had been conducted issues identified by earlier respondents but not raised by later ones also were introduced for comment and reaction. In this way, the interviews became more focused over time and the insights of one respondent could be compared to those of others. Thus, multiple constructions of issues became apparent, and confidence in the data accrued as the site visit progressed.

At the close of each SV-1 interview we routinely asked two additional questions. First, respondents were asked to identify other persons (or types of persons) who shared views similar to and different from their own. Persons who held different views could be expected to provide their unique constructions of reality on various issues; persons with similar views could be used to cross-check information. We learned, however, that even persons who held similar views always added unique insights to the issues. The second type of questioning served as a check on the interviewer's recording of information. Here, the basic question was, "Did I get this down correctly?" The interviewer read portions of his or her field notes back to the respondent to establish accuracy. This procedure served as the first of a number of measures to advance the research's trustworthiness. Additional trustworthiness measures are covered in later sections.

SECOND SITE VISIT INTERVIEWS

How the data for SV-1 were processed will be described in the next section. For now, let us assume that the SV-1 analysis has been completed. From that step, a number of products emerged that were basic to SV-2: a list of issues to be more fully explored, missing and incomplete information categories, identified conflicts or inconsistencies in the data that needed to be resolved,[7] and a list of potential interviewees who held similar or different views on particular issues that had been uncovered during SV-1.

In part, these products served to define our task for the second site visit. That is, we were to explore issues more fully, fill in missing information, resolve inconsistencies, cross-check information, and gather additional constructions of issues. Furthermore, the research team maintained a complete openness to new information. It could not be assumed that all relevant matters had been detected during SV-1, so that all that would be required during SV-2 was patching up around the edges. The research team had no delusions about the comparative simplicity of SV-2 over SV-1; they were prepared to uncover at least as much new information on the second visit as on the first.

Nevertheless, planning for SV-2 began with the residual questions stemming from SV-1. When those questions had been identified, it became possible to name the individuals (or classes of individuals) who would be in a position to answer them. Thus, whereas the intent of respondent sampling in SV-1 had been to generate as broad a sample as possible to allow for maximum variation, respondent sampling in SV-2 was intended to generate a sample that could be expected to be maximally knowledgeable about the issues that had emerged from the SV-1 data.[8]

Using the procedures described above enabled us to allow the data to emerge from the sites under study. As the interviewing progressed during SV-1 and into SV-2, questioning began to focus on those issues most characteristic or pervasive of the particular site.[9]

DATA ANALYSIS:
GROUNDED THEORY, INDUCTIVE DATA ANALYSIS

The obvious example for demonstrating how these two implications translate into practice is to explicate the data analysis process. Before proceeding with that illustration, however, two separate points need to be made. First, some comment on grounded theory would be useful.

Lincoln pointed out that the primary difference between a priori and grounded theory is the way in which data are used. In the former data are used to prove or disprove a theory. In the latter theory is derived from (grounded in) the data. However, one should not interpret the naturalists' preference for grounded theory as a total rejection of all a priori theory. In our study we did not reject theory that had been generated through previous related research. We did, however, treat it in ways that prevented it from constraining our own inquiry. Perhaps the best example of our treatment of a priori theory is the way it was used within our sampling plan. We began with site selection factors drawn from literature and experts, and we allowed for their refinement on the basis of data emanating from our sites. An example of grounding can be drawn from our data-collection procedures. We allowed the issues to emerge from our respondents by asking open-ended questions. However, we asked questions about other issues—a priori theory from other research—when respondents failed to mention them as part of their listing.

My second point is perhaps at the heart of understanding qualitative research methods. Although this section addresses data analysis, the process of data analysis occurs more than once in qualitative research. It is an ongoing process that happens at several levels and for different purposes. As we have seen, data analysis occurs in the field as data are collected. At that level the purpose is to guide subsequent data collection—during a single interview, from interview to interview on a given day, from day to day in a single site unit, and in the search for relevant documents. At its second level (the one described in this section) data analysis serves two purposes. First, like the purpose at the first level of analysis, data are used to guide subsequent data collection. At this level, however, data analysis guides data collection from site visit to site visit. Second, data analysis serves, in part, to organize the data, to bring them together under a taxonomy. A third and critically important level of data analysis occurs during the process of writing the case study report. It is addressed later in the section, "Reporting."[10]

INDUCTIVE DATA ANALYSIS

Interview and observational[11] data collected from site visits were analyzed in three steps: unitizing, individual categorizing, and team categorizing. Results of this analysis were used in two ways: as items to be considered when writing the case study (carried out after SV-2) and as sources for further questions during the second visit, as discussed in the previous section.

Unitizing

The purpose of the unitizing step is to identify and record essential information units. The definition of unit is relatively straightforward. A unit is a single piece of information able to stand by itself (i.e., interpretable in the absence of any additional information). Such a unit may be a simple sentence—"Respondent indicates she spends about 10 hours a week traveling from school to school"—or as much as a paragraph. In either case the material in the unit is completely self-explanatory. If a portion of the unit were to be removed, however, the remainder would be seriously compromised or rendered uninterpretable.

The process of unitizing was carried out by each site visit team member independently. The data source was carefully read one sentence at a time. The researcher would then ask whether the information contained in that sentence was in any sense relevant to the broad mission of the research. If it was, it was entered on a 3×5 card in sufficiently full language so that another person would be able to understand it.[12] Each card was coded with a designation for the site; the site visit; the type of respondent; the agency employing the respondent, except for parents, for whom the appropriate school and community were designated; and the interview number from which the item was drawn, so that the item's content could be traced back to raw field or interview notes.

Individual Categorizing

The essential purpose of the categorizing process is to bring those cards relating to the same content together into a loose taxonomy. The process is essentially an analytic-inductive one, but it is rule guided, although the rules emerge as part of the categorization process. Of course, it is possible to devise multiple category systems that will account equally well for the unitized cards. The purpose of this step is not to discover the set of categories that definitively encompasses the units but a set that handles the unit cards reasonably well. What is meant by reasonably well is, essentially, that an auditor would subsequently agree to the reasonableness of the category system.[13]

The process that was used is identical to the "method of constant comparisons" described by Glaser and Strauss (1968), although the purpose is somewhat different. They focus on development or specification of grounded theory. Although theory development was not a purpose of our study, the first steps of our research could not be distinguished operationally from those proposed by Glaser and Strauss.[14]

Essentially, the categorization process involves sorting the unit cards into groupings of like content and devising a rule to describe the nature of the content to be included in each one. That is, the tacit knowledge we used to judge the cards as look-alikes was translated into the propositional language of a rule for classification. As the categorization process continued, a number of cards could be placed in more than one category. This is because they contained content that was related logically to the content of established categories. These cards were duplicated in sufficient number, noted as cross-reference cards, and placed in all appropriate categories.

Team Categorizing

The categorizing steps outlined in the preceding paragraphs were carried out by each team member individually. A team meeting was then called for the purpose of combining the individual categories into a mutually agreed upon master set. At these meetings the lead researcher for the site would select a category, indicate its title, and stipulate the rule by which the included items had been classified. The other researchers would look over their own categories, and if they had developed one similar to the one announced (as was frequently the case), the cards would be combined and the rule adjusted to suit the separate formulations. The process was continued until all categories had been accounted for. This master set was then accepted as the base for subsequent steps. Additional information needed to flesh out a category (or to explore a missing category suggested by the logic of the set) was noted and built into the interview guides for the second site visit.

Analyzing Site Visit 2 Data

The SV-2 data were unitized and categorized using the same procedures that had been followed in SV-1. Now, however, the categories that had emerged from the SV-1 data and that had been mutually agreed upon by the research team were available to guide the individual categorization process. Of course, the SV-2 data sometimes required the establishment of new categories or adjustments in the old ones. Individual team members made note of these indicated changes; they were then discussed during the team categorization step, and adjustments were made by mutual agreement.[15]

REPORTING: CASE STUDY REPORTING MODE, IDIOGRAPHIC INTERPRETATION, AND TENTATIVE APPLICATION OF FINDINGS

DRAFTING THE CASE STUDIES

In our inquiry data collected during the first and second site visits provided the basic information from which the case studies were drafted. The case studies were drafted between SV-2 and the third site visit; it was the major purpose of SV-3 to obtain respondents' reactions to the draft cases prior to a final revision.

Indexing the Materials

The first step in writing any case study is to organize the materials upon which it will be based. This includes the unitized and categorized data cards and the variety of relevant documents that have been collected. To accomplish this required development of detailed indexes of cards and documents. The former was a relatively easy task, as the card categories and subcategories were all named and numbered.

The indexing task for documents was much more complex. Detailed tables of contents were developed for all relevant documents. They served as a guide to the information contained within them. Each document was assigned a number; relevant subparts within documents were noted by page number. This coding system was used to cross-reference documentary data with card categories and to relate both of these data sources to the outline of the case study.

Generating a Case Outline
and Cross-Referencing Material to It

The next step in writing each case study involved generating a highly detailed overall outline. Following provisional team agreement on the outline, the data cards and documents were cross-indexed to the proposed sections. This was accomplished by reviewing each outline item against each item of the indexes, and noting on the former the location of pertinent materials. The designation C always referred to one of the card categories; thus, C39.3 indicated category 39.3 among the cards. The designation D always referred to documents; thus, D46:14 indicated document 46, page 14.

The preliminary outline was itself organized into three major parts: description, problems/issues, and lessons to be learned. The intent was, first, to give readers a feel for what the site was like; second, to introduce them to the problems and issues as seen through the eyes of local participants; and, third, to tease out lessons that might be learned from the local experience.[16]

The second and most important information source to guide developing the substance of the report was the card category system and its subsequent refinement as the case was being written. The process of refinement amounted to a third level of data analysis.

Third Level of Data Analysis

Up to this point in preparing the case study, data had been analyzed twice: first, in the field as they were collected and, second, during the unitizing/categorizing process. In the latter case data were arranged (physically brought together) to set the stage for the third and most important step in the data analysis process: the analysis, interpretation, and synthesis of data into assertions to be presented in the case report. Although the nuances of this process are beyond the scope of this chapter,[17] it is helpful to think of the process as a translation. That is, the inquirer's task is to write what has been seen and heard so that it will make the same sense to the reader as it does to the inquirer.[18] It is at this point in the data analysis process that the tacit knowledge and values of the investigator come to bear the most on the substance of the case study. Of course the writer's understanding is to be grounded in the data, and presenting his or her understanding necessarily involves presenting those data as supporting details in the overall explanation. But it is here that qualitative research draws its heaviest criticism, because ordinarily there is no check on the researcher's interpretation or on the data sources. The consumer of the research ordinarily is asked to depend solely on the researcher's sensitivities and judgments.

Although methods of presentation may vary, most include the use of respondents' quotations to substantiate and illustrate the assertions made as well as to help the reader better understand the people and the context. There are no formal conventions for establishing truth in reporting qualitative research. The writer's task is to convince the reader of the plausibility of the presentation by including sufficient details to support the assertions he or she makes. It is at this point, however, that our study, employing the methods espoused by Guba and Lincoln, begins to differ from conventional qualitative research. An explanation of how their techniques for establishing trustworthiness in naturalistic research were operationalized and extended in our study is the primary topic of the next section. First, however, some essential mechanisms for addressing trustworthiness are described, and a concluding comment on the applicability of the case study is given.

The Audit Trail

A complete audit trail was inserted into our cases so that an auditor could subsequently trace any statements back to the original data on which they were based. The function of the auditor cannot be discharged in the absence of an audit trail, a concept not dissimilar to the audit trail in fiscal accounting. Accordingly, draft versions of the cases were documented in the right-hand margins of the pages with consecutive numbers that would lead an auditor to appropriate supporting documentation notes. For example, the number that appears in the right margin of this paragraph would lead an auditor to note number 206 in [206] an appendix. There the auditor would find the corresponding base references necessary to support the assertions made in the text of the case; for example, C22.5; C41.2; D74:12. Thus, the auditor would be directed to supporting material in card categories 22.5 and 41.2 and in document 74 at page 12.

Developing Questions for Site Visit 3

The major purpose of SV-3 was to engage local participants in testing the case study draft for accuracy and credibility. However, the task of writing the case quickly exposed informational loopholes—places where additional new or supporting data were lacking. These gaps seemed to take two forms. First, there were situations in which the case study writer was able to piece together available information into a story line that seemed reasonable, but about which the case study writer was unsure. In such instances the story was written in what seemed to the writer the most probable line. Once on site, specific informants were asked about details and interpretations. Second, there were situations in which it was obvious to the writer that basic information was missing. Typically, a bracketed note was inserted in the draft acknowledging the failing and appealing to local readers for clarification. As the writing of the case progressed, the case study writer kept a systematic record of these questions and shortcomings and suggested persons at the site who might be able to answer them. A secondary purpose of SV-3 was thus to seek out these informants and put the questions to them.

IDIOGRAPHIC INTERPRETATION
AND TENTATIVE APPLICATION OF FINDINGS

Before proceeding to the description of the trustworthiness measures we employed, some comment on the other two implications included in this section is warranted. As noted above, data for each case were interpreted idiographically (in terms of the particulars of the case) rather than in terms of broad generalizations. This is called for in naturalistic research, because of the axiomatic stance taken with respect to constructed realities, the particular investigator-respondent interaction, the local mutually shaping contextual factors, and the various local (as well as investigator) values. Because interpretations depend so heavily for their validity on local particulars, naturalists are tentative about making broad applications of their findings. The extent to which findings may be applicable elsewhere depends on the empirical similarity of both sending and receiving contexts.

Because we cannot possibly know all contexts to which our interpretations might be applied, the best we can do is to be diligent in describing the sending context. Only persons at the receiving context (who know the particulars of their context) can judge whether findings from the sending context are applicable in their case. Given this task, the case study reporting mode is the logical choice, because it is adapted to a description of the particulars of the case—multiple realities, investigator-respondent interactions, mutually shaping influences, and so on. This is less true for the scientific or technical report. The major purpose of the case study report is to provide "thick description" so that others may judge the degree of transferability of findings between sending and receiving contexts.

TRUSTWORTHINESS

The obvious implication to be included in this cluster is "special criteria for trustworthiness." The fourteenth implication, "negotiated results," is included here as well, because the procedures used to negotiate findings represent a primary means of judging one aspect of the overall trustworthiness of naturalistic research.

Guba (1981) has proposed four counterpart criteria for judging the trustworthiness of naturalist inquiries as well as specific procedures that can be used to establish that each counterpart criterion has been satisfied at a reasonable level. The counterpart criteria include: *credibility* (in place of internal validity), which addresses the truth value of the inquiry; *transferability* (in place of external validity), which addresses the basic question of applicability; *dependability* (in place of reliability), which responds to the question of consistency; and *confirmability* (in place of objectivity), which addresses the basic question of the neutrality of the inquiry.

Whereas Lincoln's chapter briefly addressed the justification for these substitutions, my task is to describe the operational techniques whereby the credibility, transferability, dependability, and confirmability of an inquiry can be addressed. Guba (1981) has listed a variety of techniques for each criterion. He notes, however, that not all techniques are equally weighty, and that it is unlikely, because of time and resource constraints, that all would ever be applied in the same study. Moreover, because of space limitations, I will not attempt to explicate each technique that was used in our study. Instead, I will describe and provide examples of some of the more powerful techniques that were used.[19] Briefly, the techniques to be addressed include the following:

(1) With respect to *credibility:*
  • Use of *persistent observation*—intense focusing on those aspects of the situation that are most characteristic or pervasive.
  • *Triangulation*—pitting a variety of data sources, investigators, perspectives (theories), and methods against one another in order to cross-check data and interpretations.
  • *Member checks*—whereby data and interpretations are continuously tested with members of the various groups and audiences from which data are solicited.
(2) With respect to *transferability:*
  • *Theoretical/purposive sampling*—intended to maximize the scope and range of information gathered and hence to illuminate the most necessary factors to take into account when comparing two contexts for similarity.
  • *Thick description*—full and dense descriptions that will provide a substantial basis for similarity judgments.
(3) With respect to *dependability:*
  • *Dependability audit*—in which an audit trail maintained by the investigator is examined by an external auditor to determine whether the research processes used fall within the domain of acceptable professional practice.
(4) With respect to *confirmability:*
  • *Confirmability audit*—the "other shoe" of the audit carried out for the sake of dependability but directed toward establishing the relation between the inquirer's claims and interpretations and the actual raw data.

CREDIBILITY[20]

The three most weighty techniques for establishing the credibility (or truth value) of an inquiry are persistent observation, triangulation, and member checks. Persistent observation was a basic characteristic of our data-collection and data-analysis procedures. With respect to data collection, issues were allowed to emerge from the sites using open-ended questions during the first site visits. In the case of data analysis, the inductive data-analysis procedures were designed both to allow issues to surface from the data and to define the issues to be pursued during the second site visit. Thus, by design, the most pervasive aspects of each site were allowed to emerge and were then focused upon during subsequent site visits.

Triangulation was one of our major focusing techniques. A variety of points of view about issues was explored by using respondents drawn from different stakeholders groups. Documents were used as a second point of reference. In some cases observations (e.g., of classrooms and board meetings) were utilized to augment what had been learned in other ways. Nonverbal cues were exploited as a base for reinforcing or questioning information gathered verbally. Different investigators challenged one another's perspectives during site interchanges and later data analyses.[21]

Member checks were carried out assiduously. They occurred at the end of each interview with a respondent, from interview to interview on a given day, from respondents of one day with those of another, during debriefing sessions that terminated each site visit, and from the first site visit to the second. Using these five levels of member checks during the study allowed us to continuously build credibility in our data. Information was checked and rechecked with the same and different respondents as well as being triangulated with other data sources and methods as described above.

The use of triangulation and member check procedures resulted in the production of draft case studies in which we were reasonably confident with respect to credibility. Of course, there were gaps in our information and understanding, as noted earlier, but these were noted specifically and slated to be called to the attention of our reviewers for clarification during the third site visit. In addition, the third visit was used primarily as a vehicle to conduct a sixth member check.

The sixth member check, or what one might call the "grand member check," was conducted under two formats. First, at each site a review committee of participants was assembled to review the draft case study and to comment on its credibility. A second set of reviewers was charged with the same task, but was composed of superintendents, ESA administrators, and LEA and ESA board members. They were scheduled to be interviewed individually.

Selecting the Review Committee

The major participants in the member check process were constituted into a local review committee. They received the case study draft in advance of SV-3 and offered their comments (in the main) through the feedback mechanism of an all-day review meeting.

Two members were selected to be representative of each of certain basic "roles" or "stakeholding audiences" (e.g., elementary classroom teachers, building administrators, parents, ESA direct service personnel). These stakeholder groups had all been represented among those respondents interviewed during the first and second site visits.

One representative from each of the stakeholding audiences was selected by the research team from among those persons interviewed during SV-1 and/or SV-2. A second person from each stakeholding audience was selected by ESA or LEA personnel from among persons who had not been interviewed during SV-1 or 2. The research team used purposive sampling procedures and selection factors as before to select its representatives as well as to specify for on-site personnel the "types" of LEAs and individuals from which they were to make their choices.

Previsit Reviewing Task

Ten days to two weeks before the grand member check was scheduled to occur a packet of materials was sent to the review committee members as well as to respondents who were to be seen individually. The packet contained a copy of the case study draft for each reviewer, letters of instructions for reviewers, consent statements tailored to the special task at hand, and reviewers' comment sheets. Although reviewers were free to comment on any aspect of the draft case study, they were asked specifically to comment on certain matters of interest to the research team. These included overall credibility, errors of fact, errors of interpretation, missing information, missing interpretations, places in which anonymity had been compromised, and the extent to which certain qualifiers, such as "many," "most," "some," and the like, were valid in the situations in which they were used (e.g., At line 5 of page 24, is the term "most" in the statement, "*Most* teachers feel that mainstreamed youngsters are stigmatized," valid?).

The Grand Member Check

A full-day review session was held with the review committee on the first day of SV-3. At this time the matters to which we had alerted members were addressed systematically. During the second day of SV-3 the site visitors conducted individual interviews using the same review procedures with the ESA administrators, LEA superintendents, and board members. It would have been possible, of course, to include these persons as members of the review committee, but it was decided to see them individually for two reasons. First, they could not be expected to devote a full day's time to the member check activity. Second, it was possible that they would dominate the proceedings, excluding the possibility of responses from persons considerably lower in the status hierarchy.

Final Revision of the Case Study

Upon return from the field, all of the materials that had been gathered were turned over to the case writer, who had always been one of the SV-3 field team. Each case was revised on the basis of the member check and other SV-3 data. A separate audit trail was established for the revisions, with the audit notes referring to specific sets of SV-3 data upon which the revision had been based. New information was also systematically provided. That information was used to develop an epilogue for each case to address new developments that had transpired between the second and third site visits.

DEPENDABILITY AND CONFIRMABILITY

An audit was carried out and is the backbone of the research team's claim to having produced a dependable study.[22] The audit took place over a three-day period in May of 1983 at Lawrence, Kansas. It tended to follow the algorithm for such audits previously developed by Halpern (1983). The major thrust of the approach is to confirm both dependability and confirmability. The algorithm requires the auditor to check, with respect to the former, appropriateness of all methodological decisions, degree of evident inquirer bias, and utility of overall design and implementation steps. With respect to confirmability, the algorithm requires the auditor to check for groundedness of findings, logic of inferences, utility of category structure, degree of evident inquirer bias, and nature of accommodation strategies.

The auditor was oriented to the project through phone conversations, several advanced mailings of materials (including three of the five draft case studies), and at an opening three-hour session on the first day of the audit. This latter orientation included a review of the project work scope, the Halpern algorithm, and the variety of audit-trail materials that had been developed for the project. These materials included the following: raw field and interview notes; site documents; decks of 3×5 cards; the category systems; all theoretical notes (working hypotheses, hunches, concepts); findings and conclusions; methodological notes detailing the nature of and rationales for emergent methodological decisions; audit trail notes (as found in the draft case margins and appendices); personal notes in journals; and the RFP and proposal. The auditor worked individually with the materials for the remaining two-and-one-half days, during which time the research team was available (on call) to answer any questions. The formal audit period ended with a one-hour debriefing with the research team by the auditor.

Although space does not permit a complete explication of the auditor's activities with respect to dependability and confirmability checks, an example of each might be instructive. In the case of dependability, the auditor reviewed our records of the steps, data sources, and results of our purposive sampling plan. The original site selection factors, the information used to modify them over time, and our rationales for selecting the sites were made available to her. Here, her purpose was not to establish that we used the best sampling plan, but that the plan we did use was methodologically sound, given our purposes and the information that was available to us.

With respect to confirmability, the auditor traced selected assertions made in the case studies back to the 3×5 unitized cards and original field and interview notes and documents. This was to determine if, in fact, those assertions were grounded in these data. The audit trail, which had been assembled for just this purpose, served as her guide.

In addition to the audit's prime use in determining the degree to which the inquiry can be said to be dependable and confirmable, we, as Halpern suggested (1983), found it useful to use the audit as a means to extend our claims for credibility. That is, we asked the auditor to assess evidence of the extent to which the techniques of persistent observation, triangulation, and member checking were actually carried out.

In the case of triangulation, this was done with a minimum of effort on the part of the auditor, as to establish confirmability she had to become familiar with the amount of triangulation for specific assertions made in the cases (these were made explicit and traceable by the audit trail materials). The extent of persistent observation was discernible by the degree to which SV-2 and SV-3 protocols (and resulting interview notes) were a logical follow-up to the issues that emerged from SV-1. Evidence for the occurrence of member checking existed in raw field/interview notes and the substantial set of materials that resulted from the grand member check, including the revised case studies.[23] Subsequently, the auditor prepared an audit report addressing the manner in which she conducted the dependability, confirmability, and credibility checks; the materials we had provided and their value in conducting the audit; and a statement of her evaluation of the study's trustworthiness. The report appears as a section in the final report of the study and is available there for public inspection.

NOTES ON METHODOLOGICAL ISSUES

Guba and Lincoln outlined in some detail the nature of the naturalistic paradigm as well as its implications for conducting research. I have attempted to provide the reader with a feel for doing naturalistic research. One should not assume from these presentations, however, that the application of the paradigm is completely understood or that the study that I have described is the end-all example of how to best do rigorous naturalistic research. There are still a number of issues to be resolved. The purpose of this section is to indicate some of the issues that arose during the conduct of our study, and, where possible, to make some suggestions about how the issues might be better handled by other researchers applying this same research paradigm under somewhat similar circumstances. The first portion of the section is devoted to the more practical issues and the second to the more theoretical.

SOME PRACTICAL ISSUES

Contract/Paradigm Disjunctions

The present study was carried out under the terms of a contract with the National Institute of Education, which has well-established and carefully monitored contract procedures. Such a process is entirely appropriate for normal contracts (say, for military hardware or office equipment). It is reasonably appropriate for research carried out within the conventional paradigm, with its a priori specification of theory and hypotheses, its carefully developed design, and its entirely predictable data collection and analysis techniques. But its utility for a study carried out naturalistically is highly questionable. As the design of such a study is by definition emergent, a number of difficulties arise.

First, it is impossible to develop a scope of work statement that conforms to typical RFP requirements. Disjunctions between contract procedures and naturalistic imperatives often can stultify the very crea- tivity with which the research act is presumed to be endowed. A second and major consequence has to do with fiscal allocations. If the work program changes, must not the fiscal allocations also change? And program changes without fiscal changes are meaningless.

If any funding agency is serious about encouraging naturalistic stud- ies, the present form of the RFP must be substantially altered. The new paradigm of thought and belief requires a new paradigm of inquiry, *and the new paradigm of inquiry requires a new paradigm of support.*

Design Problems

To say that a design is emergent covers a multitude of thoughts and actions. Designs do not emerge on their own. They must be *pulled out* of the context, the data, and the problem by the researcher who expends a considerable amount of thought and energy to get that task completed. But problems arise to militate against its completion.

Deciding on the sample of data sources to be tapped—sites, respond- ents, documents, and so on—must at times be based on the practical grounds of what data are available. Moreover, the sample that is finally selected may to varying degrees rest on judgments of parties at the research site (e.g., ESA directors, superintendents) who are not com- pletely disinterested. Unknown biases may be built into the selection process. Of course, if normal methods of checks and balances are used—triangulation, seeking out respondents who have different views from those already expressed, recycling sites and informants, and so on—the probabilities of exposing such biases (except in the unlikely event of a massive conspiracy) are high. Nevertheless, it does not pay to be naive about such matters. As long as the possibility of bias exists and there are some advantages to someone in keeping information from the researcher (or providing only biased information), it is essential to continue probing.

Arriving at an appropriate focus for the study does not occur auto- matically. It is not only the design that is emergent in a naturalistic study, but the problem as well. Indeed, critics of naturalistic inquiry frequently suggest that such research is mindless, because it does not commence with a well-defined problem in the same way that conven- tional inquiry (purportedly) does. It is one thing to say in a study such as this, "Previous research shows that rural sites suffer from certain prob- lems; indeed, one can provide a list. Now let's see whether our actual site observations bear out these earlier findings." It is quite another to say, "Let's observe the site for a time to determine what its unique dynamics are. Then we can focus on those as the basis for the rest of the study." It is the latter position that was taken here. The naturalistic inquirer must resist the press for premature closure—a press set up not only by the contractual factors already reviewed but by the researcher's own intolerance of ambiguity and need for closure. A recognition of this eventuality and patience seem to be the prime offsetting factors.

Problems in the Field

In conventional research most of the problems the inquirer is likely to encounter will confront him or her while he or she is seated in an office. The problems are mostly worked out on paper, with a computer program, or, now and then, with a telephone call. We were not so blessed. Our way of doing research required face-to-face contact with respondents on their turf. And once one is out there, numerous problems emerge.

Gaining entrée is almost entirely a political matter. There is typically no way to force an agency or an individual to be cooperative. There can be a major hiatus between getting in the door and getting what you need. Dealing effectively with gatekeepers who can deny or extend entrée may be the single most important skill that the naturalistic inquirer needs to have. Knowing that gatekeepers come in two types—formal and informal—and that both need to be dealt with is equally important.

Handling problems of trust was a major concern for us. We could hardly expect a respondent to tell us everything that ought to be known after only a brief contact. Everyone has some information that they would prefer not to share. There need not be a massive conspiracy afoot to account for reluctance to share information. On the other hand, it takes more than presenting a friendly mien on the part of the researcher to inspire confidence in the informant. Hence, the results of the member checks are even more important than they might otherwise be. The grand member check is probably the single most useful mechanism for checking out information that is received. For although the main purpose of the review is to give local participants an opportunity to tell the researcher whether "you got it right," it also is the researcher's opportunity to test whether "you gave it to me right."

Problems in Writing the Case Study

The culmination of much naturalistic inquiry—and surely of our study—is developing case studies that are the heart of the research report. Again, a number of problems emerge.

Evolving an appropriate style is difficult, because the case study has multiple objectives. It must provide the thick description needed to understand the site and to facilitate judgments of transferability to other sites. It must portray the world of the site through the eyes of the local participants, and it must provide the reader a vicarious experience of what it is like to be there. It is likely that no case description can accomplish all of these objectives well. Indeed, it is possible that they are to some extent in conflict. Thick description, moreover, may produce a mundane level of data that hardly qualifies as "seeing the world from local perspectives," nor is it likely to provide the naive reader with any feeling of excitement or identification.

The literature is not rife with examples of good case studies. It contains even fewer instances of how to best write case studies. There are no conventions for making decisions about what to include or exclude. A case ought to provide thick description, but just what is that? How thick is thick? What are some inclusion-exclusion principles that could be applied by a case study writer? There are presently no systematic answers to these questions. We relied on the convention of including as much detail as was required to explain each issue clearly. This resulted in some cases that totaled over 200 manuscript pages.

It is the nature of naturalistic research and the case study reporting method that both are more susceptible to breaches of confidentiality and anonymity than is conventional inquiry. Most naturalists are therefore very sensitive to the ethics involved. They may go to extraordinary lengths to protect respondents and sites from discovery. Of course, questions can be raised in cases of evaluation whether such protections ought to be extended, as one could argue that agents should be held accountable for their actions. But in cases of research it seems to be well-established that respondents have a right to privacy and, if they give up that right in a spirit of cooperation with the researcher, they deserve as much protection as the researcher can provide.

But such protection may be difficult to extend and impossible to guarantee. Even if all the names and places and dates are changed, it is likely that other locals will be able to pinpoint the agencies and parties involved. And that breach of confidence may have the most serious consequences of all. It is these other locals who may be in positions of authority or influence with respect to the research participants, and thus they may have the most powerful sanctions to apply. Beyond the local level, although it may not be possible to identify the agencies and participants involved, it may be possible to force disclosure should someone take umbrage. Research files have no protections against subpoena; there is no special privilege involved. Even if the researcher has guaranteed anonymity, the courts may still insist that sources be disclosed.

The respondent must be viewed as the owner of all of the data that pertain to him or her. The respondent must have the privilege of withdrawing from the study at any time, without prejudice, and taking his or her data with him or her. Finally, the researcher has the responsibility of coding and otherwise protecting the field data so that the identity of respondents cannot be inadvertently discovered. No person who is not a need-to-know member of the research team should have access to the data. Anything less constitutes unethical conduct.

Finally, there is the question of when it is appropriate to close out a case. Our draft case reports were written after SV-2, but additional information was collected during SV-3. Of course, if the information had been sought out to close a gap or clear up a misunderstanding in the case as written, it was included. But what if the new information was about occurrences that had taken place since SV-2? Should the case be updated to include that new information? To take adequate account of these developments would have meant substantial revision in the case beyond what was needed to adjust it for accuracy. We elected to append a simple epilogue to each case that would update the reader on new developments.

SOME THEORETICAL ISSUES

The Feasibility and Utility of Trustworthiness Measures

Valuable experience was gained through efforts to apply the various trustworthiness techniques proposed by Guba (1981). It seems appropriate to conclude that most of his recommended techniques could be reasonably well applied, that useful information about trustworthiness resulted from these applications, and that the weight of evidence favors their continued use.

Specifically, with respect to techniques relating to the criterion of credibility, the most useful and pervasive technique was the member check. Although certain problems exist, particularly with the kinds of massive member checks carried out in SV-3, there can be little doubt that this technique is feasible. It makes sense to participants, and it results in a variety of information that is useful for shaping the case study into its final form.

The technique of persistent observation guided our data-collection and analysis procedures. It was the mechanism that helped assure that issues would emerge from each site and that those issues would be the central focus of investigation. Each site was visited for at least eighteen person-days. This provided ample time to identify the more salient characteristics at each site that could then be subjected to persistent observation.

Triangulation is a keystone technique and was used extensively in our study. The easiest means to gain triangulation is by comparing information from respondent to respondent and from respondents to documents. The use of multiple perspectives (theories) is impossible when the theory is itself emergent. Moreover, the use of multiple investigators, although used, is also discountable (in terms of triangulation), because investigators made no effort to maintain independence. Indeed, just the opposite was true—the investigators communicated continuously in the interest of the emergent design. The use of multiple methods was limited primarily to interviews and document analyses. If more time had been available and the researchers had been able to spend more time on site, other techniques, particularly formal observation, would have been used more often.

With respect to the criterion of transferability, both techniques of purposive sampling and thick description worked well and made few extraneous demands on the researchers. The problems already described under the practical heading of the preceding section summarize most of what needs to be improved. From a theoretical point of view, all went well.

With respect to the criterion of dependability, there can be little doubt that the dependability audit is far and away the most pervasive and meaningful technique devised. Although there are some practical difficulties, and although additional experience will no doubt smooth away many of the rough spots, in principle the technique is enormously powerful. Indeed, it is so powerful that its use seems warranted not only for naturalistic studies but for all kinds of studies.

Finally, with respect to the criterion of confirmability, what has been said about the dependability audit applies equally well to the confirmability audit. These two forms of audits are two sides of the same coin and probably could not be carried out meaningfully except in concert. As a confirmability concept, triangulation probably does not warrant an independent existence from triangulation as a credibility concept. An exception would be in the sense that whereas, in the latter case, it is a step taken to enhance the probability that a report will be found to be credible and, in the former case, it is a step taken to actually confirm data. The process is a means in the case of credibility but an end in the case of confirmability. Yet it is the same process.

In all, based on the experience of the present study, the following techniques were most useful and perhaps represent a sine qua non for studies of this type: for credibility—persistent observation, triangulation, and member checks; for transferability—purposive sampling and thick description; for dependability—the dependability audit; and for confirmability—the confirmability audit. In addition, the audit proved to be useful in helping to assess the credibility of the study. It provided evidence of the extent to which the techniques of persistent observation, triangulation, and member checking were actually carried out—that is, the trustworthiness of our claims for credibility.

Fittingness of the Naturalistic Paradigm

Did the research team select the right paradigm? We think we did, for several reasons. First, there are multiple realities—the multiple constructions of the participants—which, in a very real sense, are the creations of the participants. Moreover, those realities can be understood only as wholes—to dissect them into their supposed constituent parts is to destroy them. Is there anything in the data of our study that supports that construction? Surely there existed no tangible reality at any of the sites that could be called *the* ESA. To be sure, there were buildings and equipment and organizational charts and people, but the ESA is a more elusive concept that has very different meaning depending on whom you ask. That is the case not only from site to site, as one might expect, but from different kinds of participants at the same site and from different members of the same participant group at the same site. At Site 1, for example, not all of the itinerant teachers construed the meaning of itinerancy in the same way. At Site 2 not all local superintendents viewed the advantages of being members of the ESA in the same way, and so on.

These are not simply different perceptions, as though the ESAs were some particular thing that just looked different from different perspectives; *the ESAs were different creations in the minds of different people.*

And they could not be dissected, not even the constructions of a single person. Although an individual might surmise the existence of certain parts related in certain ways, it was only in respect to his or her own single constructions that those parts and relationships could be conceptualized. Moreover, in that construction the parts and relationships all shaped and influenced one another simultaneously. If any one of them were changed, everything else would change too. The whole is more than the sum of its parts; everything interrelates.

And did the interactions between investigators and respondents make any difference? There can be no doubt of it. Whether the reactions of the locals to the member check, for example, were receptive or rejecting, they did react. The cases themselves represent the ultimate evidence of the interaction. They would not have been possible without input from the locals, and they would not be credible without their stamp of approval. Some of the issues and problems were not apparent to the locals until they had been pointed out by the research team. Thereafter, local constructions were undoubtedly different. In that sense, *the research team helped to create new local constructions—portions of which were indeterminate until they evolved from the researcher-respondent interaction.* And surely many of the questions that the researcher team ultimately took to be important emerged because they were pointed out by the locals, who in that sense played a part in creating the research.

And is there any reason to believe that generalization would be a shaky undertaking in this research? What was found at Site 1, for example, that would be generalizable to Site 2, without taking account of local contextual differences? Transportation was a problem at Site 1, mainly because that ESA had chosen to deliver service with itinerant teachers. At Site 2 it was a problem because of the variety of programs offered; at Site 3 because of the terrain; at Site 4 because of water barriers; and at Site 5 because of vast distances. The generalization, "transportation is a problem," may be true in some trivial sense, but the how and why of it depends acutely on local contextual factors.

What about causality? Can we not find instances of cause-effect relationships everywhere? Would anyone seriously question the assertion that the passage of P.L. 94-142 *caused* mainstreaming to emerge as a classroom phenomenon, or that rural isolation causes some teachers not to apply for positions there? Again, the answer seems to be that life is not so simple. If there is causality, it is mutual causality, and everything interacts to shape everything else. Causal assertions can rapidly become infinite regresses. Our experience at these sites has taught us that everything is interrelated. Although it may be possible at some instant to pull out a pair of phenomena and assert that one is the cause of the other, *it is often equally plausible to say that the purported effect is the "cause" of the purported cause.*

Finally, it seems clear that values also impinge on inquiry and could not meaningfully be excluded, even if it were possible epistemologically to do so. What was found depends on values; how what is found is interpreted depends on values. Under these conditions conventional claims for the objectivity of the researcher must give way to demonstrating the confirmability of the data, just as the conventional search for a single concrete reality must give way to representing multiple constructed realities. Moreover, it also seems that had we come onto these sites with questionnaires to be analyzed statistically, we would not have been greeted as favorably or been made privy to so much information as we were. Our values as researchers were more acceptable to local values than researchers' values typically are.

COMMENT ON THE APPLICATION
OF NATURALISTIC INQUIRY

No discussion of the potential of naturalistic inquiry for studying and improving complex organizations would be complete without calling attention to the potential threat it holds for those organizations as well as the historical inability of qualitative research per se to offer them much help.

Conventional research, with its emphasis on only parts of the whole, is not very threatening, because connections to the entire organization and, more importantly, to individuals can be made only indirectly at best. Those who are in a position to approve or disapprove research into an organization can know ahead of time where the inquiry will lead by reviewing prespecified hypotheses, samples, instruments, and so forth.

Conversely, naturalistic research, like its cousin ethnography, studies an entire context. It emphasizes the understanding of the social organization as a whole. Naturalistic researchers routinely study everyone connected with the enterprise. Moreover, because the design and the problem emerge, it is impossible to tell at the outset just where the inquiry will lead. One can only say that it will always lead to a clearer understanding of problems, precisely because it does consider the whole context. Qualitative research has never been accused of lacking relevance; indeed, most agree that this is its great strength.

Administrators of organizations who would rather not have their problems understood so clearly would do well to choose conventional over qualitative research into their operations. In fact, there are those who assert that this preference, in part, accounts for the predominance of quantitative research in education.[24]

But even when some educational organizations were forced to subject themselves to qualitative studies, as they were in the 1960s concomitant with the increased flow of federal dollars (Bogdan & Biklen, 1982), there still was a way out. Although the relevance of qualitative research was not brought into question, its perceived lack of rigor could always be used to dismiss findings that were too difficult to accept.

Naturalistic inquiry, as proposed by Guba (1978, 1981), Guba and Lincoln (1981, 1982), and Lincoln and Guba (1985) and operationalized in the study described in this chapter, differs from conventional qualitative research primarily in its attention to rigor or trustworthiness. Its potential, with respect to the current discussion, is to diminish the argument against the rigor of traditional qualitative research. Assuming that these trustworthiness measures continue to be expanded and refined, and that eventually they become accepted and institutionalized, educational organizations either would have to accept the results of rigorous naturalistic studies or increase their efforts to block such studies at the outset.

If qualitative research has relevance (can expose real problems), why have such studies historically produced useless advice? Howard Becker (1983), drawing an example from his classic study of medical student culture (Becker, Geer, Hughes, & Strauss, 1961), provides some insight into the apparent irony.

When Becker and his colleagues reported to the doctors that medical students crammed for exams and forgot what they had memorized afterward, doctors were appalled. The researchers explained that the types of exams that the doctors gave called for exactly that sort of studying. If they wanted the students to study differently, they needed to give a different kind of exam. Because the doctors wanted their students to be able to make a physical examination and plan a course of treatment, the ethnographers recommended that each student be given one or two patients to examine and treat, and then let the teachers evaluate how well they had done it. Was this a useful recommendation? Becker explains:

> The faculty looked glum when we said that. What was wrong? That, one said, would take a lot of time, and they all had their research to attend to

and their own patients to take care of. Our solution would work, of
course, but it wasn't *practical.* (1983, p. 108)

The emergent paradigm of thought and belief is beginning to provide
us with new ways to conceptualize organization and inquiry. These
newer conceptualizations of organization are providing us with a new
image of school organization and adaptability. Naturalistic inquiry—
which is, at once, more resonant with the emergent paradigm of thought
and belief and the newer conceptualizations of organization—holds the
promise of relevant and rigorous research into educational organizations. The public, government, and educators are calling for reform of
public education. The stage appears to be set. But, of course, in the end
reform is always a political matter. Whether anything comes of all this
will depend on the willingness of those who control public education at
all levels, first, to expose themselves and, second, to pay the political
costs of change—two very unlikely occurrences, given what we now
know about the functioning of institutionalized organizations.

NOTES

1. The study was carried out under contract with the National Institute of Education
(400-81-0017). The field study portion of the project resulted in five case studies and a
technical report (Skrtic, Guba, & Knowlton, 1985), from which much of the material for
this chapter was drawn. As such, Drs. Guba and Knowlton share in the credit for most of
the ideas presented in the chapter, although I assume responsibility for any of its shortcomings. The views expressed here do not necessarily reflect those of the NIE.

2. See Davis (1976) and Stephens et al. (1979) for descriptions of ESA types.
Examples include organizations such as New York's Boards of Cooperative Educational
Services, Oregon's Intermediate Education Districts, and Iowa's Area Education Agencies, as well as less formal structures in which several districts join together voluntarily to
create their own ESA.

3. Each of the substantive sections of the chapter is labeled with a particular aspect of
the inquiry and its corresponding implications, following the layout in Table 7.1.

4. Although it might seem obvious to some that the SEA should have been included
from the start, excluding the SEA was a deliberate decision on our part. It stemmed from
the NIE's original specifications and available project resources. When it became apparent
that we needed to include the SEA in our analysis, we negotiated with the NIE a reduction
in the number of sites to be studied so that we could include the SEA in the analysis at each
site.

5. Time precluded the selection of all five sites in serial order (that is, one at a time),
but we were able to select Site 1; then, when it had been explored, to select Sites 2 and 3;
then Sites 4 and 5 in the same fashion.

6. Although we used all four qualitative techniques in our study, my comments here will be limited to the interview, which was our primary means of data collection. The manner in which we used the other qualitative methods is addressed in later sections.

7. By "resolving inconsistencies" I do not mean to imply that we sought to aggregate data from multiple sources so that they would converge on a single reality. In fact, just the opposite was true: We sought to highlight multiple constructions of reality. Resolving inconsistencies in this instance refers to verifying information such as average daily membership, the distance traveled per week by the school psychologist, and the like.

8. The major difference between SV-2 and SV-1 was in the form of interview protocol. Whereas the latter had been very open-ended, those of SV-2 included an open-ended portion (much like the SV-1 protocol) and a portion that was much more structured, in line with the purposes of the second site visit. Separate protocols were devised for specific individuals or classes of individuals. Thus, there would be one for the director of the agency, one for the psychologist, one for an itinerant teacher, and so on, as the local situation dictated. By systematically including some of the same questions on various protocols, we were able to build further confidence in the data and extend our collection of multiple constructions of issues.

9. The third visit to each site was reserved primarily for determining the trustworthiness of the inquiry. Even so, SV-3 was also used to explore issues more fully, fill in missing information, resolve inconsistencies, and cross-check information, much like SV-2. The nature of SV-3 and the procedures used relative to trustworthiness will be discussed more fully in subsequent sections.

10. I do not mean to imply that there are precisely three levels of data analysis. If one had to choose, continuous data analysis is a more accurate characterization than three levels of data analysis. I have adopted the three levels convention to help organize my presentation and to distinguish between quantitative analysis, which for the most part is an event in the research process, and qualitative analysis, which is itself a process.

11. Documentary analysis was accomplished chiefly through an indexing process (see "Drafting the Case Study" below). Observational records and interview notes are treated in the same manner as interview data.

12. The general rule followed was to include everything that the researcher believed to be in any way relevant. It is easy to reject irrelevant material later, but impossible to recapture relevant material that is not recorded. The typical yield from the field/interview notes of an individual team member was between 350 and 450 unit cards for each three-day visit.

13. Our use of an auditor is discussed in the section entitled "Trustworthiness."

14. Particularly, it should be noted, the steps that were taken are not subject to criticisms of writers such as Ford (1975) and Hesse (1980), who object to grounded theory because of the well-known hazards of induction and the essential underdetermination of theory inductively derived. (There are always multiple theories that "fit the facts"; there is a serious question as to whether facts are not themselves already theory-laden, so that the process described by Glaser and Strauss may, in fact, be tautological.)

15. The typical yield (depending on the size of the site) of unit cards for both site visitors after two visits was between 2000 and 2400 cards, of which 10% to 20% were cross-reference cards. The number of categories that emerged for a given site was typically on the order of 40 to 50, each one containing multiple subcategories. Because the third visit to each site was mounted for a different purpose and thus much of the data were of a different form, SV-3 data analysis followed different procedures. The use of SV-3 data will be described under the section on "Trustworthiness."

16. Within the general sections of the outline, the illustrative research questions posed by the NIE in the research contract helped to shape the subsections that were to be included under "problems/issues." We were not bound to the questions, but they did represent the matters of concern to our sponsors and, as such, deserved our attention. Three general sets of questions were included under the headings "Organization and Governance Issues " "Special Education Service and Delivery Mechanism Issues," and "Effectiveness and Impact Issues." Information was easily included in the cases that addressed the three sets of questions.

17. See, for example, Becker (1970), Cassell (1978), Lofland (1971), Schatzman and Strauss (1973), and Spradley (1979).

18. It is critically important to understand that the case study writer is not to aggregate various participant constructions into a single reality. Rather, the task is to present multiple constructions of reality on issues. Thus, translation here means multiple translations.

19. Readers who are interested in complete descriptions of the various techniques for each counterpart criterion and how they were used (and why some were not used) in our study are referred to the technical report on the field study portion of the inquiry (Skrtic et al. 1985).

20. In this subsection and the following one I address selected techniques for three of the four counterpart criteria. The two techniques for the transferability criterion, purposive sampling and thick description, have been discussed previously.

21. In general, the rule was followed that no "fact" was cited that could not be corroborated from at least two sources, unless it had been introduced by a respondent whose expertise could not be questioned on the matter at hand (e.g., the director of an ESA on a question of how the annual budget was formulated). Even in these latter cases, however, there nearly always seemed to be multiple ways to triangulate everything. In those few instances in which an assertion could not be triangulated, an indication to that effect usually could be inserted into the case narrative. In any event, all assertions that depended on a single source were readily identifiable in the audit trail.

22. The auditor was Dr. Valerie Janesick of the State University of New York, Albany. Because an audit of this magnitude had not been conducted previously, our tack was to ask the then-current instructor for the American Educational Research Association's annual Research Training Minicourse (on qualitative research methods) to do the job for us. Dr. Janesick had served in that capacity at the 1982 and 1983 AERA meetings. As it turned out, Dr. Janesick (besides being a nationally known qualitative methodologist) had had extensive research experience in several substantive areas related to our research topics, and she had conducted ethnographic research in one of our five states.

23. The auditor had available to her both the draft and revised versions of the case.

24. For the qualitative researcher's perspective, see Becker (1983, p. 104), who argues that qualitative research is avoided in education because it threatens legitimacy. Also, see Erickson (1977) for a discussion of what he refers to as the propensity of educational administrators to avoid evidence that might prove current practices to be inadequate. He asks whether a "hidden curriculum" (p. 131) in educational administration training programs, in effect, teaches would-be administrators to tolerate only innocuous research. Moreover, institutionalization theory (see, for example, Zucker, 1977, 1981) and Meyer and Rowan's (1977) work on myth and symbol in institutionalized organizations make it clear that this sort of behavior on the part of administrators is to be expected in the interest of protecting organizational legitimacy.

25. See the Fall 1983 issue of *Anthropology and Education Quarterly,* in which several prominent qualitative researchers describe the research methods courses they offer for

educators. Although their courses concentrate heavily on qualitative techniques and methods, the question of rigor or trustworthiness receives virtually no attention. See also the Fall 1984 issue of *Anthropology and Education Quarterly* (special issue: Research Dilemmas in Administration and Policy Settings), in which guest editor Catherine Marshall (1984) summarizes several dilemmas that continue to plague field research. She addresses the rigor question rhetorically: "How much should we adhere to positivist demands for validity, reliability, replicability, and numerically analyzed findings? Do we have a well developed, agreed-upon argument that establishes a different paradigm to guide field study researchers?" (p. 197). The work of Guba and Lincoln, of course, is precisely a response to these questions.

REFERENCES

Anthropology and Education Quarterly (1983). Vol. 14 (fall).

Becker, H. S. (1970). *Sociological work.* Chicago: Aldine.

Becker, H. S. (1983). Studying urban schools. *Anthropology and Education Quarterly, 31,*(2), 99-108.

Becker, H. S., Greer, B., Hughes, E. C., & Strauss, A. (1961). *Boys in white: Student culture in medical school.* Chicago: University of Chicago Press.

Bogdan, R. C., & Biklen, S. K. (1982). *Qualitative research for education: An introduction to theory and methods.* Boston: Allyn & Bacon.

Cassell, J. (1978). *A field manual for studying desegregated school.* Washington, DC: National Institute of Education.

Davis, H. S. (1976). *Educational service centers in the USA.* New Haven, CT: Connecticut State Department of Education.

Erickson, D. A. (1977). An overdue paradigm shift in educational administration, or, how can we get that idiot off the freeway? In L. L. Cunningham, W. G. Hack, & R. O. Nystrand (Eds.), *Educational administration: The developing decades* (pp. 119-143). Berkeley, CA: McCutchan.

Ford, J. (1975). *Paradigms and fairy tales.* London: Routledge & Kegan Paul.

Glaser, N., & Strauss, A. L. (1968). *The discovery of grounded theory.* Chicago: Aldine.

Guba, E. G. (1978). *Toward a methodology of naturalistic inquiry in educational evaluation* (CSE Monograph Series, 8). Los Angeles: UCLA Center for the Study of Evaluation.

Guba, E. G. (1981). Criteria for assessing the trustworthiness of naturalistic inquiries. *Educational Communication and Technology Journal, 29.*

Guba, E. G., & Lincoln, Y. S. (1981). *Effective evaluation.* San Francisco: Jossey-Bass.

Guba, E. G., & Lincoln, Y. S. (1982). Epistemological and methodological bases of naturalistic inquiry. *Educational Communication and Technology Journal, 31,* 233-252.

Halpern, E. (1983). *Auditing naturalistic inquiries: The development and application of a model.* Unpublished Ph.D. dissertation, Indiana University.

Hesse, M. (1980). *Revolutions and reconstructions in the philosophy of science.* Bloomington: Indiana University Press.

Hofstadter, D. R. (1979). *Gödel, Escher, Bach: An eternal golden braid.* New York: Basic Books.

Lincoln, Y. S., & Guba, E. G. (1985). *Naturalistic inquiry.* Beverly Hills, CA: Sage.

Lofland, J. (1971). *Analyzing social settings.* Belmont, CA: Wadsworth.

Marshall, C. (1984). Research dilemmas in administration and policy settings: An introduction to the special issue. *Anthropology and Education Quarterly, 15*(3), 194-201.

Meyer, J. W., & Rowan, B. (1977). Institutionalized organizations: Formal structures as
myth and ceremony. *American Journal of Sociology, 83,* 340-363.

Patton, M. Q. (1980). *Qualitative evaluation methods.* Beverly Hills, CA: Sage.

Schatzman, L., & Strauss, A. (1973). *Field research.* Englewood Cliffs, NJ: Prentice-Hall.

Schwartz, P., & Ogilvy, J. (1979). *The emergent paradigm: Changing patterns of thought
and belief* (Analytical Report: Values and Lifestyles Program). Menlo Park, CA: SRI
International.

Skrtic, T. M., Guba, E. G., & Knowlton, H. E. (1985). *Interorganizational special
education programming in rural areas: Technical report on the multisite naturalistic
field study.* Washington, DC: National Institute of Education.

Spradley, J. (1979). *The ethnographic interview.* New York: Holt, Rinehart & Winston.

Stephens, E. R., Bensimon, G. A., McAdoo, H. P., & Gividen, N. J. (1979). *Education
service agencies: Status and trends* (ESA Study Series, Report 1). Burtonsville, MD:
Stephens Associates.

Weick, K. E. (1976). Educational organizations as loosely coupled systems. *Administrative Science Quarterly, 21,* 1-19.

Zucker, L. G. (1977). The role of institutionalization in cultural persistence. *American
Sociological Review, 42,* 726-743.

Zucker, L. G. (1981). Institutional structure and organizational processes: The role of
evaluation units in schools. In A. Bank & R. C. Williams (Eds.), *Evaluation and
decision making* (CSE Monograph Series, 10). Los Angeles: UCLA Center for the
Study of Evaluation.

8

EPILOGUE: DICTIONARIES FOR LANGUAGES NOT YET SPOKEN

Yvonna S. Lincoln

It should be clear, both propositionally and intuitively, that the authors of the preceding chapters are not only describing, they are in a sense creating a new world. For three of the authors, that new world is focused in a substantive manner, on organizational theory. For the other three, it is focused on the model or paradigm that guides inquiry into a variety of substantive and disciplinary arenas. The language is new, tentative. The terminology is exploratory and indeterminate rather than precise and circumscribed.

At the level of concepts (Chapters 2 and 3, by Clark and Guba) the arguments are framed at structural and epistemological levels. The overriding structures that we impose on (in this case) human organizations are undergoing radical metamorphosis. Clark's history of the "invention"—and it is truly an invention—of bureaucracy is instructive, as it explores a logic-in-use during Weber's time and in subsequent decades. At the same time, it both demonstrates a logic-in-use in the construction of a new mind set for viewing organizational theory and offers a reconstructed logic of the development of the neo-orthodox in organizational studies. The development of parallels between new theory and new terminology, particularly the terminology of Schwartz and Ogilvy, demonstrates not only that links can be found, but that those links are mutually supportive of one another, that they appear to be part of the same world view, and that they fit with an ease and comfort that we have come to call resonance.

At the same time, Guba argues that definitions of what it is we know, what it is that we think we can know, and how we will come to know it can change, and furthermore, are changing. The old rules that governed the conduct of disciplined substantive inquiry are undergoing stress and the structures are unsafe, if not indeed collapsing. As Ray Rist commented:

> There is yet a further philosophical issue here as well. Not only does the use of one methodological approach as opposed to another change the means by which one perceives the reality under study, but also the very reality to which a researcher has applied a method is itself continually in a state of change. *As all knowledge is social, so also all reality is social.* To wait for absolutes is to wait for Godot. Social systems are ongoing, regardless of how stable they may appear. Put differently, no methodology allows us to step twice in the same stream in the same place. (1977, p. 48; emphases added)

To cherish the hope that new rules for ways of knowing may be permitted (although not taken as the new orthodoxy), is the task of those working at the concept stage of theory and epistemology.

Some of the battle, however, goes on at the construct level also. In earlier work (Lincoln & Guba, 1985) the example of Orwell's *1984* was used to remind the reader that when words do not exist for concepts and constructs, there is no recognition that such states are possible. The powerful example in *1984* was the *newspeak* dictionary, which omitted words such as "freedom," "liberty," and "privacy." Without words to shape the concepts, the drive for human freedom, for liberty of thought and action slowly disappears. So it is with terminology, or even jargon. Jargon may be a particularly good example, because contemporary bureaucracies have given us so much of it. While we might be at a loss to explain the rationales behind such terms, who cannot be moved to some emotional reaction to terms like MAD (mutually assured destruction), "terminated with extreme prejudice," "delivering the mail" (as a metaphor for bombing villages in Vietnam), or "social safety net." What this doublespeak means to individuals will no doubt vary, but as part of the repertoire of everyday life they and their accompaniment of emotional freight are now embedded in the culture of Western society.

In the same way, constructs that embody the new organizational theory, and the new paradigm of inquiry that supports it, are finding their way into the research literature. Weick and I have tried to give some flavor of what those terms and aphorisms might be. In some instances they are the semantic opposites, as, for instance, when Weick proposes that one ought to "leap before you look." The statement flies in the face of cliched advice, but there is good reason to believe that it might be as useful, and perhaps more productive than looking before you leap.

Loose coupling. Organized anarchies. Fluid participation. What can these mean, save that organizational theorists are engaging, as Anne Huff terms it, in "the construction of the future." They are, in the best sense of her own market-model metaphor, "shopping ideas." They are trying out the aptness and the provocativeness of new phrases, both to describe what they are seeing and to summon others to see the same properties in organizations and inquiry paradigms.

Some of what is going on, to be sure, is shooting from the hip, as Huff calls it. It involves no inconsiderable amount of making it up as one goes along. But why should researchers apologize for engaging in the construction of their substantive world, when all the evidence points to exactly the same form of activity as characterizing the best practitioners of administration? The point she clearly makes (among others) is that the best practitioners are constantly using opportunities to "shape the premises of others' decisions"; why ought we not to do the same as reconstructors of their worlds?

Lest readers believe that we see what is not there, the game suggested in Chapter 1 can be repeated, to wit, take quite ordinary and widely accessible examples and find evidences of the constructs for yourselves. Here are several to start the game rolling: If one takes seriously the idea that reality is a constructed entity, negotiated, renegotiated, and jointly created by participants in a given situation, then take the following examples as fodder:

- Sherry Turkle's new (and bestselling) work, *The Second Self: Computers and the Human Spirit,* which argues that computers are creating a far greater revolution than originally predicted (as information processors and enablers of a return to cottage industry and the global village). The revolution, as she analyzed it, has affected "the way we think, especially the way that we think about ourselves.... Possibly the greatest change ... is that it has provoked those of us who live with it to reconsider what it means to think, to feel, and to be human." Turkle comments that her motivation to explore the cybernetic relationship, the relation of humankind to machines, was prompted by the ways in which computer experts talked about their machines and programs, and by the way they talked about their *other, human relationships.* The revolution proceeds apace in terminology, which has psychologically reversed, in some instances, the expected language. Thus, we find the expressions of fondness and affection for personal computers, and wives being described as "lousy peripherals" (1984).

- John Naisbitt's *Megatrends: Ten New Directions Transforming Our Lives* (1982), which forcefully argues (using the methodology of content analysis) that there are forces at work to move us, as a society, in directions of which we might be unaware. These forces—which might be thought of as mutually causal, in the sense in which Guba and Schwartz and Ogilvy use the phrase—are traceable, trackable, not sinister, but also not salient save to a careful observer. The ten directions promise to change the face of Western society forever, not for better or worse, but simply morphogenetically, so that totally new forms will be born from the forces. In part, those new social forms can be predicted, but in part, they must remain unknown to us, possibly because of other forces that neither we nor Naisbitt have "seen" yet.

- Michael Ignatieff's *The Needs of Strangers* (1984), which argues for a personal and collective (social) definition of needs and wants and collective visions of how they might be satisfied. But a reviewer commented, "There is, too, something rather old-fashioned about insisting on our need for a 'shared language of the good.' A shared description of reality must precede any such ethical development, and *there is scant recognition here of the great fragmentation of the real (sic) that is one of our century's central facts*. The vision of this book is pretty consistently white, bourgeois Western and male; and, as a result, a little narrow" (Manchester *Guardian,* October 25, 1984; emphasis added).

- Or consider a comment closer to home: an interview with the ubiquitous commentator on American life, Norman Mailer. In the interview Mailer was asked to comment on the then-upcoming presidential election in the United States. The battle between Reagan and the Mondale-Ferraro ticket was heating up, and Mailer found the process both cynically edifying and, at the same time, intellectually horrifying. "Of course," he says, "the press will be working for Mondale because they will have a better story if the gap between the two candidates narrows. . . . You know, you may think I'm being disrespectful, but I mean 25% of this. *I can never remember America being so mindless. It's a nation of 200m people with the inner life of Marie Antoinette"* (London *Sunday Times,* October 14, 1984, p. 11; emphasis added). Although Mailer's construction of the level and quality of the public debate that attended the reelection of Reagan will undoubtedly prove repugnant to some, it is a fascinating example of the creation of a political reality (for an eager and amused British audience, to be certain), a hyperbolic and wry attribution that nevertheless had enough ring of truth about it to give Americans abroad a queasy feeling.

If constructed realities are too simple, substitute the construct of loose coupling or heterarchy. Several more examples should serve to prove that we've mastered the game, that what we are seeing is there to be seen. Consider, for example, the following interesting illustrations:

- The confrontations between the Vatican and the bishops and priests over "theologies of liberation" are slowly simmering into revolt and rebellion among the Catholic community. While the Vatican may construe Boff and his fellow theologists as misguided, at issue is the authority of the Church and the infallibility of Papal doctrine. In fact, Boff and other liberation theologists are loosely coupled to Vatican authority, and furthermore, committed to overthrowing the oppressive hierarchies of the Church as well as those of repressive economic and political structures, according to some analysts. A regular columnist on religious affairs interprets the tensions thus:

> It reveals the thinking of a theological movement which is concerned not only with the liberation of society from economic oppression but also from religious oppression, a liberation not only by but also of the Church.

> When in his book, *Jesus Christ Liberator,* Leonardo Boff wrote of the theologian of liberation looking at society "from the bottom up" rather than, as has traditionally been the case, "from the top down," his argument is as clearly applicable to a church viewed in terms of popes, cardinals and bishops as to a state viewed in terms of presidents and generals.

> The theology of liberation is taking root in a part of the world which by the end of this century will contain more than half of the world's catholics. By that time it may have contributed to an economic transformation of a poor and underdeveloped part of the world. *But its other contribution,* which may be the one which really worries Rome, *will be a transformation of the church, from a hierarchy into a brotherly—and sisterly—community, a body of Christ in which all are members one of another, a classless society in which those old distinctions between priest and lay, and between man and woman in the church, are overcome.* (Corner, 1984; emphases added)

Clearly, unless the Church is willing to utterly change its form at or close to the beginning of the next century (an unlikely option from which any pope might willingly chose), the Father Boffs of the hierarchy will need to be brought to heel. Father Boff and his fellow liberationists are too loosely coupled with the authority of Rome. And their theologies support a universal heterarchy that in the end will defy the Roman hierarchy.

- Or consider the plight of Soviet women. In a society that makes much of the classless condition of each of its citizens, old classist structures apparently still prevail in that final small society—the family. In a report filed from Moscow, reporter Janet Price (1984) provides a catalogue of "unpalatable equality" foisted onto women in Russia:

> In spite of impressive statistics, a woman's life is overshadowed by the lingering clouds of male chauvinism. An average mother is expected to put in 8 hours at the office, then hasten home to toil away for another 4-6 hours cooking, cleaning, and washing. Meanwhile, hubby complacently sits in front of the television or goes out drinking with friends. Incredibly, the Soviet husband of the eighties does less to help in the home than he did 60 years ago.... Without a doubt, cracks are appearing in the centuries old patriarchal social order in Russia. (p. 11)

> The politics that guide economic development and foreign policy for Soviet society are obviously a bit less well coupled to private and social behavior. The Soviets might be well advised to clean up their own houses before demanding an end to Western forms of oppression!

The reader is gleefully invited to join the game, an exercise that should serve to convince that the sands are indeed shifting beneath our feet.

What this work, and the work of others in the same vein, is about can be viewed from another perspective as well. That perspective, to borrow terminology from Lather (1983), is a dialectic tension between "empowering and impoverishing ideologies." Once a vision of the new world has occurred, once one begins to see the world in a fresh and powerful way, the vision can but rarely be extinguished. In part, the arguments that exist between the neo-orthodox and the nonorthodox are concerned with what ideologies we will empower, which we will impoverish. The empowering and impoverishing occur not just at an intellectual level, but in very real political and economic contexts. As Michael Young (1971) points out:

> Existing categories . . . that distinguish home from school, learning from play, academic from non-academic, and able or bright from dull and stupid must be conceived of *as socially constructed, with some in a position to impose their constructions or meaning on others.* (p. 21, emphasis added)

Those who are in a position to do so will be those empowered, and those unable to have their ideologies considered will be those whose perspectives are impoverished. Those empowered (by contemporarily fashionable ideologies) are those who will be hired, and those impoverished (by unfashionable ideologies) are those less likely to be hired into positions of power and research. Those ideologies that are fashionable will secure funding for research programs, and those that are not currently in vogue will be unable to seize resources. The stakes are indubitably high and getting higher, with cuts in social science funding.

The question is more than just funding, however. It is, in a real and meaningful sense, an expression of the battle between hierarchy and heterarchy at the paradigmatic level. The battle is on for dominion of the positivist tradition and a hierarchy of inquiry models and preferred methods versus a choice of paradigm, non- and antipositivist models, and methods that are neither preferred nor exclusive, but that are developed and/or chosen for their aptness in exploring the particular perspectives in which we are interested.

The authors here have argued that the old paradigm is breaking down, that organizations exhibit characteristics that are neither accounted for under old constructions of organizations nor able to be explored using the older sets of inquiring glasses. The epistemologists have argued that there are new lenses through which we might see more clearly those characteristics that are now of interest in organizations. The contingency is not remarkable, considering a resurgence of interest in what makes human organizations tick, what makes them responsive to environments, why some are successful and some are not, how it is that some use resources in profitable, productive, and downright clever ways, and others seem to have resources slip through their corporate fingers (just as the opportunities also disappear).

This is a concern not only in the public sector, in schools, colleges, and universities, which must meet new demands for accountability, but also in the private and commercial sector, which has gradually lost the cutting edge in productivity to other industrialized and Third World sectors (Reich, 1983; Peters & Waterman, 1982). In order to understand why some organizations achieve excellence, quality, and productivity, we are going to have to have new descriptions of them. We need these new descriptions not only because they are different from what we imagined, and from what they were prescribed to be, but also because they are doing precisely what we never expected, what classical organizational theory said would be difficult, or relatively impossible, to do (or worse yet, what classical organizational theory never mentioned).

It is not that we have lost faith in our organizations; it is that they don't look as we imagined they would look, and we must now return to finding out what they do look like, what they are doing, how they construct organizational sagas to accomplish the missions they wish to achieve. And we need to know much more about how their leaders and participants see the world, how they construct images that produce creative and adaptive strategies.

That task for researchers involves at minimum an ideological switch that moves us from asking, "Are you doing what you're supposed to be doing?" to, "What *are* you doing, and how are your coworkers responding to it?"

In the process, members of organizations and those who do research in them will be evolving or adopting new ideologies for coherence in expression, and will be talking a new language to describe what they have found. Some researchers may explore underexplored disciplines, such as constructivist psychology. Some may be adopting perspectives that are not widely utilized in this country, such as feminism, socialism, or neo-Marxism. Some will be arguing for new versions of knowledge permission, new rules that permit other ways of seeing. That is what this book is all about.

REFERENCES

Corner, M. (1984, October 15). The Vatican's fear of liberation. Manchester *Guardian*.

Ignatieff, M. (1984). *The needs of strangers*. London: Chatto.

Lather, P. S. (1983). *Feminism, teacher education, and curricular change: Women's studies as counter-hegemonic work*. Unpublished Ph.D. dissertation, Indiana University.

Lincoln, Y. S., & Guba, E. G. (1985). *Naturalistic inquiry*. Beverly Hills, CA: Sage.

Mailer in full flow. (1984, October 14). *London Sunday Times*, p. 11.

Naisbitt, J. (1982). *Megatrends: Ten new directions transforming our lives*. New York: Warner.

Needs and greeds: A review of Michael Ignatieff's *The needs of strangers*. (1984, October 25). Manchester *Guardian*, p. 20.

Peters, T. J., & Waterman, R. H. (1982). *In search of excellence*. New York: Harper & Row.

Price, J. (1984, October 29). Unpalatable equality. Manchester *Guardian*.

Reich, R. B. (1983). *The next American frontier*. New York: Times Books.

Rist, R. C. (1977). On the relations among educational research paradigms: From disdain to detente. *Anthropology and Education Quarterly, 8,* 42-49.

Sutton, T. (1984, October 1). The first question: Does it exist? *International Herald Tribune*.

Turkle, S. (1984). *The second self: Computers and the human spirit*. New York: Simon & Schuster.

Young, M.F.D. (1971). *Knowledge and control: New directions for the sociology of education*. London: Macmillan.

ABOUT THE CONTRIBUTORS

DAVID L. CLARK is Professor of Education at Indiana University. He currently is Director of the Policy Studies Center of the University Council for Educational Administration. His recent publications include *The Changing Structure of Federal Educational Policy in the 1980s* (1983), *Effective Schools and School Improvement: A Comparative Analysis of Two Lines of Inquiry* (1984), *A Proposal for the Structural Reform of Teacher Education* (1984), and *Strength of Organizational Coupling in the Instructionally Effective School* (1985). He received his Ed.D. from Teachers College, Columbia University.

EGON G. GUBA is Professor of Educational Inquiry Methodology in the School of Education, Indiana University, where he has been for the past nineteen years. His previous academic appointments include eight years at Ohio State University and five at the University of Chicago. He has been a member of the faculties of the University of Missouri at Kansas City and Valparaiso University, and served as Visiting Professor at UCLA and Virginia Polytechnic Institute and State University. Dr. Guba received his Ph.D. from the University of Chicago in 1952, and in 1954 joined J. S. Getzels as a consultant to the Midwest Administration Center, one of the early Kellogg Centers. The well-known Getzels-Guba model of administrative staff relations was a result of this collaboration. In 1960 Dr. Guba was named Director of the Bureau of Educational Research and Service at Ohio State. After moving to Indiana University he spent six years as Associate Dean for Academic Affairs of the School of Education. With Yvonna Lincoln he has devoted himself to developing the approach known as naturalistic inquiry. Their collaboration has led to two books—*Effective Evaluation* (1981) and *Naturalistic Inquiry* (1985)—and numerous articles.

ANNE SIGISMUND HUFF is Associate Professor of Strategic Management in the Department of Business Administration, University of Illinois. Her research has focused on the process whereby senior executives reformulate strategy in the face of changing conditions and their own changing understandings of these conditions. A second subject of interest has been the extent to which organization politics affect the content and timing of organization strategy. One outcome of this line of work is evidence that politics can make a positive contribution to organization strategy. Descriptions of this research have been published in various book chapters, *Strategic Management Review, Journal of Business Research, Long Range Planning, Academy of Management Review,* and other journals. Dr. Huff currently is working on a study, funded by the National Science Foundation, focusing on the interaction of analytic and political thinking in strategy formulation.

YVONNA S. LINCOLN is Associate Professor of Higher Education at the University of Kansas. She earned a baccalaureate in history and sociology from Michigan State University, a master's in history from the University of Illinois, and an Ed.D. from Indiana University in higher education, with a minor in organizational theory and behavior. Prior to moving to Kansas, she served as Research Associate to the Vice-President of Academic Affairs at Indiana University. Dr. Lincoln serves on several editorial boards and is the author or coauthor of numerous articles and papers on program evaluation, institutional criteria for promotion and tenure decisions, administrative internships/mentoring designs, and naturalistic inquiry. With Egon G. Guba, she is coauthor of *Effective Evaluation* and *Naturalistic Inquiry.* She has been elected a member of the Executive Board of the Evaluation Network and has provided technical assistance to the Follow-Through Demonstration Projects, to Native American groups, to the Bureau of Education for the Handicapped evaluation training workshops, and to schools of education across the country. At present, she and Dr. Guba are collaborating on two books, one on fourth-generation evaluation and the other on political ideologies and emergent paradigm inquiry.

THOMAS SKRTIC is Associate Professor of Special Education at the University of Kansas, Lawrence. He holds research appointments with the Bureau of Child Research and the Institute for Research in Learning Disabilities. He held a joint appointment in the Department of Curriculum and Instruction from 1976 to 1983, and served as Danforth Associate from 1978 to 1984. His research interests have included child development, mathematics learning, cognitive development, and teacher-student relationships. More recently he has been concerned with educational policy implementation and the process of organizational change, and his latest work centers on the nature of interorganizational collaboration in the process of planned change. Dr. Skrtic is on leave during the 1985-1986 academic year as an Intra-University Visiting Professor at the University of Kansas, where his work includes multidisciplinary study in sociology, philosophy, history, and political science.

KARL E. WEICK holds the Harkins and Company Centennial Chair in Business Administration at the University of Texas, Austin, and is editor of *Administrative Science Quarterly*. He received his Ph.D. in psychology from Ohio State University in 1962, and since then has been associated with the faculties of Purdue University, University of Minnesota, and Cornell University. He also held short-term appointments at the University of Utrecht in the Netherlands, Wabash College, Carnegie-Mellon University, Stanford University, and Seattle University. His research interests include how people make sense of confusing events, the effects of stress on thinking and imagination, techniques for observing complicated events, self-fulfilling prophecies, the craft of applying social science, substitutes for rationality, and determinants of effective managerial performance. His writings on these topics are collected in four books, including *The Social Psychology of Organizing* and the coauthored *Managerial Behavior, Performance and Effectiveness*, which won the 1972 Book of the Year Award from the American College of Hospital Administration. Dr. Weick has also written numerous journal articles, book chapters, and book reviews.